Cross-National Comparisons of Social Movement Unionism

Trade Unions Past, Present and Future

Edited by Craig Phelan

Volume 18

PETER LANG
Oxford • Bern • Berlin • Bruxelles • Frankfurt am Main • New York • Wien

Cross-National Comparisons of Social Movement Unionism

Diversities of Labour Movement Revitalization in Japan, Korea and the United States

Akira Suzuki (ed.)

PETER LANG
Oxford • Bern • Berlin • Bruxelles • Frankfurt am Main • New York • Wien

Bibliographic information published by Die Deutsche Nationalbibliothek.
Die Deutsche Nationalbibliothek lists this publication in the Deutsche Nationalbibliografie; detailed bibliographic data is available on the Internet at http://dnb.d-nb.de.

A catalogue record for this book is available from the British Library.

Library of Congress Cataloging-in-Publication Data:

Cross-national comparisons of social movement unionism : diversities of labour movement revitalization in Japan, Korea and the United States / [edited by] Akira Suzuki.
p. cm. -- (Trade unions past, present and future ; 18)
Includes bibliographical references and index.
ISBN 978-3-0343-0868-7 (alk. paper)
1. Labor movement--Japan. 2. Labor movement--Korea (South) 3. Labor movement--United States 4. Social movements. I. Suzuki, Akira, 1962-
HD8720.5.C76 2012
331.88--dc23
2012031884

ISSN 1662-7784
ISBN 978-3-0343-0868-7

Hochfeldstrasse 32, CH-3012 Bern, Switzerland
info@peterlang.com, www.peterlang.com, www.peterlang.net

Contents

Acknowledgements

The chapters of this volume, except Chapter 1 (Introduction) and Chapter 6, are based on papers originally presented at the "Conference on the Cross-national Comparison of Labour Movement Revitalization," a two-day event hosted by the Ohara Institute for Social Research, Hosei University, held in Tokyo on 18–19 December 2010. Financial support for the conference was provided by the Science Research Promotion Fund and Hosei University. I would like to thank participants of the conference, including Andrew Gordon, Mark Brenner, Toru Shinoda, and Kumiko Hagiwara, for their thoughtful comments.

After the conference, I embarked on this project of editing a volume based on the conference papers. I would like to thank each author for timely submission of revised papers and Minjin Lee for permission to include an English translation of her article in the edited volume. I also would like to acknowledge Stephanie Luce and Charles Weathers for their comments on the introductory chapter and express my gratitude to Satoshi Kaneko, my research assistant, for preparing many statistical tables and figures, some of which are included in the Appendix. I am also grateful to Robert Sauté who carefully edited the book manuscript.

— AKIRA SUZUKI

AKIRA SUZUKI

1 Introduction: Theoretical and Empirical Issues of Cross-national Comparisons of Social Movement Unionism

Introduction

Labour movements in advanced industrialized countries have suffered a decline in membership and density and a weakened presence in their respective societies. The decline of organized labour is particularly pronounced in Liberal Market Economy countries (LMEs) where institutional arrangements regulating industrial relations and government social policies have weakly mediated the impact of neoliberal globalization on labour movements. Trade unions have continued losing members as they fail to keep up with the increasing speed of capital mobility when, for instance, companies in manufacturing industries, unions' traditional base, relocate plants overseas. Unions have suffered further loss of members from subcontracting/out-sourcing of business activities in domestic-oriented industries and the privatization of publicly-owned enterprises. Moreover, neoliberal states have created hostile environments for labour movements, for example, by deregulating labour markets and reforming industrial relations institutions in order to undermine the position of trade unions as legitimate representatives of workers' collective interests.

Labour movements, however, have at times gone on the offensive, and some unions have attempted to recoup their strength vis-à-vis management and states by adopting proactive policies such as organizing unorganized workers and making unions less bureaucratic and more movement-oriented organizations. Previous studies have examined conditions under which trade unions have reversed course and adopted proactive policies, what labour scholars call union or labour 'revitalization', based on the assumption that trade unions, while constrained by external economic, political and institutional contexts, have had a range of strategic choices (Turner 2005). Previous studies on union revitalization have focused their attention on locals of US-based international unions such as the Service Employees International Union (SEIU) and UNITE HERE and examined how and under what conditions these locals transformed themselves by shifting their strategy from a 'service model' to an 'organizing model' (Voss and Sherman 2000). Here, the service model refers to the maintenance of existing unions based on the provisions of 'services' to union members and is associated with an allegedly obsolete model of business unionism, while the 'organizing model' refers to aggressive organizing campaigns based on mobilization of activists and rank-and-file members.

Social movement unionism (SMU), the subject of this volume, shares many characteristics with the organizing model, and some studies use the two concepts interchangeably. It can be argued, however, that SMU is not merely a prescriptive model of active union organizing, but 'encompasses a vision that extends beyond a particular workplace to the labor movement and society as a whole' (Schenk 2003: 251). In other words, SMU-oriented unions are not only concerned with a numerical increase in union members through organizing campaigns but also recognize their role in broad society-based campaigns for alleviating economic inequality and addressing economic injustice.

The concept of SMU was originally developed to explain militant labour movements involved in community-based struggles and political movements against authoritarian developmental states such as South Africa and Brazil (Webster 1988; Seidman 1994; von Holdt 2002, 2003). Researchers introduced the new concept of unionism in the 1980s because the existing concepts of unionism in industrialized countries such as business unionism and social democratic unionism assumed the institutionalization of trade unions and could not account for militant union movements against authoritarian regimes. Later, in the 1990s, researchers adopted this concept to explain the revitalization of union efforts in North America to counter the negative effects of neoliberal globalization (von Holdt 2002,

2003; Moody 1997). Studies of US (and to a lesser extent, Canadian and Australian) union revitalization efforts relied on the concept of SMU in analysing organizing campaigns of immigrant workers and other low-paid, service-sector workers. Those studies also explored alliances between trade unions and social movements to achieve policy goals such as living wages (Lopez 2004; Luce 2004; Milkman 2006).

This volume expands the geographical scope of studies on union revitalization and social movement unionism and examines cases in Japan, South Korea (hereafter Korea) and the United States. One of the chapters also covers a comparison of Australia, Japan and the United States. Labour movements in those countries have different historical trajectories and policy orientations (see discussions of the contexts of SMU in the three countries below) and raise the question of comparability. They face, however, similar trends in changing industrial structures: a declining proportion of employment in the manufacturing sector where union presence was once relatively strong and an increase in the service sector where union presence has been relatively weak (see Table A.1 and Figures A.1 and A.2 in the Appendix). In addition, the labour movements of these three countries with decentralized bargaining structures suffered from a decline in their organizational power under the impact of neoliberal globalization, although the timing and intensity of the impact varied with the countries. In the United States, employer and state offensives against labour based on a neoliberal creed started in the late 1970s. In contrast, the pressures of neoliberal globalization and labour market deregulation began to weaken labour movements in Japan and Korean from the early 1990s (the impact of neoliberal globalization in Korea came in a dramatic form with the IMF bailout in late 1997). Although neoliberal globalization put the labour movements in the three countries on the defensive, we have also seen efforts by some segments of the labour movements to revitalize their power in alliance with social movements and/or by reframing their goals in broader terms. Revitalization efforts took on new forms of organizing the unorganized in the United States and new forms of union organization in Japan and Korea. The main targets of organizing campaigns were workers who fell outside the usual coverage of mainstream unions: immigrant workers in low-paying service sector jobs in the United States and in Japan and Korea non-regular workers and workers in small firms. The new trends in Japan and Korea, particularly the former, have received insufficient attention in previous studies of cross-national union revitalization[1] and social movement unionism.[2] This volume will contribute to the sociology of labour movements by filling the lacunae in comparative studies of union revitalization and SMU and shed light on how institutional and social contexts, such as the structures and policy orientations of labour movements and the state of civil society and social movements, have influenced the forms and goals of SMU in the United States, Japan and Korea.

This introductory chapter is organized as follows. The first section discusses definitional, conceptual and theoretical issues of social movement unionism and presents a broad framework encompassing SMU in both late-industrializing and industrialized countries. The second section gives brief outlines of the chapters in this volume. The chapters are organized by three theoretical issues raised in the first section: the impact that SMU has on the existing labour movement, discussions of SMU from a cross-national perspective, including cases of 'non-Western' countries, and elaborations of how neoliberal globalization (the macro context of SMU) are mediated by meso-level factors. The third section outlines the historical backgrounds and contexts of SMU in Japan, Korea and the United States.

1 Major studies of cross-national comparisons of union renewal or revitalization include the volume edited by Fairbrother and Yates, which compares cases of five Anglo-American countries whose social-economic systems are relatively similar (Fairbrother and Yates eds 2003), the volume edited by Cornfield and McCammon, which compares actions taken by labour movements in eight countries in the Global North and South, including Korea, 'to strengthen themselves' in the social contexts of 'labor organizations' relationship and interactions with workers, employers, and the state' (Cornfield and McCammon eds 2003: 3–4), and the volume edited by Frege and Kelly, which systematically compares six different union revitalization strategies in the United Kingdom, the United States, Germany, Spain and Italy (Frege and Kelly eds 2004).

2 Korea has received more attention in previous studies of social movement unionism (e.g. Chun 2009; Webster et al. 2008).

Conceptual Framework and Theoretical Issues of Social Movement Unionism

Social Movement Unionism in Industrialized and Late-industrializing Countries

Researchers tend to define social movement unionism by identifying common characteristics of innovative strategies trade unions adopt in the countries they observe. According to Kim Voss, a small group of union activists in service sector unions in the United States started to 'experiment with a new model of unionism' for union revitalization in the 1990s. She termed this new model 'social movement unionism' and pointed out three of its characteristics:

> This model marked a radical shift from business unionism...in at least three ways. First, it emphasized rank-and-file leadership and direct action as the source of collective power. Second, it stressed social justice, linking labor movement revival to a broader movement for expanded citizenship in the US and anti-corporate struggles internationally. Third, it introduced a new repertoire of social action, including corporate campaigns and alternatives, such as 'card-check neutrality', to the state-sanctioned (National Labor Relations Board) union recognition process (Voss 2010: 375).

Gay Seidman, in her study of militant labour movements in Brazil and South Africa, two late-industrializers in the semi-periphery, defined SMU in the following way:

> Theoretically, social-movement unionism is perhaps best defined as an effort to raise the living standards of the working class as a whole, rather than to protect individually defined interests of union members...Social-movement unionism, broadly speaking, consists of precisely such [class] struggles over wages and working conditions, and also over living conditions in working-class areas...These campaigns link factory-based unions and communities, and they lead to challenges to states as well as to individual employers. Strikes over factory issues receive strong community support; conversely, community campaigns for improved social services and full citizenship are supported by factory organizations as labor movements redefine their constituencies to include the broader working class (Seidman 1994: 2–3).

The two researchers assumed labour movements in different national contexts and at different stages of industrialization in defining SMU. Their definitions, however, have in common the assumption that labour movements/ unions seek broad goals beyond the narrowly-defined goals of business and economic unionism. These goals may include social justice, expanded/full citizenship, improvements in social services in working-class areas, anti-corporate campaigns on a global scale, or other challenges to states. SMU-oriented movements/unions pursue these broad goals often in coalitions with social movements (as implied by the second characteristic in the Voss's definition) and community-based movements (as explicitly stated in the Seidman's definition). Furthermore, SMU-oriented movements/unions contest the legitimacy of institutionalized industrial relations by pursuing an alternative way of union recognition (as indicated by the third characteristic of Voss's definition) or by getting involved in community-based issues unconstrained by factory-based labour-management relations (as indicated by Seidman's definition). The extra-institutional tendencies of SMU-oriented movements/unions in both late-industrializing and industrialized countries correspond with pre-institutionalized and de-institutionalized stages of industrial relations, respectively. In other words, the development of SMU in the former countries reflects contentious labour-management and/or labour-state relations under authoritarian developmental states, while the development of SMU in the latter countries reflects labour's proactive policies to the weakened institutional positions that hard-line management and neoliberal state policies have wrought (see Table 1.1 below).

If SMU tends to develop in labour movements in both the pre-institutionalized and de-institutionalized stages, we can argue that SMU in industrialized countries is not a new strategy. Trade unions of semi-skilled workers in the United States and European countries during the rapid industrialization of the early 20th century (corresponding to the pre-institutionalized stage) adopted SMU-oriented strategies by forming coalitions with working-class communities and by making broad demands such as industrial and social citizenship rights for workers and their families (see Seidman 1994: 5). We should also note that the institutionalized stage does not necessarily mean the total absence of SMU in the labour movement.

Table 1.1 Comparison of Social Movement Unionism in Late-industrializing (1) and Industrialized Countries (2)

	Late-industrializing Countries (1) (authoritarian developmental states)	Industrialized Countries (2)
Seeking broad goals	Yes	Yes
Forming coalitions with social movement organizations	Yes	Yes
Extra-institutional tendency	Yes	Yes
SMU's relations with the institutionalization of IR	Pre-institutionalized stage	De-institutionalized stage
Target of struggles	Management + Negative aspects of authoritarian developmental state	Management + Negative aspects of Neoliberal globalization
Relationship between unions and social movement organizations	Unions playing 'vanguardist' role in coalitions with social movement organizations	Unions and social movement organizations on a relatively equal footing
Workers involved in labour movement oriented toward SMU	Semi-skilled male workers in metal industries	Non-regular, precariously-employed workers, esp. those engaging in low-paid service sector jobs

For example, Isaac and Christiansen argued that newly-developed social movements may have 'militancy spillover and penetration' effects on 'a mature, institutionalized movement' (Isaac and Christiansen 2002: 726). According to them, some trade unions in the United States in the 1960s, particularly those in the public sector, came under the radicalizing influence of civil rights movements and adopted SMU-oriented policies (Isaac and Christiansen 2002).

Different Stances on the Nature of Social Movement Unionism

Although there are common features in definitions of social movement unionism, i.e., broad goals, coalition-building between labour and social movements and extra-institutional tendencies, we notice researchers take different stances on the nature of labour-social movements/labour-community coalitions and on the nature of mobilization of union members. Concerning the nature of coalitions, one group of researchers characterizes SMU basically as a class-based movement against authoritarian or neoliberal capitalist states. They posit that labour movements should play a 'vanguard' role in coalitions with social movements, build a stronger relationship among coalition partners based on 'a class vision' and 'imprint' demands of community-based groups 'with a distinct class character' (Frege et al. 2004: 141–2; Seidman 1994: 276; Moody 1997: 276). Some are even critical of the concept of SMU itself because they take SMU to mean that trade unions formed coalitions with 'post-materialist' new social movements and thus weaken their class-orientations (Schiavone 2007: 378; Upchurch and Mathers 2011). Another group of researchers, based on the assumption that the power of trade unions has been considerably weakened under neoliberal globalization, regarded support from social and community-based movements as a necessary condition for union revitalization and consider the relationship between the two movements as being more or less equal. They are concerned with more practical issues of how to sustain durable and effective coalitions (Waterman 1999; Frege et al. 2004: 139–41; Tattersall 2005, 2010).

Researchers also have different views on the nature of the mobilization of union members: whether initiatives of mobilizations should be taken by rank-and-file members or union leaders. Kim Voss points out that 'social movement unionism in the US is evolving into two separate models', 'worker-centered unionism' and 'leverage-centered unionism'. The former 'focuses on individual empowerment and deliberative democracy', while the latter 'stresses building enough associational power within the union to make economic democracy viable' (Voss 2010: 371). Advocates of 'worker-centered unionism' had strong distrust of top-down, bureaucratically-operated union organizations as quintessential characteristics of business unionism (Moody 1997; Schenk 2003; Clawson 2003).

Advocates of 'leverage-centered unionism' recognize the importance of rank-and-file mobilization, but argue that such mobilization should be coordinated by union leadership, if unions exercise organizational power vis-à-vis management and states. These researchers regarded top-down and bottom-up approaches not as 'strategic alternatives'. Rather, they regard these approaches as 'contradictory elements in any route to union revival' or as complementary union strategies that should be effectively combined (Hyman 2004: 344; Milkman 2006: 153). Some take a clearer stance that strong initiatives should come from union leaders, at least under certain institutional environment. Kim Voss argues that, in the United States with employers' strong anti-union attitudes and institutional arrangements hostile to trade unions, 'skilled leadership and sophisticated research in union organizing' are required to implement SMU-oriented union strategies (Voss 2010: 379).

In comparing characteristics of social movement unionism between late-industrializing and industrialized countries, previous studies suggest that SMU-oriented unions in the former countries are more likely to adopt 'vanguardist' approaches to coalitions with social and community-based movements than those in the latter countries. The difference in the tendency can be explained by the relative strength of trade unions in their respective struggles against authoritarian, developmental and neoliberal states. As suggested by previous studies of SMU in South Africa and Brazil, trade unions that lead workplace- and community-based struggles have been unions of semi-skilled workers in metal industries that held 'strategic positions' in both labour-management and labour-state relations and have had more mobilizing capacity than other organizations (Seidman 1994; von Holdt 2002, 2003; Webster 1988).[3] This contrasts with the situations in industrialized countries where neoliberal globalization has considerably weakened the economic and political power of labour movements.

3 It should be noted that von Holdt does not necessarily support 'the vanguardist' approach of SMU. He rather characterizes the relationship between trade unions and community-based popular movements as 'an interpenetration of movements, a complex and dynamic network of political, community and workplace struggles' connected by 'a discourse of national liberation struggle' (von Holdt 2003: 147–8).

Table 1.1 (above) summarizes similarities and differences in SMU in late-industrializing and industrialized countries.

Where are cases of SMU in Korea located in the two different types of SMU outlined in Table 1.1? Previous studies have treated the militant Korean labour movement since the mid-1980s as a typical case of social movement unionism in late-industrializing countries (Seidman 1994; Moody 1997). Militant labour disputes fought by semi-skilled workers in manufacturing industries in the Great Worker Struggle in 1987 laid the foundation for the movement of independent and democratic trade unions (see a discussion of the context of SMU in Korea below). Researchers such as Hagen Koo, however, argue that Korean trade unions are different from their counterparts in South Africa and Brazil, because Korean unions did not develop relationships with community-based movements but were mainly concerned with 'their factory-specific problems' such as the improvement of workers' status within enterprises (Koo 2001: 204–5). Thus, it is more appropriate to consider Korean SMU as having the characteristics of SMU in industrialized countries, especially when we examine the movement of non-regular and women workers after the IMF crisis in the late 1990s that developed outside the mainstream unions of semi-skilled workers in manufacturing industries.

We should not overlook, however, the legacy of social movements against the authoritarian state prior to the mid-1980s on the development of SMU in a later period. Labour and student activists who had fought against the authoritarian regime later supported the movement of disadvantaged workers under neoliberal reform (Chun 2009). Another point to note is the development of SMU in Korea is not necessarily associated with a 'de-institutionalized stage' of industrial relations. Industrial relations in the post-authoritarian period did not develop into well-established institutions. While unions of large *chaebol* firms established relatively stable relations with management in the 1990s, labour, management and the state were unable to reach a formal or quasi-formal class compromise on which industrial relations could be institutionalized, as in the case of other industrialized countries. Before institutionalization based on class compromise was achieved, the Korean economy came under the strong pressure of neoliberal globalization.

Theoretical Issues of Social Movement Unionism

This chapter raises three theoretical issues inadequately addressed in previous studies of social movement unionism. First, while previous studies were mainly concerned with examining conditions under which particular unions adopted SMU-oriented strategies and/or whether such strategies were successful in organizing the unorganized (Bronfenbrenner and Juravich 1998; Voss and Sherman 2000; Lopez 2004), they did not closely consider the extent to which SMU presents a country's labour movement with viable revitalization strategies. In the case of industrialized countries, does SMU offer viable alternatives to stagnant unions embedded in industrial relations institutions, or is SMU relegated to a minority of unions that organize non-regular and precariously employed workers? If the influence of SMU remains limited, what factors prevent its spread, and what strategies can unions and their allies take to overcome these factors? Forces outside and inside the labour movement constrain the influence of SMU. For example, extra-institutional tendencies promote SMU-oriented unions to adopt unconventional strategies and tactics in confrontation with management and states, which in turn provoke 'hostility on the part of economic and political elites' (Robinson 2000: 113–14). Institutional factors inside the labour movement may also prevent the spread of SMU among a majority of unions. Ruth Milkman, in her study of the labour movement in Los Angeles, argues that the unions originally affiliated with the American Federation of Labor (AFL) were more likely to adopt SMU-oriented strategies than those originally affiliated with the Congress of Industrial Organizations (CIO) because former AFL unions, less constrained by existing institutional arrangements, are able to adopt more innovative organizing strategies than the institutionally-embedded former CIO unions (Milkman 2006).[4] Her study suggests the uneven

4 According to Milkman, since former AFL unions had experienced the pre-institutionalized stage of industrial relations (i.e., the period prior to 'the establishment of the NLRB and the broader New Deal regulatory framework'), they were able to make flexible responses to the hostile environments due to the de-institutional stage of industrial relations (i.e., the decline of New Deal framework) by adopting

spread of SMU-oriented unions is due to 'organizational inertia' or the path-dependency of unions' historical origins (see Martin and Dixon 2010: 100).[5] Other studies of US SMU similarly point out its limited impact on the labour movement due to unions' internal constraints. According to Rick Fantasia and Kim Voss, in 2004, only six national unions (SEIU, HERE, UNITE, CWA, AFSCME and the higher-education division of the UAW) out of the sixty-five unions affiliated with AFL-CIO were committed to SMU-oriented strategies, and 'resistance [was] also strong within both local and national unions [including these six unions], where many leaders and members remain bound to a business union model and "servicing" mentality that it creates' (Fantasia and Voss 2004: 133–4, 206).

Second, previous studies on social movement unionism (in industrialized countries) have tended to focus on cases in the United States (and to a lesser extent in Canada and Australia), based on an implicit assumption that a set of social contexts unique to these Anglophone countries, such as relatively active civil societies and large-scale influxes of migrant workers, promoted the development of SMU. Although there are some important exceptions (Chun 2009), previous studies have not extended their analytical scope to cases in 'non-Western' countries, nor have they developed cross-national, comparative frameworks comprehensive enough to cover these countries. As mentioned in the introduction to this chapter, and as chapters in this volume will show, some sectors of labour movements in non-Western LME countries, including Japan and Korea, have adopted SMU-oriented strategies to cope with the negative impact of globalization and neoliberal policies on workers and their movements even under social, political and institutional contexts different than those of Anglophone countries. We should also note cross-national variations

---

innovative strategies such as region-based organizing. Former CIO unions, having experiencing union growth only within the New Deal framework, remained embedded in the increasingly perfunctory institutions of industrial relations, rigidly sticking to the conventional strategy of workplace-based organizing (Milkman 2006).

5 Milkman, however, gives a rather optimistic view of the spread of SMU due to the shift of the main force of the labour movement in the United States from former CIO unions to former AFL unions.

among LME countries: SMU-oriented unions differ in such aspects as their organizational forms, their repertoire of collective action, the way they form coalitions with social/community-based movements, their relationships with mainstream labour movements and their effectiveness in articulating demands to management and states.

Third, related to the second issue, previous studies have associated the development of SMU with macro contexts such as neoliberal globalization, deregulation and anti-labour state policies (Robinson 2000; Clawson 2003) but have not elaborated how these contexts are mediated by meso-level factors. To make a systematic explanation of the cross-national variations of SMU, we need to explain in more detail how meso-level factors mediate between the macro contexts and nationally specific forms of SMU. Meso-level factors include legal and institutional contexts of industrial relations, the extent of union incorporation into the dominant structures at firm and state levels, strategic choices of union leaders, the relationships between labour movements and political parties, the state of civil society, especially the availability of social movement partners that can form coalitions with unions and the extent ethnic, gender and other forms of social discriminations are superimposed on labour market polarization along the core-periphery divide.

Outline of Chapters

Part One of this volume (Chapters 2 to 4) is concerned with the first theoretical issue of SMU: the extent to which social movement unionism influences a country's labour movement. In Chapter 2, Jennifer Jihye Chun theoretically discusses 'the limits and possibilities of innovative forms of labour contention', particularly those based on symbolic leverage and public drama. Chun's discussions draw on Charles Tilly's theory of popular contention, which is rather pessimistic about the occurrence of 'repertoire innovation', and William Sewell's agency-based analysis of structures 'in terms of the relationship between schemas and resources', which is more optimistic about structural changes. She argues that while 'workers located at the margins of the economy and society' adopted innovative forms of labour contention based on symbolic leverage in the United States and Korea, these worker struggles have been marked by obstacles and difficulties, i.e., the reestablishment in the United States of service model unionism that allocates resources to 'top-down, strategic organizing' and in Korea the resistance and criticism of innovative forms of labour contentions by unions of regular workers.

In Chapter 3, Akira Suzuki examines social movement unionism in Japan in the context of industrial relations institutions dominated by cooperative enterprise unions. Suzuki shows that individually-affiliated unions (community unions) that organize workers not covered by the mainstream enterprise unions have characteristics of social movement unionism. He argues that, although there are possibilities that a fusion of labour and livelihood issues will promote future development of community unions, these SMU-oriented unions have not had much impact on the labour movement as a whole, not only due to the small-scale human and financial resources of community unions but also because of resistance to community unions within the labour movement, particularly from mainstream, cooperative enterprise unions.

Joohee Lee's contribution in Chapter 4 examines the 'exceptional' case of the enterprise unions of E-land Group (the New Core enterprise union and the E-land general union) which engaged in prolonged struggles against the dismissals of non-regular workers. These unions built solidarity between regular and non-regular workers based on socio-economic similarities and a shared sense of injustice and fought, with the support of political and social movement organizations, a 17-month long labour dispute. Lee, however, argues that social movement unionism, as exemplified by the E-land unions' struggles against neoliberal restructuring, is unlikely to spread in the Korean labour movement as a whole due to the deep-rooted divide between regular and non-regular workers and the indifference of regular workers' unions to discrimination against non-regular and in-house subcontract workers.

Part Two of this volume (Chapters 5 and 6) is concerned with cross-national comparisons of SMU. Nobuyuki Yamada makes a preliminary attempt in Chapter 5 to compare systematically social movement unionism in the United States and Japan based on six variables of union revitalization (subjects, organizations, tactics, industries, directionality and policy). In applying these variables to the SMU in the two countries, Yamada asks the following questions: whether there have been changes in leaders and primary actors in the labour movements, whether organizations of unions/labour movements have expanded and gone through internal transformations, whether unions have adopted innovative organizing tactics, whether unions have taken community- and/or global-oriented strategies and how unions articulate their political interests at the national and local levels.

In Chapter 6, Minjin Lee, using the conceptual framework of community unionism, compares three individually-affiliated unions (community unions) in Japan and three regional general unions in Korea. Community unionism and social movement unionism have many characteristics in common, for example, seeking broad goals and coalition-building with social movements, but the former emphasizes community-based organizing and involvement in community-related issues more than the latter. In comparing community unionism in Japan and Korea, Lee argues that regional general unions in Korea are closer to the cases of community unionism in other industrialized countries (e.g., the United States, Canada, Australia) than community unions in Japan because the former are more active in community-related issues and coalition-building with social movement organizations.

Part Three of this volume (Chapters 7 to 11) addresses the third theoretical issue of SMU: how meso-level factors mediate the macro contexts of neoliberal globalization/labour market deregulation and specific SMU forms. Stephanie Luce analyses four case studies in Chapter 7 of the limitations and challenges faced by labour-community coalitions in the United States. Labour-community coalitions have been formed in more than 100 cities and have achieved living wage ordinances and other legislation and public policies benefitting workers, their families and local residents in general. Luce points out, however, that labour-community coalitions have internal challenges, such as coalition partners coming together on minimally agreeable issues (the 'least common denominator' issue), the historically-rooted distrust of African-American communities toward labour unions and the issue of leader-driven coalitions with weak rank-and-file involvement, as well as the external challenges of economic constraints and constraints imposed by state and federal politics. She argues that coalition partners need to engage in debates to work out 'an alternative "counter narrative"' to neoliberal ideologies so that coalitions can build 'larger movements and deeper power'.

Charles Weathers compares the relationships between labour movements and political parties in the United States, Australia and Japan in Chapter 8. He shows that, although labour movements in the three countries scored victories from 2007 to 2009 in electoral campaigns in support of the political parties with which they have long been allied, they adopted different political strategies. While unions in the United States and Australia adopted SMU-oriented strategies in electoral campaigns, major unions in Japan, being embedded in 'corporate and policymaking realms', took a 'technocratic' approach toward union-party relations. Moreover, even with the strong presence of major unions in the DPJ- (Democratic Party of Japan) led government, the unions have not been able to realize major pro-labour policies. He also shows the union-party relations varied across countries: the union-party relationship in Australia was more distant than in the United States and Japan.

In Chapter 9, Koshi Endo examines how gender-based discrimination against women workers in Japanese firms promoted the development of women's labour NGOs (commonly called NPOs [not-for-profit organizations] in Japan) outside male-dominated enterprise unions that were indifferent to gender issues. Taking the Working Women's Network (WWN) and its predecessors as examples of such NPOs, Endo shows how they fought to eliminate discrimination against women in pay and promotions by making appeals to a UN committee on gender equity and by supporting nine women workers who sued their employers (three Sumitomo companies). He notes that the nine women litigants supported by WWN won settlements in their favour without any cooperation from the enterprise unions to which these workers belonged.

Heiwon Kwon's contribution in Chapter 10 analyses the strategic capacities of unions fighting against the privatization and restructuring of the public sector in post-IMF-crisis Korea. Focusing on the case of the Korean Railway Workers' Union (KRWU), Kwon shows that, despite the inhospitable institutional contexts, the KRWU succeeded in preventing the privatization of the railroad because it exercised three kinds of strategic capacities: internal mobilization of union members; leadership skills to take advantage of political opportunity structures and coalition-building; and joint struggles with other public-sector unions, political parties and social movement organizations.

Hirohiko Takasu provides a detailed examination of the historical development and current state of region-based amalgamated unions in Japan in Chapter 11. He shows that the Japanese labour movement addressed issues associated with the dual structure of labour markets, first organizing workers in SMEs into region-based amalgamated unions from the mid-1950s to the mid-1970s, then organizing non-regular workers into a new type of region-based amalgamated union (community unions) since the early 1980s and into amalgamated unions established by the national confederations (regional unions and local unions) since the mid-1990s. He shows the challenges amalgamated unions (community, regional and local unions) currently face include limited financial resources, over-reliance on the activities of dedicated organizers, and difficulties in the generational succession of organizers.

The Historical Background and Context of Social Movement Unionism in Japan, Korea and the United States

Japan

The dominant characteristic of industrial relations in Japan is enterprise-based, cooperative labour-management relations. Enterprise unions, the dominant form of union organization, cooperate with management on improving productivity and increasing firm competitiveness. Cooperative industrial relations were firmly established from the late 1960s to the mid-1970s, especially among large firms in key export-oriented industries in the private sector such as steel, electronics, automobile and shipbuilding industries. Although some union members have been critical of cooperative labour-management relations and have advocated more arm's length relations with management, they have been relegated to minority groups and deprived of opportunities to express their voices, at least within their companies. The stability of enterprise-based industrial relations has been maintained by a system of labour-management consultation at the enterprise level where management has relied on 'mutual-trust' and consulted with union leaders on a wide range of corporate policies. Until the late 1980s, enterprise unions have been able to negotiate wage increases and ensure union members with employment security in the annual *shunto* [spring offensive].

Unions in small- and medium-sized enterprises (SME) and in the public sector, also enterprise-based, have had arm's length relations with management and occasionally engaged in labour disputes throughout the 1970s (especially in the first half of the decade). SME unions often formed solidarity across enterprises at the regional level through affiliations with general amalgamated unions as well as with regional labour councils [*chikuro*] (see Takasu in this volume). Public sector unions maintained militant and politicized stances because their labour rights (especially the right to strike) were restricted by the government. In the late 1970s, SME firms faced strong market pressures and unions chose to cooperate with management to avoid bankruptcies at their firms. Militant public-sector unions, especially those of the Japanese National Railways (JNR), were considerably weakened in the mid-1980s by government policies that divided the JNR into seven privatized railway companies (JRs). The JNR authority instituted hard-line policies that weakened militant JNR unions by refusing to hire active union members in the privatized companies. The establishment of Rengo (Japan Trade Union Confederation) in 1989 brought together ideologically-divided labour confederations under a dominant confederation and symbolized the rise of cooperative enterprise unionism to a hegemonic position in the Japanese labour movement (Weather's chapter in this volume, for example, shows its implications for political action in Japan).

The Japanese economy went into a long-term recession in the early 1990s, as seen in the decline in GDP growth (see Table A.2 in Appendix), and came under the increasing influence of neoliberal globalization.[6] As Japanese firms came under intense pressure to cut the wage bill to stay competitive, they increasingly relied on non-regular workers as a source of inexpensive and flexible labour. Non-regular workers as a percentage of employees increased from 20.2 in 1990 to 29.4 in 2002 to 34.4 per cent in 2010. Women accounted for about 70 per cent of non-regular workers in 1990, 2002 and 2010, while the rate of non-regular women workers in the total of women workers increased from 38.1 per cent in 1990 to 49.3 per cent in 2002 to 53.8 per cent in 2010 (MIAC each year). Government policies to deregulate labour markets also facilitated the rapid increase in non-regular workers. The revision of the Labour Standards Law in 1998, for example, extended the maximum fixed-term employment contract for workers with highly-specialized skills and expertise from one year to three years. The revised Worker Dispatching Law (enacted in 1999) liberalized in principle worker dispatching businesses, which used to be limited to twenty-six types of jobs. The Worker Dispatching Law was revised again in 2003, extending the dispatching period from one year to three years and lifting a ban on dispatching workers to manufacturing jobs. The Labour Standards Law, revised in the same year, extended the maximum fixed-term employment contract to three years in principle (five years for workers with highly-specialized skills and expertise).

Neoliberal globalization and labour market deregulation polices since the 1990s put the labour movement at a disadvantage. The policies brought about a decline in membership and density (see Figure 1.1 below and Tables A.3 and A.4 in the Appendix) and undermined labour's ability to negotiate wage increases and insure member employment security. Large,

6 One indication of neoliberal globalization is relocation of production facilities overseas. An increasing number of manufacturing firms, especially automobile and electronics industries, have relocated their production facilities overseas, undermining the domestic manufacturing base. The overseas production ratio (in terms of Japanese manufacturing firm sales) increased from 7.9 per cent in 1994 to 17.2 per cent in 2009, and the ratios are especially high in the automobile industry (39.3 per cent in 2009) and electronics industry (26.1 per cent in 2009) (METI 2006, 2011).

private-sector, enterprise unions accepted wage restraints and/or wage cuts and redundancy measures such as 'voluntary' retirements of union members but remained deeply embedded in institutionalized, cooperative industrial relations (see Suzuki, Chapter 3, in this volume). Moreover, since enterprise unions were comprised of regular workers at specific firms and were mainly concerned with protecting members' interests, they had little incentive to organize the ever-increasing, non-regular workers. Exceptions were enterprise unions in retail industries, where part-time workers accounted for a majority of the workforce. In the latter industries, some supermarket and department store enterprise unions organized part-time workers with the consent of management, i.e., within the framework of cooperative union-management relations.

Industrial relations institutions in Japan have entered a 'de-institutionalized stage' since the 1990s, at least from the perspective of employers. Mainstream enterprise unions, however, did not share such a perspective and were still committed to the existing institutions. Efforts to organize the unorganized and to reassert 'the movement dimension' of trade unions (see von Holdt 2002), mainly came from outside of mainstream unions, i.e., from individually-affiliated general unions and labour NGOs. Individually-affiliated general unions have a regional structure with members drawn from a number of firms. These unions, variously referred to as 'community unions', 'regional unions', or 'local unions', generally cover workers who fall outside the coverage of enterprise unions, such as part-time and other non-regular workers, workers in small firms, or foreign workers. Nationwide, these unions total around 300, and their size is small, about 290 members on average. They usually organize new members by counselling workers having disputes with employers. After these workers become union members, the unions engage in collective bargaining on members' behalf to resolve disputes. Although they are concerned with broad social issues, such as the poor working conditions of non-regular workers or gender discrimination, and form mutual support networks among themselves, they tend to be inactive in coalition-building with community and social movement organizations. They frequently lack community/social movement partners with which to form coalitions because of the relatively weak state of Japanese civil society (Suzuki 2008). Beside the individually-affiliated general unions, there are small labour NGOs concerned with assisting individual workers who have brought legal actions against employers over gender-based discrimination and other employment issues. These NGOs developed because enterprise unions sided with employers and offered no assistance to the workers involved in legal disputes, even when they were union members. What individually-affiliated unions and labour NGOs have in common is that both seek broad goals such as economic justice for workers and question the legitimacy of enterprise-based industrial relations (see Suzuki, Endo and Takasu in this volume).

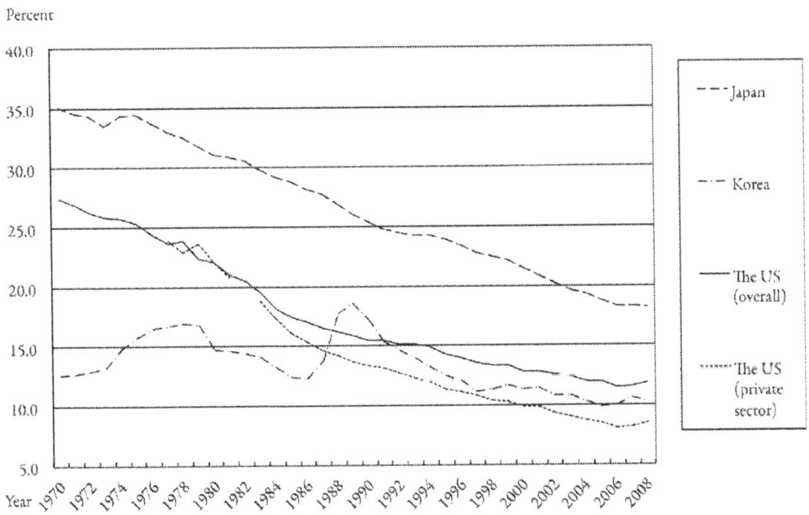

Figure 1.1 Union Density

Korea

The military regimes of Park Chung Hee and Chun Doo Hwan severely repressed unions independent of the control of management and the state in the 1970s and 1980s. The regimes allowed only those unions affiliated with the state-sanctioned FKTU (Federation of Korean Trade Unions), most of whose affiliates were *oyong* (company-controlled) unions that instead of representing workers suppressed them on behalf of employers and the state. It was only after the Great Worker Struggle in 1987, occasioned by the political transition from an authoritarian to democratic state, that the movement of independent and democratic trade unions became fully active; workers either established new independent unions or removed *oyong* union leaders from the union leadership. From 1986 (a year before the Great Worker Struggle) to 1989, the number of unions and union members increased by 297 and 186 per cent, respectively. In the same period, union density increased from 12.3 per cent to 18.6 per cent, the highest density recorded (see Figure 1.1 above and Table A.4 in Appendix). The main force in the movement of independent unions consisted of the enterprise unions at large *chaebol* firms such as Hyundai. Like their Japanese counterparts, Korean unions were formed on the basis of the enterprise, but unlike Japanese unions, they were militant; these unions of male, semi-skilled workers demanded large-scale wage increases, better working conditions and, above all, 'humane treatment and human dignity' through the abolition of 'despotic industrial relations' (Koo 2001: 158–60, 205).

In the 1990s, the movement of independent unions experienced a series of setbacks as the government took repressive measures against militant unions, especially against the newly-established NCTU (the National Congress of Trade Unions, a federation of independent unions of SMEs and their regional councils established in 1990), and as 'new managerial strategies' adopted by large *chaebol* firms met with success in making enterprise unions more pragmatic and accommodative. Moreover, Korean labour laws continued to restrict the activities of independent unions. Labour laws bestowed legitimacy only on unions affiliated with the FKTU by prohibiting multiple unions at the industry and enterprise levels. Despite these difficulties and restrictions, independent trade unions succeeded in establishing their own national confederation, the KCTU (Korean Confederation of Trade Unions), in 1995 through the merger of the NCTU, a federation of large *chaebol* enterprise unions, and a federation of white-collar unions (Koo 2001: 193–7). The prohibition of multiple unions meant the KCTU started as an 'illegal' confederation. It was only after the revision of labour law in 1997 that recognized multiple unions at the industry level that the KCTU attained its legal status.

It was not long after independent unions increased their presence in the Korean labour movement that the Korean economy felt the strong pressure of neoliberal globalization. The Kim Young Sam government (1993–1997) sought to de-regulate labour markets and weaken the power of trade unions. In the absence of opposition party members, the ruling party railroaded through the National Assembly a labour law reform bill 'designed to give more power and flexibility to employers in laying off workers and hiring temporary workers or strike replacements' in late 1996 (Koo 2001: 199). Unions (both KCTU- and FKTU-affiliates) and their allies in civil society mobilized large-scale general strikes (involving about three million workers) to force the government to retract the bill and reintroduce a bill based on democratic procedures. The new labour reform bill passed the National Assembly in March 1997 but was not very different from the original bill fiercely opposed by the labour movement. The new laws recognized multiple unions at the industry level (therefore the legalization of the KCTU), but kept the controversial provisions of granting employers the right to lay off workers (albeit with two years' delay in implementation) and hiring replacement workers during strikes (Koo 2001: 199–200; Gray 2008: 96–8).

The IMF bailout in the late 1997 and the subsequent economic crisis (see Table A.2 in the Appendix for the sudden drop of GDP growth in 1998) added further pressure for neoliberal labour market reforms and brought about a drastic increase in precariously-employed, non-regular workers. The Kim Dae Jung government (1998–2003), through an accord of the newly-established tripartite body and the revision of the Labour Standards Law in February 1998, immediately legalized laying off workers (jettisoning the two year delay in implementation), which led to a drastic increase in the unemployment rate from 2.6 per cent in 1997 to 7.0 per cent in 1998 (see Table A.5 in the Appendix). Women and migrant workers represented a disproportionate share of those workers laid-off early in the economic crisis (Koo 2001: 202; Chun 2009: 39–41).

The number of non-regular workers grew rapidly in the early 1990s and accelerated once the economic crisis was underway. Companies, particularly those in the expanding service sector, reduced the number of regular workers but to secure a flexible labour force and reduce labour costs increased non-regular workers. The proportion of non-regular workers (classified by the government as either temporary or daily workers) increased from 41.8 per cent in 1995 to 51.6 per cent in 1999. Government's labour statistics introduced a new (and more accurate) system of categorizing employment arrangements starting with its 2001 survey. According to the new survey, the proportion of non-regular workers from 2001 to 2009 ranged from 54 to 56 per cent.[7] Analyses of the 2001 and 2008 data show that women accounted for about 51 per cent of non-regular workers in both years, and the proportion of non-regular workers among female workers in 2001 and 2008 was 70.9 per cent and 66.3 per cent, respectively (the corresponding figures for male workers were 45.5 per cent for both years) (Chun 2009: 52; Lee 2010: 121–3). Although the numbers of male and female non-regular workers were almost equal, Yokota (2011) points out that there was a 'gender structure' among non-regular workers because male non-regular workers were concentrated in specialized jobs with relatively stable employment and good working conditions.

The economic crisis weakened the influence of the labour movement. From 1996 to 1998, the number of unions and union members declined by 13 and 12 per cent, respectively. The decline was most pronounced in the SME sector where enterprise unions lost members because they were unable to resist 'corporate restructuring or plant relocation', and some even dissolved because of company bankruptcies. The impact of the economic crisis on enterprise unions of large *chaebol* firms was limited, but these unions became more inward looking as their main concerns shifted to

7 Non-regular workers under the new system of categorizing employment arrangements include temporary workers, part-time workers, on call workers, independent contractors, dispatched workers, subcontracted workers and at home workers. The Korean government and trade unions use different definitions in calculating the proportion of non-regular workers: while the government treats temporary workers employed over long-term periods as regular workers, trade unions regard these workers as non-regular workers. Thus, the proportion of non-regular workers calculated by the government is lower than that calculated by trade unions. For example, the proportion of non-regular workers in 2001 calculated by the government and trade unions were 26.8 per cent and 55.7 per cent, respectively. The proportions and numbers of non-regular workers used in this chapter are those calculated by trade unions (see Joohee Lee in this volume; Lee 2010: 121).

'the immediate problems of protecting jobs and preventing wage cuts for their own members' (Koo 2001: 159, 203). The retreat of the labour movement under the impact of the economic crisis made union leaders at the national level realize the limits of enterprise-based unions in coping with critical situations such as corporate restructuring, mass unemployment and the rapid increase in non-regular workers. Thus, both the KCTU and FKTU put forward the transformation of union structures into industrial unions as their official policy goal. In the case of the KCTU, two industrial-level federations transformed themselves into industrial unions in the late 1990s and early 2000s: the Korea Health and Medical Workers Union (KHMWU) and the Korea Metal Workers Union (KMWU) were established in 1998 and 2001, respectively. The labour movement, in promoting industrial unionism, aimed not only to consolidate organizationally hitherto decentralized union structures but also to organize the unorganized, especially non-regular workers (Im 2006: 3–5). In other words, the Korean labour movement adopted the construction of industrial unions as a major strategy for union revitalization.

The industrial union strategy, however, was unsuccessful in building solidarity between regular and non-regular workers or in overcoming the 'plant egotism' of union members in large *chaebol* firms. For example, enterprise unions in large auto manufacturing companies, including in Hyundai Motor Company (HMC), dissolved themselves and joined their industrial union (the KMWU) in 2006, but remained *de facto* enterprise unions as enterprise-based locals (Kim 2007; Park 2006). Moreover, non-regular workers have been regarded as 'an expendable, buffer labour force' and have faced social discrimination from regular workers in the workplace. Regular workers often opposed the unionization of non-regular workers as a threat to their relatively superior working conditions and employment security (Kim 2007; Lee and Frankel 2004; Gray 2008: 491). Thus, trade unions, especially enterprise unions (or enterprise-based locals) in large *chaebol* firms, came under public criticisms due to their allegedly 'self-centred' orientations. Social (civic) movement organizations concerned with broad, social issues distanced themselves from the labour movement because they regarded trade unions as 'self-serving and only seeking private goods within the company' (Shin 2010: 226).

It was outside the mainstream labour movement that efforts to organize non-regular workers developed often with the support of social movement organizations. Social movement unionism in Korea, in other words, developed 'at the margin' of the labour movement, as in the case of its Japanese counterpart. The organizational forms of SMU-oriented unions are also similar to those in Japan: region-based general unions that organize non-regular workers, workers in small firms and women workers. These general unions establish locals at the firm level and promote class- and/or gender-based solidarity across firms. They also accept members on an individual basis, but individually-affiliated members account for a smaller proportion of membership than in the case of community unions in Japan. Examples of SMU-oriented unions include three women's unions,[8] 21 region-based general unions,[9] and unions of workers in 'special forms of employment' (independent contractors) such as a union of educational workers in the private tutoring industry (Chun 2009; Chang and Chae 2004: 444; see also Minjin Lee in this volume). In addition, a small minority of enterprise unions that organize non-regular as well as regular workers and engage in struggles on behalf of non-regular union members are examples of SMU-oriented unions. The New Core Enterprise Union and the E-Land General Union are such SMU-oriented enterprise unions (see Joohee Lee in this volume). The struggles of non-regular workers for economic justice led by SMU-oriented unions are supported by social movement organizations that regarded the rapid increase in non-regular and precariously-employed workers as a serious social problem (Shin 2010). The support of social movement organizations for SMU-oriented unions

8 The three women's unions are the Seoul Women's Trade Union, the National Federation of Women's Trade Unions and the Korean Women's Trade Union (KWTU). The KWTU, with a membership of 6,500 in 10 regional branches and 70 local branches, is the largest and most effective among the three unions (Chun 2009: 91–2).

9 These region-based general unions offer 'umbrella union membership, legal consultation and support to irregular workers without regard to the sort of occupations' and 'set up branches...in small size firms where the number of employees is too small to be organized under the individual enterprise union' (Chang and Chae 2004: 444).

is a legacy of pre-1987 social movements against the authoritarian state. Many of these leaders/activists were former student and labour movement activists in the democratization movement against the authoritarian regime. Although they distanced themselves from the mainstream labour movement and were concerned with non-class issues such as social welfare and consumer rights, their concerns with economic injustice led them to support and/or (re-) join the newly developed movement to expand the rights of non-regular workers (Koo 2001; Kim 2006; Chun 2009; Shin 2010).

Besides the SMU-oriented unions concerned with organizing non-regular workers, public-sector unions, such as those of the national railways and the electric corporation, adopted SMU-oriented strategies. After the IMF crisis, the government adopted policies to restructure and privatize state-run enterprises and public corporations. In response, railway and electrical unions engaged in struggles against the government policies, not only by mobilizing rank-and-file members but also by forming coalitions with other public-sector unions and social movement organizations and re-framing the restructuring and privatization issues as the protection of public goods (Chang and Chae 2004; see Kwon in this volume).

The United States

The labour movement in the United States from the late 1940s to the 1970s had 'a postwar accord' with employers after organized labour's defeat in Congress in the late 1940s. The passage of the Taft-Hartley Act in 1947 depoliticized trade unions and narrowed the sphere of union activities to 'an increasingly insular collective-bargaining regime' (Lichtenstein 2002: 115). Under the accord, employers accepted 'the existence of unions, learning to work with them', while unions 'became bureaucratic staff-driven entities… concerned…to win wage increases for workers and to function as lawyers/social workers who effectively handled grievances [rather than challenging employers by raising issues related to corporate management]' (Clawson 2003: 32). Moreover, the post-war accord was 'a limited and unstable truce, largely confined to a well-defined set of regions [with strong union presence] and industries [key manufacturing industries such as auto and steel]'

(Lichtenstein 2002: 99). Unions in the industrial sector covered by the accord negotiated agreements with employers that brought economic benefits to members that included not only steady wage increases but also 'a private system of social provisions' such as health insurance and additional unemployment compensation (Clawson 2003: 30–1; Fantasia and Voss 2004: 19).[10]

The post war accord was sustained by the superior position of the US economy in international markets, a position eroded in the course of the 1960s and 1970s as Japan and West Germany regained economic power. Employers of unionized firms, especially those in manufacturing, went on the offensive from the late 1970s to the early 1980s to weaken the power of unions, demanding concessions from unions in contract bargaining, shifting major production facilities from unionized plants to non-unionized plants built on greenfield sites in the United States or overseas and adopting whipsaw tactics to play unionized plants against each other or non-unionized plants. Leaders of 'service model' unions in these industries could do little but make concessions in wages and benefits to employers because they had been 'well-schooled in the language of the social contract' and regarded concessions as necessary measures to 'stem the tide of industrial decline' (Fantasia and Voss 2004: 64–5). The government's policies to deregulate domestic-oriented industries, the most noted example of which was the deregulation of the trucking industry in 1980, also put trade unions on the defensive and promoted the de-unionization of those industries (Milkman 2006: 97–8). As the post-war accord between unions and employers disintegrated, overall union density declined, particularly in the private sector (see Figure 1.1 above and Table A.4 in the Appendix).[11]

10 While labour scholars characterize the period of the post-war accord as a period of stable and institutionalized industrial relations, we should note that the level of strikes was higher than that in the post-accord period (since the 1980s) (see Lichtenstein 2002: 136–7).

11 In contrast to the private-sector, union density in the public sector (from the late 1970s to the mid-1980s) remained stable and even slightly increased (in the range of 43–5 per cent).

While many union leaders, particularly those who had been 'well-schooled' in business unionism under the social contract, remained passive in the face of the hostile contexts, some union leaders acted proactively to stem the further decline of the labour movement. The latter leaders, many of whom had been activists in social movements and community organizing movements in the 1960s and 1970s, entered the labour movement 'with experiences in social combat that were utterly foreign to most union staff members and functionaries' (Fantasia and Voss 2004: 116). They introduced, in a top-down manner, innovative strategies aimed to organize low-wage service sector workers outside the institutional routes (i.e., the NLRB elections), as exemplified by the Justice for Janitors campaigns of SEIU. Despite the pros and cons of the top-down decision-making process, research by Kim Voss and Rachel Sherman on local unions showed that 'the presence in the local of staff with social movement experience outside the labor movement' was one of the three factors that fully revitalized locals (Fantasia and Voss 2004; Voss and Sherman 2000: 326; Milkman 2006).[12] The AFL-CIO and some of its affiliates undertook other innovative strategies. 'Union Summer', modelled on 'Freedom Summer' in the 1960s, gave college students opportunities to get involved in organizing campaigns. The Union Cities Program aimed at revitalizing 'the structure and practice of the [country's] six hundred central labor councils (CLCs)'. The latter program also promoted coalitions between trade unions and community groups including 'Jobs with Justice', a group that had been shunned by the previous leadership of the AFL-CIO due to its militancy (Fantasia and Voss 2004: 109–11, 132; Clawson 2003: 43–5).

Labour-community coalitions played an important role not only in providing community-based support for union organizing campaigns but also in promoting the involvement of unions in community-wide issues such as campaigns for living wage ordinances and community benefit agreements (see Luce in this volume). In contrast to the cases of Japan and Korea, where SMU-oriented unions developed forms different than

12 The other two factors were 'the experience of an internal political crisis' in locals and 'support from the international union' for local revitalization efforts (Voss and Sherman 2000: 326).

those of mainstream unions, SMU-oriented unions such as SEIU, CWA, HERE and UNITE emerged within the established labour movement. Union officials and activists with social movement backgrounds worked 'within the very union structures that had long sustained business unionism', trying to 'build a new labor movement within the shell of the old' (Voss and Fantasia 2004: 127; see also Clawson 2003: 43).

Table 1.2 compares the characteristics of social movement unionism in the three countries.

Table 1.2 Comparison of Social Movement Unionism in Japan, Korea and the United States

	Japan	Korea	United States
SMU relations with mainstream unions	SMU developed outside mainstream unions	SMU developed outside mainstream unions (except SMU-oriented public-sector unions)	SMU developed within some established unions
policy orientations of mainstream unions	cooperative enterprise unionism	militant enterprise unionism	business unionism
organizational forms of SMU	individually-affiliated general unions (community unions), labour NGOs	general unions that organize workers across firms, enterprise unions that represent interests of non-regular workers	some locals of SEIU, CWA, HERE and UNITE led by leaders with social movement backgrounds
coalitions between trade unions and community-based and/or social movements	not widespread, coalition partners not widely available	increasing support of social (civic) movement organizations for SMU efforts to improve conditions of non-regular workers	widespread, with wide availability of coalitions partners

Conclusion

This volume aims to expand the geographical scope of comparative studies of social movement unionism by analysing the cases of Japan and Korea as well as the United States. Those labour movements face the common challenge of a decline in their organizational and social power. SMU has sought to organize workers disadvantaged in labour markets by moving beyond the institutional constraints the labour movement faces. The strategies and organizational forms of revitalization vary among the three labour movements. While these efforts developed within some of the established unions in the United States, often in alliances with social movement organizations, such efforts, in the form of small-size region-based trade unions, developed mainly at the margin of the labour movements in Japan and Korea. Although the labour movements in the latter two countries developed relationships with social and civic movement organizations in their revitalization efforts, the Korean labour movement, because of a relatively active Korean civil society, sought to build stronger coalitions with actors than the Japanese labour movement did. Thus, we can argue that there are varieties in the forms and strategies of social movement unionism even among countries exposed to the common pressures of neoliberal globalization and deregulation; likewise, concrete SMU forms and strategies are mediated by various meso-level and country-specific institutional and social factors.

The chapters in this volume examine union revitalization and social movement unionism in Japan, Korea and the United States not through systematic comparisons of SMU but based on the authors' research questions and analytical frameworks This introductory chapter, however, seeks to highlight a broad conceptual framework and set of theoretical issues that can serve as a common baseline for discussions and analyses of issues the chapters in this volume address. This chapter also brings together the two types of SMU that have been discussed separately in previous studies, i.e., SMU in late-industrializing and industrialized countries, into a single conceptual framework, and associates those two types of SMU with pre-institutionalized and de-institutionalized stages of industrial relations, respectively. Based on this framework, we observe that the characteristics of

SMU in Korea are closer to those in industrialized countries than to those in late-industrializing countries. Although such a broad framework may be criticized for being too sweeping to make cross-national comparisons grounded in unique historical and sociopolitical contexts, the framework is a starting point for further cross-national studies of SMU and union revitalization whose geographical scope is broader than that covered by this volume.

References

Bronfenbrenner, K., Juravich, T. (1998). 'It Takes More Than House Calls: Organizing to Win with a Comprehensive Union-Building Strategy'. In K. Bronfenbrenner, S. Friedman, R.W. Hurd, R.A. Oswald, R.L. Seeber (eds), *Organizing to Win: New Research on Union Strategies*. Ithaca, NY: ILR Press.

Chang, D., Chae, J. (2004). 'The Transformation of Korean Labour Relations Since 1997', *Journal of Contemporary Asia*, 34 (4), 427–48.

Chun, J.J. (2009). *Organizing at the Margins: The Symbolic Politics of Labor in South Korea and the United States.* Ithaca, NY: Cornell University Press.

Clawson, D. (2003). *The Next Upsurge: Labor and the New Social Movements.* Ithaca, NY: ILR Press.

Cornfield, D.B., McCammon, H.J. (eds) (2003). *Labor Revitalization: Global Perspectives and New Initiatives.* Oxford: Elsevier Ltd.

Fairbrother, P., Yates, C.A.B. (eds) (2003). *Trade Unions in Renewal: A Comparative Study.* London: Continuum.

Fantasia, R., Kim, V. (2004). *Hard Work: Remaking the American Labor Movement.* Berkeley: University of California Press.

Frege, C.M., Kelly, J. (eds) (2004). *Varieties of Unionism: Strategies for Union Revitalization in a Global Economy.* Oxford: Oxford University Press.

Gray, K. (2008). *Korean Workers and Neoliberal Globalization.* New York: Routledge.

Hyman, R. (2004). 'Union Renewal: A View from Europe', *Labor History*, 45 (3), 340–7.

Im, Y. (2006). 'Kankoku ni okeru Sanbetsu Roso Kensetsu Undo: Seika to Kadai' (Achievements and Problems of the Movement to Establish Industrial Unions in Korea), *Ohara Shakai Mondai Kenkyujo Zasshi*, 573, 1–12.

Isaac, L., Christiansen, L. (2002). 'How the Civil Rights Movement Revitalized Labor Militancy', *American Sociological Review*, 67 (5), 722–46.

Kim, D. (2006). 'Growth and crisis of the Korean Citizens' Movement', *Korean Journal*, 46 (2), 99–128.

Kim, W. (2007). 'Gendai Jidosha Rodo Kumiai no Sangyoroso eno Tenkan ga Imisurumono' (Significance of the Transformation of the HMC Union into an Industrial Union), *Konodai Keizai Kenkyu*, 18 (3), 73–189.

Koo, H. (2001). *Korean Workers: the Culture and Politics of Class Formation*. Ithaca, NY: Cornel University Press.

Lee, B. (2010). 'Hiseiki Rodo no Genjo to Kadai' (The Current State and Problems of Non-Regular Workers). In J. Woo (ed.), *Kankoku no Keiei to Rodo*. Tokyo: Nihon Keizai Hyoronsha.

Lee, B., Frankel, S.J. (2004). 'Divided Workers: Social Relations Between Contract and Regular Workers in a Korean Auto Company', *Work, Employment and Society*, 18 (3), 507–30.

Lopez, S. (2004). *Reorganizing the Rust Belt: An Inside Study of the American Labor Movement*. Berkeley: University of California Press.

Lichtenstein, N. (2002). *State of the Union: A Century of American Labor*. Princeton: Princeton University Press.

Luce, S. (2004). *Fighting for a Living Wage*. Ithaca, NY: Cornell University Press.

Martin, A., Dixon, M. (2010). 'Changing to Win? Threat, Resistance, and the Role of Unions in Strikes, 1984–2002', *American Journal of Sociology*, 116 (1), 93–129.

METI (Ministry of Economy, Trade and Industry). (various years). *Kaigai Jigyo Katsudo Kihon Chosa* (Basic Survey on Overseas Business Activities). Tokyo: METI.

MIAC (Ministry of Internal Affairs and Communications). (various years). *Rodoryoku Chosa* (Labour Force Survey). Tokyo: MIAC.

Milkman, R. (2006). *L.A. Story: Immigrant Workers and the Future of the U.S. Labor Movement*. New York: Russell Sage Foundation.

Moody, K. (1997). *Workers in a Lean World: Unions in the International Economy*. London: Verso.

Park, C. (2006). 'Keizai Kiki Ikono Kankoku Roshi Kankei' (Labour Relations in Korea after the Economic Crisis), *Ohara Shakai Mondai Kenkyujo Zasshi*, 572, 17–32.

Robinson, I. (2000). 'Neoliberal Restructuring and U.S. Unions: Toward Social Movement Unionism?', *Critical Sociology*, 26 (1–2), 109–38.

Schenk, C. (2003). 'Social Movement Unionism: Beyond the Organizing Model'. In P. Fairbrother, C.A.B. Yates (eds), *Trade Unions in Renewal: A Comparative Study*. London: Continuum.

Schiavone, M. (2007). 'Social Movement Unions and Political Parties (in South Africa and the Philippines): A Win-Win Situation?', *African and Asian Studies*, 6 (4), 373–93.

Seidman, G.W. (1994). *Manufacturing Militance: Workers' Movements in Brazil and South Africa, 1970–1985*. Berkeley: University of California Press.

Shin, K. (2010). 'Globalisation and the Working Class in South Korea: Contestation, Fragmentation and Renewal', *Journal of Contemporary Asia*, 40 (2), 211–29.

Suzuki, A. (2008). 'Community Unions in Japan: Similarities and Differences of Region-based Labour Movements between Japan and Other Industrialized Countries', *Economic and Industrial Democracy*, 29 (4), 492–520.

Tattersall, A. (2010). *Power in Coalition: Strategies for Strong Unions and Social Change*. Ithaca, NY: ILR Press.

Tattersall, A. (2005). 'There is Power in Coalition: A Framework for Assessing How and When Union-Community Coalitions Are Effective and Enhance Union Power', *Labour & Industry*, 16 (2), 97–112.

Turner, L. (2005). 'From Transformation to Revitalization: A New Research Agenda for a Contested Global Economy', *Work and Occupations*, 32 (4), 383–99.

Upchurch, M., Mathers, A. (2011). 'Neoliberal Globalization and Trade Unionism: Toward Radical Political Unionism?', *Critical Sociology*, 37 (5), 1–16.

Von Holdt, K. (2003). *Transition from Below: Forging Trade Unionism and Workplace Change in South Africa*. Cape Town: University of Kwazulu Natal Press.

Von Holdt, K. (2002). 'Social Movement Unionism: The Case of South Africa', *Work, Employment and Society*, 16 (2), 283–304.

Voss, K. (2010). 'Democratic Dilemmas: Union Democracy and Union Renewal', *Transfer: European Review of Labour and Research*, 16 (3), 369–82.

Voss, K., Sherman, R. (2000). 'Democratic Dilemmas: Union Democracy and Union Renewal', *American Journal of Sociology*, 106 (2), 202–49.

Waterman, P. (1999). 'The New Social Unionism: A New Union Model for a New World Order'. In M. Ronaldo, P. Waterman (eds), *Labour Worldwide in the Era of Globalization: Alternative Union Models in the New World Order*. New York: Palgrave Macmillan.

Webster, E. (1988). 'The Rise of Social-movement Unionism: The Two Faces of the Black Africa'. In P. Frankel, N. Pines, M. Swilling (eds), *State, Resistance and Change in South Africa*. London: Croom Helm.

Webster, E., Lambert, R., Bezuidenhout, A. (2008). *Grounding Globalization: Labour in the Age of Insecurity*. Hoboken, NJ: Wiley-Blackwell.

Yokota, N. (2011). '1990-nendai Iko no Kankoku ni okeru Josei Rodo no Hiseikika to Genda Kozo' (Non-Standardization of the Labour Force and Its Gender Structure in Korea Since the 1990s), *Ohara Shakai Mondai Kenkyujo Zasshi*, 632, 18–39.

PART ONE

The Impact of Social Movement Unionism on Existing Labour Movements

JENNIFER JIHYE CHUN

2 The Power of the Powerless: New Schemas and Resources for Organizing Workers in Neoliberal Times

The struggles of workers located at the margins of the economy and society have thrust the issue of social justice to the forefront of labour movements around the world. In perhaps the most well-known case, janitors, many of whom are immigrants, people of colour and women employed in low-paid, precarious and subcontracted jobs in the United States, have successfully organized under the morally-charged banner, 'Justice for Janitors' (not 'compensation for custodians' as Rudy Preston (2004) puts it). Socially disadvantaged workers in other low-paid occupations such as homecare aides, hotel cleaners, nursing care workers, security guards and domestic workers have also joined organized labour's ranks, highlighting the overlapping nature of economic struggles with 'struggles for recognition' – that is, symbolic-cultural struggles aimed at revaluing the identities and worth of devalued groups in society (Fraser 1995). Across the Pacific, the struggles of workers in the rapidly growing *pijonggyujik* [non-standard employment] sector, many of whom are women in low-paid work, have made the poor, the excluded and the marginalized increasingly central to the aims and concerns of the Korean labour movement. No longer willing to accept the stigma and chronic poverty associated with work on the 'lowest rungs of the social hierarchy', some of the most invisible and unexpected groups of workers have joined unions and engaged in workplace strikes and street protests. This includes golf caddies, home study tutors and truck drivers misclassified as independent contractors; assembly workers, hotel room cleaners, cafeteria workers and train attendants employed in triangulated subcontracting arrangements; and telephone operators and cashiers hired under fixed short-term contracts.

The colourful and dramatic struggles of some of the most vulnerable, as opposed to the most powerful, segments of the working-class have captivated the interests of a new generation of labour scholars. A cursory survey of books published over the past decade, particularly in US labour studies, reveals the depth and breadth of new areas of inquiry. Book monographs and edited volumes chronicle new union tactics and strategies to 'organize the unorganized' (Delgado 1993; Bronfenbrenner et al., eds, 1998; Milkman, ed., 2000; Turner, Katz and Hurd, eds, 2001; Clawson 2003; Lopez 2004; Fantasia and Voss 2004; Milkman and Voss, eds, 2004; Milkman 2006). Labour scholars have researched the development of alternative organizational forms and practices for advancing the interests of working people such as living wage campaigns (Luce 2004), worker centres (Fine 2006), regional labour councils (Dean and Reynolds 2009) and transnational networks and campaigns (Brooks 2007; Seidman 2007). Interest in studying new labour struggles, especially those involving migrants and women in precarious employment, has also burgeoned in other countries, including Australia (Tattersall 2010; Webster, Lambert and Beziudenhout 2009), Canada (Choudry et al. 2009; Basok 2009), England (Wills 2001, 2005), Japan (Suzuki 2010), South Korea (Chun 2009; Gray 2008) and South Africa (Webster and Von Holdt, eds, 2005; Von Holdt and Webster 2008).

Paradoxically, burgeoning interest in new forms of labour politics and organization has coincided with the persistent decline of unionism on a national and global scale. In the United States, where studies on union revitalization and new forms of labour organizing have been the most prolific, union membership rates have dwindled from 30.9 per cent in 1960 to 11.4 per cent in 2010. Although the rates of decline vary, union membership rates have also steadily declined in Japan, the United Kingdom and Canada during this period, with the steepest decline in Australia. In South Korea, where we see a growing interest in the struggles of women workers and irregular workers, union density levels dropped from 17.2 per cent in 1990 to 10 per cent in 2010.[1] Alongside these facts and figures, organized

1 Figures taken from OECD Statistics Database. See http://stats.oecd.org/Index.aspx?DataSetCode=UN_DEN (accessed November 30, 2010).

labour has lost political and moral ground. Business groups repeatedly highlight the unsustainable costs of union wages and benefits on corporate profitability and growth in a highly competitive global economy, resulting in a weaker regulatory climate for workers. The broader public also tends to criticize unionized workers for being selfish during strikes and labour disputes, especially when compared to non-union workers who have few benefits and earn lower wages.

How do we understand this paradox – the decline of unions alongside the rise of new labour studies? How do we make sense of the vibrant interest in new forms of labour organizing, especially in relation to marginalized sectors of the workforce, when figures on union membership are at their lowest ebbs in countries as divergent as South Korea and the United States?

One plausible explanation relates to labour studies as a field of knowledge production. Observing similar trends in the subfield of labour history, Charles Bergquist (1993: 758) notes that 'labor historians have always empathized with the democratic struggles of working people' and have endeavoured to write history 'from the bottom up', especially in the face of historic transformations such as the industrial revolution and the rise of market capitalism. This is particularly true for labour sociologists and other critical social scientists that came of age during and after the social movements of the 1960s. For this generation, academic research went hand-in-hand with alternative forms of knowledge production that profiled the everyday struggles of ordinary people fighting for racial, gender and sexual equality, social and political liberation and economic opportunity and advancement.

A related explanation is linked to what Michael Burawoy (2010) describes as the 'false optimism of global labor studies'. Confronting the collapse of state communism and welfare capitalism, left-oriented labour scholars began searching for hopeful examples of resistance against the accelerated drive for capital accumulation and global market integration. Inspired by anti-systemic protests around the world – from the Zapatistas in Mexico to anti-WTO protests in Seattle and Hong Kong, labour scholars began applying Karl Polanyi's critique of market fundamentalism to explain the dynamics of new labour struggles in the neoliberal era. However, by adopting a Polanyian lens which inadequately theorizes the role of the state and capital in suppressing counter-movements, Burawoy argues that global labour studies scholars have tended to overstate the power of local struggles, leaving us with flawed and decontextualized accounts.

While the political inclinations of some labour scholars may partially explain the current paradox in labour studies, the resurgence of interest in workers' struggles is more aptly connected to the shifting dynamics of labour's contentious politics. Rather than traditional scholarship on industrial relations, new labour scholars are exploring transformations occurring at the *periphery* of mainstream labour movements. It is at the outer edges of existing union tactics and strategies that we observe examples of innovation and dynamism. What we find is a concerted effort by a relatively small group of unions and labour activists to expand the conception of labour politics beyond the workplace and beyond narrowly defined labour-management struggles. This includes expanding the organizational terrain of workers' struggles to include students, community organizations and transnational allies and broadening union demands to include basic livelihood and citizenship entitlements. What we also find is growing interest in a new political subject of labour. Rather than narrowly representing the interests of native (male) workers in higher paid trades and manufacturing sectors, new labour struggles include women, immigrants, people of colour, low-paid service workers and precarious workers among others – groups that have been historically excluded from the moral and material boundaries of union membership. While these shifts still remain partial and limited, they are part of a growing effort to prioritize the struggles of workers located at the margins of the economy and society and transform understandings of who and how labour unions should organize the working class (Chun 2009).

Theorizing the Struggles of Workers at the Margins: Charles Tilly and the Dynamics of Popular Contention

The struggles of workers at the margins have the potential to create new horizons of organizational and structural transformation. However, how do we evaluate this potential without exaggerating its broader impact? What frameworks help identify concrete prospects for change while accounting for the extraordinary capacity of ruling institutions and groups to resist change from below?

One approach to addressing these questions is to analyse the spatial and temporary dynamics of workers' struggles at the margins vis-à-vis dominant forms of popular contention. Charles Tilly (1986; 1995) asserts that 'popular contention' encompasses the array of extra-legal tactics that ordinary people utilize to express their grievances and make claims on decision-making authorities. By cultivating new means for influencing political power such as holding public meetings and organizing mass protests, repertoires of popular contention expand the boundaries of politics beyond the formal arena, thereby changing the meaning of politics itself. While such repertoires provide ordinary people with potentially powerful alternatives for challenging power, Tilly emphasizes that its forms and expressions are circumscribed. Most aggrieved individuals and groups draw on a limited set of repertoires when acting collectively and making contentious claims, whether directed at landlords, government officials or employers. This is largely because people 'learn only a rather small number of alternative ways to act collectively' (Tilly 1995: 42). Thus, when innovation occurs, it usually happens at the 'perimeter of the existing repertoire rather than breaking entirely old ways' (Tilly 1995: 44). Consequently, most innovations either fail or disappear in the long-term; the rare few that remain leave traces of their presence such as a 'memory of the interaction' or a 'changed web of relations within and among participating sets of people' (Tilly 1995: 41).

Tilly (1986: 4) attributes the relatively fixed and durable features of collective action practices to the constraining character of the repertoire itself:

> The repertoire actually constrains people's actions; people generally turn to familiar routines and innovate within them, even when in principle some unfamiliar form of action would serve their interests much better.

To put it another way, he argues that the 'prior path of collective claims-making constrains its subsequent forms, influencing the very issues, actors, settings, and outcomes of popular struggle' (1995: 37). Tilly points to France, a country with a history of over four centuries of popular contention, to support his argument about the path-dependent character of repertoires of contention. Despite considerable regional variation and historical change, people across different historical periods and geographic regions have been connected to each other by their use of strikingly similar forms of public protest. Thus, he (1995: 37) emphasizes that we must recognize that

> Struggle has its own partly autonomous history, a history that does not reduce simply to a reflection of the changing organization of production or of the changing structure of state power, a history that in itself influences the organization of production and the structures of state power.

His analysis provides an important starting point for evaluating the struggles of workers at the margins. By acknowledging that repertoires of contention have the capacity to structure other aspects of social life, Tilly emphasizes that repertoires themselves should be acknowledged as separate meaning-making structures, independent from politics and the economy. Repertoire innovation represents exceptional moments when claims-making practices depart from existing norms and create the potential for the assertion of new symbolic understandings and social relations, albeit under considerable constraints. Repertoire reproduction represents historical continuity in the way contentious publics express their grievances and engage in collective action, even in the face of external pressures for change. Given that the dynamics of innovation and reproduction generate internal tension and conflict, examining the shifting dynamics of cultural meanings and practices provides concrete empirical insight into the relationships of power and authority that influence the structure of the repertoire itself.

In the case of new labour struggles, this means recognizing that labour movements do not simply signify the aggregate behaviour of labour unions or even the entire universe of actors and organizations that strive to represent and advance the collective interests of workers. Labour movements represent power-laden structures at multiple scales – from locally-situated relations in the family and community to national and international organizations – that tend to reproduce, rather than transform, existing patterns of labour contention. Thus, at the same time we see innovation and change in the kinds of workers being organized and the strategies being used, we also see a concurrent tendency by social actors who rely on historically- and culturally-entrenched methods for responding to innovation and change.

Towards a Structural Analysis of Repertoires of Labour Contention

Although Tilly's framework provides a useful departure for examining the dynamics of new labour struggles, his relatively static notion of culture hinders our understanding of the dynamic relationship between repertoire innovation and repertoire reproduction. For Tilly, repertoires of contention rarely change because people's everyday understandings and behaviours rarely change. By assuming that the arena of culture is relatively impenetrable to the historical forces of change, he fails to examine the 'structuring' influence of social practices and social relationships. When and under what conditions is innovation possible? What defines the parameters for how local innovation and transformation take place? To more adequately address these questions, we need to identify the mechanisms that both facilitate and suppress alternatives. To do this, I draw on William Sewell's theory of 'structure'.

Sewell (1992; 2005) proposed a framework for analysing structure in terms of the relationship between schemas and resources. Schemas represent a set of cultural understandings and practices that influence how social actors respond to a given situation. In anthropological terms, cultural schemas consist of 'binary oppositions but also various conventions, recipes, scenarios, principles of action and habits of speech and gesture'

(2005: 132). Schemas are 'generalizable' and 'transposable' in the sense that they can be applied to any number of cases outside the context in which they are initially learned, but they are also contingent and creative responses to an infinite and unpredictable range of circumstances (2005: 140–1). Resources represent a combination of both human and non-human elements that can be used to enhance or maintain power, which include everything from physical strength, dexterity, knowledge and emotional commitments to money and technology (2005: 133).

While the application of schemas and their resource consequences are never fixed or entirely predictable, given the elements of human agency, local divergence and historical contingency, Sewell (2005: 137) argues that they can form the basis of historically durable and causal structures in social life:

> If schemas are to be sustained and reproduced over time – and without sustained reproduction they could hardly be counted as structural – they must be validated by the accumulation of resources that the enactment engenders. Schemas not empowered or regenerated by resources would eventually be abandoned and forgotten, just as resources without cultural schemas to direct their use would eventually dissipate and decay. Sets of schemas and resources may properly be said to constitute *structures* only when they mutually imply and sustain each other over time.

Placing the relationship between schemas and cultures at the centre of a concept of structure underscores the importance of agency in explaining structural change. By emphasizing that reproduction is never automatic, Sewell views every new case as an opportunity to either innovate or re-instantiate familiar practices, but he does so by situating agency in the context of mutually constraining sets of schemas and resources. The degree to which schemas and resources influence the organization of structures varies along the dimensions of depth and power. Depth, according to Sewell, reflects the pervasiveness of the schema. Schemas that are applied without thought or purpose are deeply rooted in the organization of structures. Likewise, resources that are allocated without question or reservation to enact particular schemas are usually the product of individuals and organizational agents that are empowered to make such decisions and thus, influence overall patterns of labour contention.

Sewell's framework for analysing structures in terms of schemas and resources provides constructive approaches for studying the limits and possibilities of innovative forms of labour contention. In every workplace dispute there are mutually constraining schemas and resources that influence the course of action. For example, a strike is a schema used by workers and labour unions to respond to a grievance in the workplace. The decision to strike is usually viewed as a way to gain leverage over a belligerent employer, and appropriate resources are allocated to support the enactment of the strike, be they the bodies of actual workers on the picket lines or organizational resources deployed to support striking workers. The power of strikes as a schema gained efficacy historically in the struggles of industrial workers. As industrial workers across different sectors began using their collective power at the point of production to affect employers' business operations and revenue streams, strikes became increasingly common and pervasive. Unions created strike funds and allocated other organizational resources in support of the capacity of workers to strike, which in turn, reinforced the power of strikes as a dominant schema in organized labour's repertoires of contention. The influence of strikes as schemas, however, waned when workers chose not to strike in response to a labour dispute or when unions decided not to support striking workers. Their influence further deteriorated as the legal parameters determining when workers were allowed to strike without incurring sanctions and penalties began to narrow.

In my comparative study of new forms of labour organizing in South Korea and the United States (Chun 2009), I found that strikes – the most familiar schema of working-class resistance – were becoming less central in the struggles waged by immigrant and women workers employed in low-paid, precarious employment.[2] This was largely due to significant shifts in the nature of employment relationships for workers on the bottom rungs of the labour market. Rather than hire workers under full-time contracts, employers were increasingly utilizing non-standard contractual arrangements such as part-time work, temporary agency employment,

2 For detailed empirical discussion of the cases I studied, see Chapters 5 and 6 in *Organizing at the Margins* (Chun 2009).

subcontracted work and independent contracting. As employment relationships became triangulated and structurally ambiguous, striking workers began to face obstacles in achieving their collective demands. It became less clear exactly who represented the target of a strike action when the source of workers' pay came from multiple sources, and it also became less clear what labour rights workers had when they were classified as independent contractors or self-employed workers. These dilemmas were also exacerbated for workers who faced limited mobility in the broader labour market due to inequities based on race, gender, immigration status, education, social networks or age.

The case of subcontracted work is a clear example of the creation of new schemas and resources beyond the industrial strike in organized labour's repertoires of contention. Subcontracting is a business practice in which labour needs are outsourced to an external firm. It is one of the oldest forms of labour exploitation, but it has experienced a rebirth in a wide array of service industries in the context of neoliberal economic restructuring, including the janitorial sector. The practice of subcontracting creates a legal distinction between the entity that pays for and benefits from a particular form of labour and the entity that establishes and manages the terms of compensation. For workers, this means that they are no longer directly employed where and for whom they work. Consequently, subcontracting practices create a new classificatory scheme that complicates how workers can generate leverage during the course of a workplace strike. The subcontracting company may serve as the legal employer-of-record, but it often rejects demands for higher wages and benefits and better working conditions based on the rationale that its labour costs are already fixed in cleaning contracts with customers, and, thus, it has no financial resources to meet union demands. The building owner also commonly rejects responsibility for meeting union demands based on the rationale that it is not the official employer-of-record and, thus, has no legal responsibility to negotiate with the union, even if it is the economic employer and dispenses the funds that indirectly pay workers.

Despite these challenges, various case studies I conducted of janitors' organizing struggles in both South Korea and the United States revealed that unions were not derailed by the barriers to unionism presented by triangulated employment arrangements. Rather, they developed new schemas for shifting the balance of power between workers, subcontracting companies and building owners. Specifically, they waged public dramas to pressure building owners to accept moral responsibility as employers, regardless of whether they were legally liable. While laws often prohibited directly targeting third party entities such as building owners, unions circumvented these barriers by redefining what it meant to be an 'employer' in the eyes of broader publics, rather than the narrow confines of legal interpretation. Unions drew upon an array of material and symbolic resources and social relationships to strengthen the moral authority of their public dramas. They allocated financial resources to hire more organizers and researchers to escalate public dramas. They appealed to the collective morality of past social movement struggles, especially those of socially and economically disadvantaged groups of workers, to undermine more recognized forms of authority, such as university officials or contractual law. Unions also recruited the support of progressive student groups and other labour and community activists to validate the union claims that labour disputes not only represented workplace disputes but broader struggles over what is just and fair in a given community.

In many ways, symbolic leverage is in direct opposition to conventional forms of worker power. Historically, industrial workers have wrested concessions from employers from a place of structural power – due to their strategic position in the economy or in tight labour markets. They have also fought bitterly for the creation of national labour laws and labour market institutions that formally guarantee the power of their collective associations, regardless of employer or region. However, for workers employed in peripheral jobs and sectors *and* excluded from basic labour rights protections, these forms of worker power are no longer sufficient. For these workers, symbolic leverage offers an important alternative: it seeks to overcome the absence of structural power and strengthen the basis of workers' associational power by reclassifying the very nature of the employment relationship in moral and symbolic terms, as well as economic and political terms. In other words, symbolic leverage invokes new schemas and new resources for shifting the balance of power between workers and employers during the course of a collective struggle.

The Dilemmas of Symbolic Leverage

Since the late 1990s, there has been a proliferation of new union struggles that utilize symbolic leverage to attempt to shift the balance of power against employers and the state during the course of a labour dispute. In the current neoliberal climate, perhaps it is no surprise that workers and unions in countries as different as South Korea and the United States have once again resorted to morally-driven, public dramas that are reminiscent of earlier historical periods of working-class insurgency. Like during the pre-New Deal era in the United States and the state-led authoritarian developmental era in Korea, workers are confronted with mounting employer (and state) resistance when they attempt to exercise basic labour rights. The ambiguous and contradictory features of non-standard employment arrangements also complicate the ability of large sections of the workforce from accessing labour protections and benefits, resulting in their exclusion from existing regulatory frameworks. When existing institutional channels for adjudicating workers' grievances are blocked or constrained, the cases that I examined reveal that workers and their collective organizations are innovating their repertoires of contention by developing new schemas and resources aimed at generating more potent forms of symbolic leverage.

While my cases highlighted the empirical and theoretical significance of symbolic leverage in the struggles of workers at the margins, it would be naïve and presumptuous to assume that profound and multi-faceted crises facing organized labour in different countries can be resolved by simply unleashing the power of public dramas. All my cases demonstrate that workers at the margins of society and economy do not have power in the conventional sense. Not only is their ability to exercise basic labour rights commonly disputed on legal and contractual grounds, but their location at the lower tiers of labour market hierarchies exposes them to repeated forms of mistreatment and exploitation that are either all too familiar or tucked away from the public eye. Marginalized workers that face overlapping conditions of economic and social subordination also lack the ability to exercise recognized forms of authority or command resources.

Immigrants in low-paid work, for example, who are often most vulnerable to rights violations and employer abuses, have limited access to political authorities that pass labour legislation or regulate labour standards enforcement. Women workers in South Korea are also a marginalized group and thus face difficulties accessing existing resources in the labour market, in organizations and in the formal political arena.

There have also been numerous examples of new labour struggles in which the appeal to the symbolic dimensions of labour politics has not resulted in union victories. In South Korea, in particular, we have seen many failed examples of public and dramatic struggles as the public protests of irregularly-employed workers has increased over the past decade. Two of the earliest examples include the 516 day struggle of the Korea Telecom Fixed Contract Workers Union and the over two-year fight led by Chun Bong-hui of the KBS Broadcasting Irregular Workers Union to fight discriminatory layoffs. Later examples include protracted struggles waged by the KTX Crew Workers Union and the Kiryung Workers Union – the former which lasted over 1,000 days and the latter which is still on-going and represents the longest continuous worker protest in Korean history. Each of these struggles involved an array of highly symbolic and dramatic tactics and the intensification of such tactics over time; however, they were unable to generate the kind of leverage that could effectively shift the balance of power and result in the reinstatement of protesting workers or the elimination of irregular employment practices.

The risks of waging indefinite symbolic struggles raise profound challenges for individuals and organizations that rely on extra-legal tactics and strategies to challenge unequal power relationships for subordinated social groups such as low-paid and precarious workers. According to Bourdieu (1990: 239–40), differences in the symbolic recognition of dominant versus subordinate actors require that the latter 'wage a symbolic struggle of all against all'. In other words, subordinated workers must wage highly mobilized symbolic struggles to acquire the 'belief, credit, perception and appreciation, knowledge and recognition' to adequately challenge the legitimacy of more recognized authorities such as businesses and universities or the state more generally (Bourdieu 1984: 251–2). This not only entails devoting organizational resources towards supporting workers' symbolic struggles, but it also entails enlisting the participation and support of a broader array of social actors to help recast narrow labour disputes into broader moral battles. Consequently, while it is possible to convert symbolic capital into effective forms of economic capital, it can be an extremely resource- and time-intensive process, especially for subordinated actors that confront belligerent opponents that will not easily be swayed by symbolic struggles or moral arguments. Its power to persuade must also be continually renewed and reinforced in the face of contestation, creating the potential for indefinite resource demands on unions.

Given the intensive nature of waging 'symbolic struggles of all against all,' each new attempt to generate symbolic leverage for subordinated groups of workers exposes the kinds of schemas and resources that are necessary to innovate existing repertoires of contention. While such empirical research needs to be conducted, I briefly outline important trends taking place in the United States and South Korea that highlight the disjunctures between innovating schemas and resources and reinforcing more familiar understandings and practices.

In the case of the United States, the risks of escalating union struggles based on symbolic leverage have generated several tendencies that re-inscribe more familiar practices. First, there has been a tendency to re-establish the model of service-oriented business unionism in the form of top-down, strategic organizing, which maintains a clear gap between union leaders who make decisions about how resources are allocated and decisions are made and rank-and-file members who pay union dues. The growth in union budgets for strategic research, in contrast to member education, is one sign of this tendency. Investment in training educated organizers from outside the labour movement over dues-paying union members is another indication of emphasis on creating a tier of professional leaders in union bureaucracies. Second, unions tend to view their relationships with community organizations and other allies and supporters in an instrumental and one-way fashion. By failing to develop more genuine and reciprocal relationships with broader publics, unions tend to focus on ends over means, which weaken the legitimacy of new schemas based on symbolic leverage. They also privilege material struggles over economic redistribution over more abstract goals such as social solidarity and a more activated civil society. Third, the vast majority of unions continue to prioritize electoral support and political campaigns over movement-oriented strategies that promote oppositional positions against employers and the state. Given the highly unequal terrain of political power in favour of corporations and the private sector in the US, many argue that the focus on the formal political arena has resulted in a continued erosion rather than strengthening of workers' collective power.

Stephen Lerner, architect of the historic Justice for Janitors campaign and a former leader of the Service Employees International Union (SEIU) strongly articulated the need to change existing parameters of labour contention in his piece, 'A New Insurgency Can Only Arise Outside the Progressive and Labor Establishment', published by the *New Labor Forum* in Fall 2011. Lerner (2011: 9–10) identifies unions themselves as the major obstacle to achieving more effective forms of change for working people:

> Unions have the money, members, and capacity to organize, build, and fuel a movement designed to challenge the power of the corporate elite. But despite the fact that thousands of dedicated members, leaders, and staff have worked their hearts out to rebuild the labor movement, unions are just big enough – and just connected enough to the political and economic power structure – to be constrained from leading the kinds of activities that are needed.

Rather than jeopardizing relationships with particular employers and politicians, or threatening the financial solvency of their pension funds and union investments, for example, many unions still refrain from engaging in more oppositional and intensive public protests. But, Lerner argues that one of the most potent forms of worker power is 'prolonging protest' – that is, 'intensive escalating activities – designed to challenge and disrupt unfair corporate abuses of power' that 'go on for weeks, growing in size and intensity'.

By focusing on the necessity for on-going escalation, Lerner emphasizes the importance of adopting a 'movement-based organizational model', which encompasses but is not necessarily limited to tactics such as public dramas. Lerner describes this step as a 'leap of faith', but another way to characterize it is to emphasize the importance of allocating the kinds of resources necessary to support new schemas for organizing workers – which is a site of conflict and resistance. The example of SEIU's 2006 janitors' strike in Houston illuminates these tensions. Lerner (2011: 11) explains:

> With the SEIU's 2006 janitors' strike in Houston, we built incredible momentum – a Houston-based mini-movement – by tapping into issues that went way beyond the specificities of the strike. We won the strike because it was seen as part of a bigger fight that scared the hell out of Houston's business elite. If we had taken it a step further – engaging and supporting other organizations with the capacity to expand the fight beyond janitors – the movement would have grown (instead of having dissipated) when the strike settled.

By drawing our attention to SEIU's decision not to continue devoting resources, Lerner shows how the allocation of resources is a crucial component to enacting new schemas as more enduring forms of organizational change. However, the problem in enacting new schemas and resources is not necessarily just SEIU's limitation. He views it as endemic to the vast majority of unions who make decisions on 'how to protect the 7 percent of private sector workers who are unionized (instead of the 93 percent of private sector workers who aren't in unions)'.

In the case of South Korea, resistance to the adoption of new schemas and resources is also linked to the sharpening divides between a small number of unionized workers and the vast proportion of non-union workers, especially those employed as *pijonggyujik* (irregular or non-standard) workers. In almost every case involving an irregular workers' union struggle, there has been a parallel story of rejection and often, active opposition by their regularly-employed counterparts. The consequences of such divisions were most recently apparent in the struggle that began on December 20, 2010 in response to the announcement by Hanjin Heavy Industries and Construction Co. Ltd. that the company would be dismissing hundreds of workers at its shipyard in Yeongdo, Busan in the near future. In response, the labour union at Hanjin Heavy Industries and Construction Co. (HHIC) retaliated by waging a full-scale strike. After six months, the union leadership signed an agreement with company management to officially end the strike in exchange for retirement benefits for workers who chose to retire voluntarily.[3] However, approximately 60 union members refused to sign the agreement, arguing that the union leadership made a unilateral decision without the support of its members and commenced a militant public protest in which dissenting unionists 'tied themselves to a 50-meter crane' at the shipyard. The company elicited the support of the Busan District Court which authorized riot police to forcibly remove protesting workers;[4] however, police were unable to remove one protester, Kim Jin Suk, who proceeded to stage a one-woman protest at the top of a 35 meter crane for 309 consecutive days without running water and only a bucket for a toilet, enduring a heat wave, typhoon winds and snowstorms.

Although the union dispute was not initially about the struggles of *pijonggyujik* workers, Kim Jin Suk's protest became a symbolic representation of the cumulative struggles facing the South Korean working class and a call to action to the broader public to challenge the growing gap between the rich and poor, government repression against striking workers and the struggles of the vast majority of workers employed in lower-paid and more insecure non-standard jobs. Kim Jin Suk, a former welder in the shipyards and a Direction Committee member of the Busan office of the Korean Confederation of Trade Unions (KCTU), earned a reputation as a strong democratic union leader during the 1980s when she became one of the only elected women leaders in a male-dominated industrial workplace (See Nam 2009). Her union involvement eventually resulted in the loss of her job, but she continued to be an outspoken critic of neoliberal economic restructuring and the erosion of job security in the 1990s and an advocate for the rights of irregular workers in the 2000s.

Kim's struggle on Crane No. 85 was laden with symbolic meaning right from the start. Crane no. 85 was the site of the suicide of Kim Ju-ik, a 40-year-old father of three, who hanged himself in the crane's control

3 Choe He-Suk, 'Hanjin Heavy Chief Under Fire For Lying Low Over Labor Crisis' *The Korea Herald* August 3, 2011 http://www.koreaherald.com/national/Detail.jsp?newsMLId=20110803000519 (accessed August 31, 2011).

4 Kim Tae-Jong, 'Hanjin Heavy Union Calls Off Strike' *The Korea Times* June 27, 2011 http://www.koreatimes.co.kr/www/news/nation/2011/06/113_89738.html (accessed August 31, 2011).

room after waging a three month protest against unjust dismissals and the debilitating fines that striking workers were required to pay under Criminal Code 314, the 'obstruction of business' clause.[5] The symbolic representation of Kim's struggle greatly intensified in the context of burgeoning public support, namely in the form of 'Hope Buses', in which thousands of people from across the country travelled to the Yeongdo shipyard to show their solidarity with Kim Jin Suk. Workers from a wider range of different unions, students, Democratic Labor Party members, Buddhist, Catholic and Protestant religious leaders, movement activists from a wide range of civil society organizations from human rights and women's groups to disability and queer LGBT activists, university professors, lawyers and others not only travelled on Hope buses in support of Kim Jin Suk but also for 'a world without redundancy dismissals and precarious work' (Robinson 2011). The arrival of striking irregular workers, who had previously worked for companies such as Hyundai Motors, seeking some source of 'hope' for their on-going protests strengthened the symbolic framing of Kim Jin Suk's struggle.

The fact that Kim Jin Suk's harshest critics were from the HHIC union itself indicated the widening gulf between the thousands of supporters that mobilized in support of Kim Jin Suk and a few hundred unionists who berated Kim for jeopardizing negotiations between the union and Hanjin Heavy Industries management. When Kim Jin Suk finally agreed to come down from the crane after 309 days, she was able to secure deals with company management to reinstate 94 dismissed workers and drop all legal action against protesting workers and the union. While it is unclear whether the reinstatements will occur or whether the union will face severe punitive consequences for waging a so-called 'illegal action', the broader impact of the struggle points to the potential for more enduring realignments in the terrain of labour contention. Rather than point towards the

5 See John M. Glionna and Jung Yoon-Choi, 'South Korea Activist's Protest on Cargo Crane to Enter 8th Month' *Los Angeles Times*, August 04, 2011 http:// articles.latimes.com/2011/aug/04/world/la-fg-south-korea-crane-protest-20110805 (accessed August 31, 2011).

possibility of increasing unity among unionists employed in regular and irregular employment, this case highlights the consolidation of tremendous human resources from wide sectors of the public in support of the escalation of public protests for irregular workers and the struggles of working people more broadly.

Conclusion

In outlining a systematic approach to assessing the struggles of workers located on the margins of the economy and society, I argue that the current state of labour studies is rightly focused on the struggles of socially disadvantaged workers with diminished forms of power and leverage. However, it has done so by neglecting the influence of meaningful transformations in the structures of labour contention. This is largely because much of the current literature treats union revitalization and social movement unionism as independent variables and then proceeds to analyse their impact on the success or failure of campaigns.[6] While it is important to identify the impact of innovative practices and strategies, it is also crucial to examine how new ways of engaging in worker protests influence changes in the repertoires of labour contention themselves since they also play a critical role in structuring the limits and possibilities of transformation.

The spatial and temporal dynamics of workers' struggles at the margins reveal that such struggles are emergent and peripheral to more dominant ways of engaging in collective action. As such, their long-term transformative potential is necessarily conditioned by their ability to transform the schemas and resources patterning existing repertoires of contention. Symbolic leverage represents a new schema of labour contention aimed at reconfiguring the relations of power and authority between low-paid,

6 Important exceptions are Clawson (2003), Fantasia and Voss (2004), Lopez (2006), Milkman (2006) and Ganz (2009).

precarious and socially disadvantaged workers and the entities that use and benefit from their labour. It is a schema that redefines labour disputes as broader struggles against injustice and discrimination and hence is waged not just in the workplace but in the contested arena of culture and public debates about values. As a form of collective action that requires what Bourdieu terms 'a symbolic struggle of all against all', it is also an extremely risky and time- and resource-intensive schema to enact. It requires legitimating the authority of subordinated social groups with the moral weight of mobilized publics and thus reconfiguring who participates in and under what conditions labour contention takes place. It also requires a prolonged escalation of public protest that not only reproduces existing patterns of waging collective action but also brings in a wide array of other social actors and groups that help broaden the stakes of labour disputes. Thus, an important consequence of the adoption of new schemas and resources in organized labour's repertoires of contention is the realignment of support and solidarities between workers and other social actors, be they community organizations, faith-based groups, students and university professors and various social movement groups from the women's movement to the disability rights movement.

Trends in South Korea and the United States both point to the existing tensions and constraints facing innovation in repertoires of contention, as well as genuine possibilities for change and transformation. In both countries, unions themselves seem to be the major force against innovation and change. The reasons differ in each country, however. In the United States unions exhibit a tendency to disengage, rather than escalate, the kind of oppositional public pressure that is key to generating symbolic leverage. This criticism has been most fervently made by Stephen Lerner but others have also emphasized the need for unions to redefine their priorities and re-allocate their resources to revitalize the practice of social movement unionism and strengthen the power of mobilized publics to change the balance of power between workers, neoliberal states and corporate actors. The recent participation of labour unions in various 'Occupy Protests' – from Occupy Wall Street to Occupy Wal-Mart – signals that these shifts may already be taking place.

In South Korea, regularly-employed workers' unions seem to be exerting the most visible forces against innovation and change. Highlighting regular workers' unions should not detract attention from the overdetermining role of the repressive apparatus of the state in support of anti-union employers. However, it is still necessary to pay attention to the constraining role of regular workers' unions, which routinely settle their disputes with employers without including the demands of irregular workers as well as actively resist efforts by irregularly-employed workers to intensify and escalate their struggles after they are abandoned by their regularly-employed counterparts. Despite their influence, or perhaps in part due to it, we are witnessing the emergence of new forms of solidarity between protesting irregular workers and a diverse array of civil society groups. While regularly-employed workers in large enterprises continue to dominate the actions and priorities of most unions, deepening alliances and solidarities such as those activated to support Kim Jin Suk's 309-day aerial protest are redefining the horizons of existing repertoires of contention and forging the basis of a new kind of social movement in South Korea, one that is not just about social movement unionism but about constituting a broad-based popular movement for more genuine social, economic and political transformation.

References

Basok, T. (2009). 'Counter-Hegemonic Human Rights Discourses and Migrant Rights Activism in the U.S. and Canada', *International Journal of Comparative Sociology*, 50 (2), 179–201.

Bergquist, C. (1993). 'Labor History and Its Challenges: Confessions of a Latin Americanist', *The American Historical Review*, 98 (3), 757–64.

Bourdieu, P. (1990). *In Other Words: Essays Towards a Reflexive Sociology.* Stanford, CA: Stanford University Press.

Bourdieu, P. (1984). *Distinction: A Social Critique of the Judgement of Taste.* Cambridge, MA: Harvard University Press.

Bronfenbrenner, K., Friedman, S., Hurd, R.W., Oswald, R.A., Seeber, R.L. (eds) (1998). *Organizing to Win: New Research on Union Strategies.* Ithaca, NY: ILR Press.

Brooks, E.C. (2007). *Unraveling the Garment Industry: Transnational Organizing and Women's Work.* Minneapolis: University of Minnesota Press.
Burawoy, M. (2010). 'From Polanyi to Pollyanna: The False Optimism of Global Labor Studies', *Global Labour Journal*, 1 (2), 301–13.
Choudry, A., Hanley, J., Jordan, S., Shragge, E., Stiegman, M. (2009). *Fight Back: Workplace Justice for Immigrants.* Halifax: Fernwood Books Ltd.
Chun, J.J. (2009). *Organizing at the Margins: The Symbolic Politics of Labor in South Korea and the United States.* Ithaca, NY: Cornell University Press.
Clawson, D. (2003). *The Next Upsurge: Labor and the New Social Movements.* Ithaca, NY: ILR Press.
Dean, A., Reynolds, D.B. (2009). *A New New Deal: How Regional Activism Will Reshape the American Labor Movement.* Ithaca, NY: Cornell University Press.
Delgado, H.L. (1993). *New Immigrants, Old Unions: Organizing Undocumented Workers in Los Angeles.* Philadelphia: Temple University Press.
Fantasia, R., Voss, K. (2004). *Hard Work: Remaking the American Labor Movement.* Berkeley: University of California Press.
Fine, J. (2006). *Worker Centers: Organizing Communities at the Edge of the Dream.* Ithaca, NY: ILR Press.
Fraser, N. (1995). 'From Redistribution to Recognition? Dilemmas of Justice in a "Post-Socialist" Age', *New Left Review*, Iss. 212 (July/August), 68–93.
Ganz, M. (2009). *Why David Sometimes Wins: Leadership, Organization, and Strategy in the California Farm Worker Movement.* New York: Oxford University Press.
Gray, K. (2008). *Korean Workers and Neoliberal Globalization.* London: Routledge.
Lerner, S. (2011). 'A New Insurgency Can Only Rise Outside the Progressive and Labor Establishment', *New Labor Forum*. 20(3), 9–13.
Lopez, S. (2004). *Reorganizing the Rust Belt: An Inside Study of the American Labor Movement.* Berkeley: University of California Press.
Luce, S. (2004). *Fighting for a Living Wage.* Ithaca, NY: Cornell University Press.
Milkman, R. (2006). *L.A. Story: Immigrant Workers and the Future of the U.S. Labor Movement.* New York: Russell Sage Foundation.
Milkman, R. (ed.) (2000). *Organizing Immigrants: The Challenge for Unions in Contemporary California.* Ithaca, NY: Cornell University Press.
Milkman, R., Voss, K. (eds) (2004). *Rebuilding Labor: Organizing and Organizers in the New Union Movement.* Ithaca, NY: ILR Press.
Nam, H. (2009). 'Shipyard Women and the Politics of Gender: A Case Study of the KSEC Yard in South Korea'. In R. Barraclough, E. Faison (eds), *Gender and Labour in Korea and Japan: Sexing Class.* London: Routledge.
Preston, R. (2004). '"Justice for Janitors," Not "Compensation for Custodians": The Political Context and Organizing in San Jose and Sacramento'. In R. Milkman,

K. Voss (eds), *Rebuilding Labor: Organizing and Organizers in the New Labor Movement.* Ithaca, NY: Cornell University Press.

Robinson, T.K. (2011). 'South Korea's 300 Day Aerial Sit-in Strike Highlights Plight of Precarious Workers in Korea and the Philippines', *The Asia-Pacific Journal*, 9 45 (4).

Seidman, G.W. (2007). *Beyond the Boycott: Labor Rights, Human Rights, and Transnational Activism.* New York: Russell Sage Foundation.

Sewell, W.H. Jr. (2005). *Logics of History: Social Theory and Social Transformation.* Chicago: University of Chicago Press.

Sewell, W.H. Jr. (1992). 'A Theory of Structure: Duality, Agency, and Transformation', *American Journal of Sociology*, 98 (1), 1–29.

Suzuki, A. (2010). 'Institutional Contexts and Characteristics of Social Movement Unionism in Japan', Paper Presented at XVII ISA World Congress RC 44 Session 8 (July 11–17 2010, Gothenburg, Sweden).

Tattersall, A. (2010). *Power in Coalition: Strategies for Strong Unions and Social Change.* Ithaca, NY: ILR Press.

Tilly, C. (1995). *Popular Contention in Great Britain, 1758–1834.* Cambridge, MA: Harvard University Press.

Tilly, C. (1986). *The Contentious French.* Cambridge, MA: BelKnap Press of Harvard University Press.

Turner, L., Katz, H.C., Hurd, R. (eds) (2001). *Rekindling the Movement: Labor's Quest for Relevance in the Twenty-First Century.* Ithaca, NY: ILR Press.

Von Holdt, K., Webster, E. (2008). 'Organising on the Periphery: New Sources of Power in the South African Workplace', *Employee Relations*, 30 (4), 333–54.

Webster, E., Lambert, Rob., Benzuidenhout, A. (2008). *Grounding Globalization: Labour in the Age of Insecurity.* Hoboken, NJ: Wiley-Blackwell.

Webster, E., Von Holdt, K. (eds) (2005). *Beyond the Apartheid Workplace: Studies in Transition.* Scottsville: University of Natal Press.

Wills, J. (2001). 'Community Unionism and Trade Union Renewal in the UK: Moving Beyond the Fragments at Last?', *Transactions of the Institute of British Geographers*, 26 (4), 465–83.

Wills, J. (2005). 'The Geography of Union Organising in Low Paid Service Industries in the UK: Lessons From the T&G's Campaign to Unionise the Dorchester Hotel, London', *Antipode*, 37 (1), 139–59.

AKIRA SUZUKI

3 The Limits and Possibilities of Social Movement Unionism in Japan in the Context of Industrial Relations Institutions

Introduction

This chapter examines the limits and possibilities of social movement unionism (SMU) in Japan in the context of its industrial relations (IR) institutions. I will contribute to the literature on cross-national comparisons of social movement unionism by examining cases in Japan where institutional arrangements regulating industrial relations are different from those countries covered by previous studies of social movement unionism.

Previous studies have tended to focus on the United States. Although anti-union and neoliberal policies of management and the state since the late 1970s have drastically weakened the organizational and socio-economic influence of the US labour movement, unions such as SEIU and HERE have attempted to counter their decline by aggressively organizing lower-paid, service sector workers. SEIU's Justice for Janitors Campaign, which began in the late 1980s, was typical of such aggressive, organizing campaigns. Efforts to reform the labour movement in a more activist direction reached the national level when the New Voice slate took control of the leadership of AFL-CIO in 1995. Observers and labour scholars, impressed by a series of innovative programs adopted by the AFL-CIO, such as Union Summer, Union Cities, and New Alliances, and by successful cases of union organizing by SEIU and HERE in the second half of the 1990s, expected that the national confederation and its affiliates would revitalize their organizational and mobilization power. Many case studies of union revitalization and social movement unionism have been published in monographs, edited volumes and journal articles since the mid-1990s (Bronfenbrenner, et al., eds, 1998; Turner, Katz and Hurd, eds, 2001; Voss and Sherman 2000; Clawson 2003; Milkman and Voss, eds, 2004; Fantasia and Voss 2004; Lopez 2004; Milkman 2006).

The literature on union revitalization also extended its scope: it covered not only cases in the United States, but also those in other industrialized countries, such as the United Kingdom, Canada and Australia, where the labour movements had been weakened by neoliberal economic and political systems (Fairbrother and Yates, eds, 2003; Cornfield and McCammon, eds, 2003; Kumer and Schenk, eds, 2006). With regard to East Asian countries, while there are studies that have examined social movement unionism in South Korea as country-specific studies or as part of cross-national comparative studies (Gray 2008; Webster et al. 2008; Chun 2009), there are fewer studies (especially in English) that have examined the Japanese labour movement in the framework of social movement unionism.

Although previous studies of union revitalization have defined social movement unionism differently, I argue that by synthesizing these definitions four strategies of SMU can be identified: trade unions that (1) extend their activities beyond the framework of existing institutions and, in that process, redefine narrowly-defined goals into broadly-defined ones; (2) form alliances with social movement and community-based organizations; (3) transform their internal organizations so as to increase involvement of rank-and-file members in union activities; and (4) promote grass-roots cross-national union solidarity (Suzuki 2005). Trade unions need not necessarily have all four aspects to become part of social movement unionism. Previous studies suggest that the first and second aspects are more important requisites than the fourth (i.e., not all SMU-oriented unions are practicing grass-roots cross-national union solidarity). Concerning the third aspect, labour scholars have engaged in debates over whether organizing campaigns should be led by rank-and-file members or by professionally-trained activists sent by union headquarters (Voss and Sherman 2000; Milkman 2006; Moody 2007; Voss 2010; see also Introduction to this volume).

In pursuit of activities beyond the framework of existing institutions – the first strategy – industrial relations institutions constitute restrictions on SMU-oriented unions. In fact, previous studies tend to treat existing institutional arrangements as exogenous constraining factors. For example, studies of the United States regard industrial relations institutions, especially National Labor Relations Board (NLRB) union certification elections, as obstacles that SMU-oriented unions can circumvent through union-community alliances that pressure employers to recognize unions voluntarily (Voss and Sherman 2000; Martin 2008). Some recent studies of SMU, however, suggest the importance of institutions as endogenous contexts of social movement unionism. For example, Lowell Turner in his study of SMU in Germany (Turner 2009) posits that institutions not only place constraints on the development of SMU but also provide opportunities for its development. Since trade unions in Germany are embedded in industrial relations institutions much more than those in the United States, trade unions tend to be slow in adopting SMU-oriented strategies, even when they are put on the defensive by anti-union policies of service sector employers. Innovative leaders of HBV (the banking, insurance, and retail union later merged into Ver.di), however, took advantage of codetermination rights enshrined in German industrial relations institutions and engaged in strategies based on labour-community coalitions to pressure management of Schlecker (a nation-wide drug store chain with strong anti-union attitudes) to allow their employees to establish works councils.

Previous studies give little consideration to the influence of industrial relations institutions on social movement unionism or to the impact of SMU on IR institutions. These studies tend to focus on successful organizing campaigns that incorporate union-community alliances and membership mobilization, ending 'the stories' at the point of union victory. Concerning the impact of SMU on the existing institutions, these studies provide mildly optimistic predictions for the radical transformation of the institutions through the spread of SMU-based union strategies and successful organizing in other parts of the country. For example, Ruth Milkman, in her study of social movement unionism in Los Angeles (Milkman 2006), associates the revitalized union movement in Los Angeles with the concentration of Hispanic immigrant workers in the city and with the rising influence of former AFL unions capable of comprehensive and region-based organizing of service-sector workers (with the concomitant decline in influence of former CIO unions which are institutionally embedded in workplace-based organizing in manufacturing industries). She predicts that the LA-style social movement unionism will spread in other cities of the United States because of the geographical dispersion of Hispanic immigrant workers and because of the growing influence of former AFL unions such as SEIU in the US labour movement. Dan Clawson examines cases of 'fusion' between labour and social movements and takes a cautiously optimistic position that these cases may be early signs of the 'next upsurge' of the US labour movement (Clawson 2003). These studies, however, do not examine how widely innovations in organizing and labour-community alliances will be accepted as viable strategies by trade unions, other than a few revitalized unions, or the extent to which the development of social movement unionism will undermine the NLRB-based institutional arrangements (see Martin 2008 for the limited spread of non-NLRB organizing).

This chapter examines how industrial relations institutions influenced, and in turn were influenced by, the development of social movement unionism in Japan. The analytical focus of the chapter is community unions. Community unions [*komyuniti yunion*][1] have a regional representation structure with members drawn from a number of firms. They generally cover workers who fall outside the purview of enterprise unions, such as part-time and other non-regular workers, workers in small firms, and foreign workers. Representing workers at the 'margins' of labour markets, they are widely regarded as SMU-oriented.[2] This chapter also considers

1 Region-based, individually-affiliated unions are commonly called 'community unions' [*komyuniti yunion*] but are also called 'regional unions' [*chiiki yunion*] and 'local unions' [*rokaru yunion*]. The latter two are used to refer to region-based unions established by Rengo (Japanese Trade Union Confederation) and Zenroren (National Confederation of Trade Unions), respectively. To be exact, community unions refer to those affiliated with CUNN (Community Union Nationwide Network, a loose federation of 74 region-based unions, many of which are not affiliated with either of the two national confederations). For the sake of simplicity, however, this chapter uses the commonly used term, 'community unions', to refer to region-based unions.

2 It should be noted that, although community unions carry 'community' in their names, not all unions are involved in addressing community-based issues (see the discussion below).

how enterprise unions, which are located at the core of industrial relations institutions in Japan, react to the development of social movement unionism at the institutional margins. It argues that some aspects of industrial relations institutions promote, while others constrain the development of social movement unionism in Japan. It also argues that although community unions challenge the institutional arrangements dominated by cooperative enterprise unions, the community union movement has a limited effect on enterprise-based industrial relations and the labour movement as a whole. The second section of the chapter briefly examines the current state of community unions, such as their organizational characteristics, policy-orientations, and activities. The third section, based on a review of previous studies, identifies three approaches to the relationship between industrial relations institutions and social movement unionism and applies them to cases in Japan. The fourth section considers the limits and possibilities of social movement unionism in Japan from a long-term perspective.

The State of Social Movement Unionism in Japan

Community unions were first organized in the first half of the 1980s by regional labour councils [*chikuro*], semi-autonomous regional federations of trade unions affiliated with Sohyo (the leftist, national confederation that dissolved in 1989 when it joined the newly established confederation, Rengo). Some of these councils organized workers in their respective regions, particularly part-time workers and workers in small firms. These councils established individually-affiliated unions to engage in collective bargaining with their respective employers (see Takasu in this volume). The establishment of individually-affiliated community unions was made possible by the liberal union recognition procedures of Japanese labour law. Any group of workers, even those working for different firms and a minority in their respective firms, may form a trade union with the right to engage in collective bargaining with the management of their respective firms (Suzuki 2008: 501–2). It should be noted, however, that employers do not necessarily respect the legal right of community unions.[3]

By 1989, the number of community unions increased to about 50. In 1990, 60 community unions representing 10,000 workers established a loose nationwide network, the CUNN (Community Union Nationwide Network). Currently, CUNN has 74 affiliates and represents about 15,000 workers. Besides community unions affiliated with CUNN (many are not affiliated with either of the two major national confederations, Rengo or Zenroren),[4] there are community unions established by the regional organizations of the two national confederations. Rengo adopted a new organizing policy in 1996 and gave its prefecture-level organizations the authority to establish community unions. As of 2009, 45 prefecture-level organizations established community unions with a total membership of about 15,000 (Takasu 2010: 50, 53). The line separating CUNN and Rengo was blurred somewhat when eight community unions affiliated with CUNN formed a formal federation, the Japan Community Union Federation (JCUF [*Zenkoku Yunion*]) in June 2002 and joined Rengo the following year. Zenroren, the leftist confederation, adopted a policy promoting the establishment of community unions in 2002. As of 2009, there were 135 Zenroren-affiliated community unions with a membership of 10,000 (Takasu 2010: 57–8). Besides these three groups of community unions, there are community unions affiliated with Zenrokyo (a loose national-level federation of leftist unions), and individually-affiliated unions established by some industrial-level union federations. It is estimated that there are about 300 community unions in Japan. Their total member-

3 For example, community unions filed 267 of 395 cases of illegal labour acts before labour commissions in 2009 (Doko 2010: 75).

4 Rengo, the dominant confederation, has a membership of 6.8 million. The membership of Zenroren, the leftist rival of Rengo, is about 1.3 million. Zenroren has a close relationship with the Japan Communist Party. These membership figures are based on each confederation's own surveys in 2008. Besides these confederations, there is another federation, called Zenrokyo (National Trade Union Council), whose membership is 144,000 (as of 2008). Zenrokyo does not characterize itself as a confederation, but as a loose nation-level federation of various types of (non-communist) leftist unions.

ship is estimated to be from 30,000 to 100,000, depending on the definition of community unions.[5] The membership of community unions, however, is a tiny fraction of the total union membership as a whole (10 million).

A survey of individually-affiliated (community) unions conducted by the Ohara Institute for Social Research (OISR) from the late 2009 to early 2010 found community unions have on average 292 members (70.4 per cent of whom are individually-affiliated) with 1.3 full-time staff members.[6] Female members and members who are non-regular workers account for 36.4 per cent and 44.2 per cent of the membership, respectively. These proportions are above the figures (as of 2009) for all trade unions (29.1 per cent and 7.0 per cent [part-time workers only], respectively). Community unions operate on small budgets: 76.4 per cent of responding unions have an annual budget of less than ¥3 million. Their main source of income is membership fees, but they are supplemented by donations of a proportion of 'compensation money' that union members receive at the time of dispute settlements[7] (61.5 per cent of the unions answered they received

5 If community unions are defined to include region-based unions affiliated with general unions [*ippan roso*] that organize SME workers, their total membership becomes about 100,000 (Takasu 2010: 64; see also Takasu in this volume). These general unions are often loose federations of enterprise unions established at SMEs but have a minority of individually-affiliated members.

6 We sent survey sheets to 298 individually-affiliated unions (a more general term for community unions) in November and December 2009, and 161 unions answered the survey by April 2010 (a response rate of 54 per cent). The survey questions consisted of three parts. In the first part, the survey asked organizational characteristics of unions, such as membership size, founding year, number of paid staff members, and annual budgets. The second part asked about counseling activities on labour issues, such as number of cases handled by unions per month, number of persons available as counselors, contents of complaints, and percentage of those who become union members of the total number of workers seeking counselling services. And the third part asked activities unions engage in besides labour-issue counseling, such as collective bargaining, labour education, or involvement in problems of community and/or social problems in general.

7 In cases of dismissals, community unions often make compromises with employers in such a way that that employers pay 'compensation money' to dismissed workers in return for the acceptance of the dismissal by unions and concerned workers.

such donations) and by financial assistance from federations with which community unions are affiliated (18.0 per cent of the unions answered that they received such financial support) (OISR 2010).

The following section outlines activities of community unions based on three out of the four strategies of social movement unionism discussed above: (1) seeking broad goals, (2) alliance-formation with social movement and community organizations, and (3) rank-and-file participation.

Seeking Broad Goals

While the goals of mainstream enterprise unions are bound by enterprise-based industrial relations and tend to give priority to cooperative relationships with management and the economic competitiveness of their firms, community union goals are not bound by such an institutional framework. Community unions organize workers who are in disadvantageous positions in labour markets and bargain with employers on behalf of union members with individual grievances, such as dismissals, harassment, arbitrary changes in working conditions and employment status (e.g., from regular to non-regular status) or wage discrimination based on employment status and/or gender. Thus, a sense of economic injustice shapes the discourse of their policy goals. For example, the JCUF framed the different treatment of regular and non-regular workers as an issue of economic injustice and regarded redressing it as one of its core missions. A passage from the policy statement adopted by the JCUF's founding convention states:

> The JCUF will fight against discrimination. Currently, we witness a glaring wage gap based on employment status. The wage gap has widened to such an extent that it has become a sort of social discrimination, and we need to seek to establish socially equal treatment through legislation...We will actively engage in a movement to establish workers' rights in any forms of employment relations under which workers may work (JCUF 2002).

Despite broad economic and social justice goals, the day-to-day activities of community unions are relatively 'mundane' and include counselling services on labour issues,[8] organizing workers who seek counselling services into unions, and engaging in collective bargaining with employers. Through collective bargaining, community unions resolve a fairly high proportion of labour disputes that union members have with their employers (Oh 2010: 54, 61). These day-to-day activities may be seen as constituting indispensable elements of the broader social movement to redress discriminatory treatment of non-regular and other workers disadvantaged in labour markets. If community unions, however, specialize only in labour-issue counselling and dispute resolutions without forming networks with other organizations, they become mere providers of services rather than parts of a broader social movement based on economic justice.

Alliance-formation with Social Movement and Community Organizations

Previous studies of social movement unionism regard alliances between trade unions and social movement/community organizations as their core characteristic. I, however, argued elsewhere that the forms and extent of labour-social movement and labour-community alliances are influenced by the state of civil society: while SMU-oriented unions in countries where civil society is relatively strong, such as the United States and Canada, tend to form such alliances, alliance-formation across the boundary of labour and social movements occur less frequently where civil society is relatively weak, such as in Japan (Suzuki 2008; see Minjin Lee in this volume). According to survey reports of activities in 2006 and 2007 of CUNN-affiliated community unions, an overwhelming majority of unions either did not undertake 'activities reaching out to communities' [*chiiki no torikumi*] or participated in such activities through 'regional labour council centres' [*chikuro senta*], small-scale regional federations voluntarily established by labour unions (mainly former Sohyo affiliates) concerned with peace issues and committed to the movement to protect the Constitution of Japan. A small

8 Results of the OISR survey show that almost all of the 161 responding unions (98.2 per cent) provide counselling services on labour issues (OISR 2010).

minority of community unions, however, reported coalitions with local residents' movements on environmental issues and with social movements on such issues as opposition to US bases, gender equality, assistance to foreign workers, and occupational health and safety (Suzuki 2008: 505).

Although coalition-building with social movement organizations is not a key characteristic of social movement unionism in Japan, community unions are active in forming networks among themselves. CUNN is a typical example of networks among community unions. It is a loose nationwide grouping of 74 community unions without any hierarchical relationship between its headquarters and member unions. It publishes newsletters and holds annual meetings where activists of community unions form personal networks and exchange information and opinions on various issues. Community unions in certain regions (e.g., areas around Tokyo or Osaka) form smaller networks among themselves (Takasu 2010: 46).

Community union activists initiate networks with activists of various social movements and with experts such as lawyers and academics. Unlike coalitions between organizations, these personal networks are fluid and lack solid organizational structures, such as liaison committees of activists involved in networks. The OISR survey shows that labour-issue counselling, one of the main activities of community unions, is supported by counsellors' personal networks with specialists in other fields (38.5 per cent of the unions answer that their counselling activities are supported by such networks) (OISR 2010). Community union activists also form networks to tackle policy issues such as the deregulation of the Labour Standards Law and social issues such as the increase in the working poor among young people. These networks are often based on loose personal networks among community union activists, those of labour-related NGOs, labour lawyers and academics (Takasu 2010; Shinoda 2009; Azuma 2009). Such a personal network played an important role in the movement to set up an emergency camp at Hibiya Park in the centre of Tokyo (called *Hakenmura*, literally 'a village of [jobless] dispatched workers') during the 2008–2009 end-of-year/New Year holiday period. Community union activists of the JCUF were key players in the *Hakenmura* movement. The emergency camp provided food and shelter for about 500 unemployed non-regular workers who had lost their jobs and housing because of the economic and financial crisis.[9] The camping-out of 500 unemployed workers, supported by about 1,700 volunteers, became a sort of 'public drama' (Chun 2009), drew wide media attention and created wide support from the general public. As a result, the movement put strong pressure on the government to reconsider its neoliberal labour market policies, particularly de-regulation of manpower dispatch businesses (for details, see Shinoda 2009; Endo 2009).

Involvement of the Rank and File in Union Activities

In contrast to the bureaucratized organizational structures typical of enterprise unions where there is little rank-and-file activism, community unions have high levels of member participation. The high levels of participation reflect that community unions cannot hire many full-time activists (according to the OISR survey, a community union, on average, hires 1.3 full-time activists) and have to depend on members' support to engage in activities. In some unions, active members participate in activities performed in enterprise unions by full-time activists, for example, by volunteering as labour-issue counsellors for other workers and as union representatives in other members' collective bargaining (Kotani 1999; Kotani 2001). According to the OISR survey, 31.7 per cent of the unions reported rank-and-file members volunteer as labour-issue counsellors. In addition, rank-and-file members, other than those who are union officials or members directly involved in labour disputes, participated in collective bargaining as union representatives: 18 per cent of the unions had rank-and-file members who participated 'often' and another 46 per cent 'sometimes' (OISR 2010).

9 Many dispatched factory workers in manufacturing industries lived in dormitories or apartments owned by manpower dispatching companies near the factories where they worked. When the economic and financial crisis hit the Japanese economy, many factories reduced the scale of operations and stopped receiving dispatched workers. When employment contracts with manpower dispatching companies were not renewed or cancelled in the middle of contract terms, these workers had to leave their dormitories and apartments.

In sum, community unions in Japan have characteristics associated with social movement unionism but somewhat different than SMU-oriented unions in the United States and other industrialized countries. Community unions seek broad goals, typically redressing discriminatory treatment of non-regular workers and other issues of economic injustice through the daily activities of labour-issue counselling and collective bargaining. Community unions are less active in coalition-building with community and social movement organizations. They, however, are active in creating networks among themselves, and their activists often form personal networks with specialists in labour-related fields and supportive individuals. The level of rank-and-file participation in union activities among community unions is higher than in bureaucratized enterprise unions.

Institutional Contexts of Social Movement Unionism in Japan

The development of community unions, discussed in the second section, does not occur in an institutional vacuum. Community unions hold a marginal position in the industrial relations institutions dominated by enterprise unions. Their institutional position is marginal in two senses. First, community unions organize workers on a regional basis, outside of the dominant sectors of the economy that enterprise-based industrial relations generally serve. Second, the policy orientations of community unions, characterized by 'arm's-length' and potentially conflictual relations with employers, are diametrically opposed to the dominant ideology of cooperative enterprise unionism. Thus, the institutional contexts of community unions and social movement unionism in general in Japan are unfavourable. Before examining the institutional contexts of community unions, let us first review studies on the relationship of industrial relations institutions and social movement unionism.

Three Approaches to the Relationship Between Industrial Relations Institutions and Social Movement Unionism

Previous studies have taken three approaches to the relationship between industrial relations institutions and social movement unionism. The first approach is that social movement unionism develops when mainstream trade unions have become embedded in industrial relations institutions and become conservative and bureaucratized organizations whose interactions with management and the state are routine and rule-based. SMU-oriented unions attempt to 'de-institutionalize' these labour-management relations by challenging the dominance of bureaucratized unions through labour-community coalitions and rank-and-file mobilization (e.g., Martin 2008). This approach tends to assume a radical institutional transformation, or what historical institutionalists call 'a strong punctuated equilibrium model'. In this model, 'long periods of institutional stasis' are 'periodically interrupted by some sort of exogenous shock that opens things up, allowing for more or less radical reorganization' (Streeck and Thelen 2005: 1). Clawson's study on union revitalization in the United States is based on this model. Although he confines his argument to the US labour movement, he posits that '[h]istorcially, unions...have grown in explosive bursts rather than in steady increments', noting that there were two previous periods (between 1898 and 1904 and between 1934 and 1945) of such rapid growth or upsurge. A period of upsurge entails a drastic transformation of institutions, redefining 'what we mean by "the labor movement"' and changing '...the form that unions take, laws, structures, and accepted forms of behavior' (Clawson 2003: 13, 16). He suggests a possible collapse of the outdated 'New Deal Labor System' from 'a new upsurge', which may take the form of a 'fusion' between labour and new social movements.

The second approach pays attention to cross-national differences in institutional conditions for the development of social movement unionism. According to the second approach, social movement unionism develops in those countries where the institutional position of trade unions is weak, while such unionism is unlikely to develop in countries with strong institutional support for trade unions. In the former countries, typically the United States, trade unions have not been institutionally protected from employers' anti-union policies, and a rapid decline in union density has created a deepening sense of crisis among union leaders. That unions are not deeply embedded in institutional arrangements provides opportunities for the adoption of 'innovative' union strategies such as rank-and-file mobilization and union-community alliances. In the latter countries, typically Germany, trade unions hold a relatively advantageous position as they are embedded in industrial relations institutions through industry- or region-wide collective bargaining and works councils at the enterprise level. Thus, despite declining union density, a sense of crisis among leaders of German unions is weak, and they are not strongly oriented to adopting organizing strategies that move beyond the institutional boundary (Frege and Kelly 2003; Baccaro et al. 2003; Turner 2003). Studies of a recent development in German industrial relations, however, indicate that national-level institutional differences in promoting the development of SMU have become somewhat less significant. Turner's previously mentioned study shows that, in the retail sector where the influence of unions is weak, they have adopted SMU-oriented strategies by taking advantage of the existing institutional arrangements as 'a viable basis on which to build' innovative union strategies (Turner 2009: 300–1).

The third approach to the relationship between industrial relations institutions and social movement unionism is that social movement unionism exercises only a minor influence on labour movements and is incapable of drastically transforming the labour movement and/or industrial relations institutions. The existence of a small minority of SMU-oriented unions may create opportunities for active debates over organizing and organizational strategies within the labour movement which may bring about minor institutional transformations but have little impact on the institutionalized, 'mainstream' part of the labour movement. While the first and second approaches regard industrial relations institutions as a causal factor of SMU, the third approach reverses the relationship and pays attention (but not exclusively) to the effect of SMU on IR institutions. This approach is applicable even to the United States. Although the second approach predicts that the weak institutional position of organized labour in the US would promote the diffusion of non-NLRB organizing, the third approach posits that such campaigns are unevenly spread among trade unions and concentrated in a small number of SEIU and HERE locals (Martin 2008). According to Rick Fantasia and Kim Voss, only six national unions out of the sixty-five unions affiliated with AFL-CIO as of 2004 were committed to SMU-oriented strategies, and 'resistance is also strong within both local and national unions [including these six unions], where many leaders and members remain bound to a business union model and "servicing" mentality that it creates' (Fantasia and Voss 2004: 133–4).

The Relationship Between IR Institutions and SMU in Japan

How do these three approaches to the institution-SMU relationship apply to social movement unionism in Japan? Industrial relations institutions in Japan are similar to those in the United States in that they share characteristics of a decentralized structure without any encompassing institutional arrangement regulating firm-level industrial relations. In a decentralized structure of industrial relations, the institutional position of trade unions is weak (Turner 1991). Contrary to the expectation of the second approach, however, the weak institutional position of organized labour does not seem to promote the development of social movement unionism in Japan as much as in the United States. This is because enterprise unions, the basic units of trade unions in Japan, are deeply embedded in enterprise-level industrial relations. Industrial relations in large private-sector firms can be characterized by what Andrew Gordon calls 'ultra-cooperative' relations (Gordon 1998). These unions have developed relationships based on 'mutual trust' with management. They engage in consultation rather than collective bargaining with management and seldom resort to industrial disputes. Although leaders of these unions 'voice' their views on a wide range of corporate policies including personnel policies through a system of labour management consultation (Inagami ed., 1995), these leaders share with managers the values that prioritize corporate performance and market competitiveness. Thus, the rapid decline in union density has not caused a strong sense of crisis among union leaders at the enterprise level.[10] It is out of the question for these leaders that enterprise unions adopt SMU-based strategies, for example by mobilizing union members or in collaboration with community unions, to organize new members such as non-unionized part-time workers in their enterprise or workers in non-unionized subcontracting companies. In other words, mainstream unions in Japan (i.e., enterprise unions in large private-sector firms) behave as institutionally-embedded unions despite the industrial relations institutions that put the position of trade unions at a disadvantage.

This does not mean that social movement unionism has not developed at all within the Japanese labour movement. As expected by the first approach, a counterweight in the form of community unions has developed against the institutionally-embedded mainstream enterprise unions. Community unions have regionally organized those workers, such as non-regular workers and workers in small firms, who fall outside the coverage of mainstream enterprise unions. Community unions contrast with mainstream enterprise unions not only in their organizational forms but also in their policy orientations. Community unions criticize not only management for discrimination against non-regular workers in wages and employment security but also enterprise unions that give management tacit approval for such discrimination. While community unions developed as a counterweight to the institutionalized part of the labour movement, it should also be noted that the IR institutions provide community unions with the legal underpinnings for their development. In other words, the liberal union recognition procedures of Japanese labour law provide the 'institutional openings' for the countermovement at the margins of the institutions.

As expected by the third approach, the institutional influence of community unions is weak, despite their 'relatively high profile' in the news media. The media often cite leaders of community unions as 'knowledgeable

10 Union density was 34.5 per cent in 1975. It declined to 28.8 per cent in 1985, to 24.0 per cent in 1995, and to 18.8 per cent in 2005 (see Table A.4 in the Appendix). Union density in the private sector declined from 20.8 per cent in 1995 to 16.4 per cent in 2005.

or expert sources on labor problems'. They portray community unions as 'innovators of labor strategies and models of progressive Japanese-style unionism' (Weathers 2010: 69). Some observers and academics, in line with the somewhat inflated media image of community unions, expect community unions to play a role revitalizing the labour movement as a whole. For example, Takeo Kinoshita (2007) argues that community unions have the potential of transforming enterprise unions from the outside by infusing members with an organizing principle of individual-based affiliation. We, however, should be aware of the difficulties of the countermovement at the 'margins' of institutions against the institutionally-embedded enterprise unions and need to be cautious about an overly optimistic view of the capability of community unions to revitalize the labour movement.

Evidence of community union's weak institutional impact is indicated by their difficulty in increasing membership. Community unions mainly organize non-regular workers experiencing low wages, poor working conditions, and precarious employment security. Although those at the 'margins' of labour markets have increased rapidly since the mid-1990s, now accounting for about one third of the workforce, community unions have been unsuccessful in expanding their share of irregular workers.[11] The oft-cited reasons for the slow growth in membership are internal to the organizations, such as high membership turnover, small organizational size, and limited financial resources.[12]

11 For example, CUNN (Community Union Nationwide Network) had 60 affiliates with a total membership of about 10,000 in 1990 when it was established. The membership of CUNN increased to 15,000 in the early 2000s but has stayed at this level ever since. The JCUF (the Japan Community Union Federation), the federation of community unions affiliated with Rengo, saw its membership decline from about 5,000 in 2002 (when it was established) to about 3,300 in 2009, even though the number of affiliated unions increased from 7 in 2002 to 11 in 2009.

12 While a community union organizes a certain number of members each year through counselling services on labour issues, many of them leave the union when their individual disputes with employers are resolved. In addition, their small organizational size and weak financial base make it difficult for community unions to allocate enough financial and human resources to proactively organizing new members (Suzuki 2008: 500–1; Weathers 2010: 68).

Besides the organizational problems of community unions, another, less noticed challenge community unions face is resistance from within the labour movement. The resistance derives from ideological differences between leaders of enterprise unions of large private-sector firms who are committed to cooperative relations with management and better corporate performance and leaders of community unions who are more attentive to workers' grievances and have arm's length relations with employers. Because of the ideological differences, some mainstream union leaders do not hide their hostility toward community unions. For example, a vice president of UI Zensen Domei (the largest, private sector union that organizes in service industries) stated that, while industrial relations should be based on mutual trust between unions and management, community union activities were based on distrust. According to this union leader, community unions formed only temporary relations with employers. They bring labour disputes into the enterprise from the outside and bargained with employers only to win financial settlements for individual workers in labour disputes (Koido et al. 2005: 25–6). Some enterprise unions are motivated to organize part-time workers in their firms lest community unions disrupt enterprise-level industrial relations by organizing these workers from the outside (Oh 2004: 43). For example, the enterprise union of 'I Department Store', one of the major affiliates of JSD (Japan Federation of Service and Distributive Workers Union) organized part-time workers in order to 'safeguard' the union and the company from 'outside organizations' (i.e., community unions) that would organize aggrieved part-time workers and extract financial settlements for individual labour disputes through negotiations with management (Interview with I Department Store Union, 12 September 2003).

In sum, industrial relations institutions in Japan provide both constraints on and opportunities for the development of social movement unionism. The institutionally embedded positions of enterprise unions make the development of SMU within the mainstream of the labour movement almost impossible but prompt the development of community unions as a counterweight to mainstream unions at the institutional margins. This development has been also helped by liberal union recognition procedures. Community unions, however, do not have much impact on mainstream

IR institutions, let alone cause a rupture in industrial relations institutions. This lack of influence is not only because of union organizational problems but also because of inter-union politics that pit a small minority of SMU-oriented unions against a large majority of cooperative enterprise unions.

The Limits and Possibilities of Social Movement Unionism in Japan

The examination of the relationship between industrial relations institutions and social movement unionism in the previous section led to a rather pessimistic view of the future development of community unions and social movement unionism in Japan. I base this assessment on the continued domination of enterprise-based, cooperative union-management relations.

The institutions of enterprise-based industrial relations seem as stable as ever, as leaders of enterprise unions remain strongly committed to the existing system, typically labour-management consultation through which union leaders and management share information based on mutual-trust (Inagami and Whittaker 2005; Mori 2003). The institutions have been stable, despite that even in large private-sector firms, employment of full-time workers has become less secure and wage levels of many workers have remained stagnant or even declined. Confidence in this stability is indicated by statements of enterprise union leaders in the 2000s who remain strongly committed to the 'politics of productivity'. They believe industrial relations should contribute to the competitiveness and productivity of their firms and accept downsizing employment for the sake of firm development as difficult but inevitable choices. They also readily accepted the reforms of labour management in the direction of performance-based and individually-oriented systems that reward high achievers. Some leaders even argue that one of the future missions of enterprise unions is to assist union members who have accepted voluntary retirement make a smooth transition to their 'second career' (Suzuki 2009a: 38–43; Imai 2011: 130).

The commitment of mainstream union leaders to enterprise unionism was made clear in their reaction to the recommendation made by the Rengo Assessment Committee. In September 2003, the committee of seven external members (a lawyer, three academics, a journalist, an NGO activist, and a writer), submitted its final report to Rengo. The report made critical comments on the current state of Rengo and its affiliates and made proposals for the future direction of the labour movement. One section of the report, devoted to criticism of enterprise unions stated that enterprise unions were no longer able to adapt themselves to rapid social and economic changes and called upon the labour movement to break away from enterprise unionism and become more independent as a social movement. To realize this goal, the report proposed that Rengo adopt a new organizing policy that would promote the establishment of trade unions that organized workers across enterprises, such as unions of part-time workers, craft unions, and community unions. It also recommended that Rengo and its affiliates revise membership rules to allow members to join two unions at the same time. For example, the report proposed that part-time workers organized by enterprise unions be allowed to join part-time workers' unions organized at the regional level (Rengo 2003; Suzuki 2009b: 184–5).

When the Committee presented the draft report to a meeting of Rengo-affiliated leaders, leaders of major affiliates, such as UI Zensen Domei, JSD, and JAW (Confederation of Japanese Automobile Workers' Unions) argued that enterprise unions were basic units of the labour movement and that its revitalization should be achieved not through overcoming enterprise unionism but through strengthening the functions of enterprise unions. After the submission of the final report, top leaders of Rengo held meetings with leaders and members of its affiliate unions to exchange opinions on how to revitalize the labour movement. In these meetings, leaders of Denki Rengo (Japanese Electrical, Electronic and Information Union) argued that, although the report emphasized that trade unions should organize those workers who were disadvantaged in labour markets, enterprise unions should protect the employment security of current members and could not afford to organize such disadvantaged workers. Leaders of Kikan Roren (Japan Federation of Basic Industry Workers' Unions) argued that, although they agreed in principle with the basic message of the report, they disagreed on the report's call for breaking away from enterprise unionism (Suzuki 2009b: 185). Although Rengo incorporated some of the Committee's basic ideas, because of affiliate objections it avoided adopting policy recommendations that would challenge enterprise union legitimacy.

The industrial relations institutions dominated by cooperative enterprise unions at large private-sector firms will continue into the foreseeable future. This does not necessarily mean, however, that social movement unionism at the institutional margin has no transformative effects. Activities of SMU-oriented unions such as community unions may have some 'de-institutionalizing' effects on the labour movement, by partially revitalizing the labour movement. In the following, I discuss two scenarios of such partial revitalization that may have the long-term effect of undermining the existing enterprise-centred IR institutions: (1) the involvement of community unions in the problems of the social security system, and (2) Rengo's policies to strengthen regional labour movements.

The Involvement of Community Unions in the Problems of the Social Security System

The economic and financial crisis of fall 2008 caused havoc in labour markets in Japan, increasing the unemployment rate from 4.0 per cent in 2008 to 5.1 per cent in 2009 (see Table A.5 in the Appendix) and drastically lowering the job-offers-to-seekers ratio from 0.88 in 2008 to 0.47 in 2009. Non-regular workers such as part-time workers and dispatched workers took the brunt of the deterioration in employment conditions, and the above-mentioned emergency camp to assist these workers (the *Hankenmura* movement) dramatically demonstrated the dire state of these workers to the general public. Although social and labour movement activists, policy-makers, concerned citizens and academics have long recognized the working poor's lack of sufficient social security protection to be a serious social problem, it was not until the mass dismissals of non-regular workers, particularly dispatched factory workers, in the aftermath of the economic and financial crisis that the general public came to realize the seriousness of poverty among non-regular workers. That many non-regular workers who suddenly lost their jobs also lost places to live pointed to the social problems associated not only with the precarious employment of these workers but with the social security system's incapacity for providing these workers with necessary assistance.

Problems with the ways in which social security policies are implemented particularly relevant to the working poor are a result of the malfunctioning of unemployment insurance and livelihood protection systems. Concerning the former, many non-regular workers, even though they are eligible for unemployment insurance, do not receive unemployment benefits because employers have evaded paying employment insurance fees. Among all unemployed workers only 21.6 per cent received unemployment benefits in 2006 (Yuasa 2008: 25, 31). As for the latter, unemployed or under-employed workers are often denied benefits under the system of livelihood protection, a system of public assistance for low-income households to maintain minimum standards of living. Local government officials, in means-testing applicants for livelihood protection, exclude from assistance those whom they judge as having an ability to work. It is estimated that only 15 to 20 per cent of those who live below the minimum standards of living receive livelihood protection allowances (Tange 2009: 63).

Community unions, through their labour-issue counselling, address 'cutting-edge' problems faced by workers, i.e., cases involving the malfunctioning of social security system. Results of the OISR survey show that 14 unions, 8.7 per cent of the total, experienced a rapid increase in cases related to housing and other livelihood problems in the previous twelve months. The survey also shows that 33 unions, 20.5 per cent of the total, are involved in activities addressing housing and other livelihood problems. Thus, a minority of community unions expanded their scope of activities into workers' livelihood issues, for example, by advising unemployed or extremely-low paid workers on applying for livelihood protection allowances. The 'fusion' of labour and livelihood issues provides opportunities for community union activists to form networks with activists involved in various anti-poverty movements (Azuma 2010: 221–2; see also Takasu in this volume). The most famous example of such a network is the 'Anti-Poverty Campaign' (*Han Hinkon Net*), a Tokyo-based network that led the *Hakenmura* movement. The network consists of activists of various anti-poverty movements, union activists and officials, lawyers and other concerned individuals and seeks to realize humane livelihood and labour conditions based on social and political solutions to poverty issues (*Han Hinkon Net* website, accessed on 7 June 2010). Although it is not yet clear to what extent similar networks of activists will spread to other parts of Japan, such networks bridging the boundary of labour and livelihood issues may become the basis for the future growth of social movement unionism.

Rengo's Policies to Strengthen Regional Labour Movements

Leaders of national confederations such as Rengo have a stronger sense of crisis about the current state of trade unions than those at the enterprise level, because their positions as officials of the national-level union organization require them to take a broader perspective on the position of organized labour in society. The idea of setting up the Rengo Assessment Committee came out of this sense of crisis among top leaders. As mentioned above, criticisms from leaders of affiliated unions prevented Rengo from adopting policies to 'break away' from enterprise unionism, one of the key proposals of the Committee's final report. Rengo, however, tried to implement another key proposal, strengthening regional labour movements. More specifically, at its 2005 convention, it adopted a policy to consolidate functions of its regional councils [*chikyo*] by reorganizing 481 regional councils (established at the municipal level) into 300 councils.[13] The newly reorganized councils would have their own offices and staff. Although they remain

13 Rengo's policy to strengthen regional councils did not proceed without opposition. UI Zensen Domei, which has been active in organizing part-time and other non-regular workers into cooperative enterprise unions, was one of the vocal opponents of the policy. The union expressed concern that the policy would promote autonomous activities of regional councils and that regional councils might escape Rengo leadership control (e.g., some councils might become active in organizing non-regular workers by establishing SMU-oriented community unions). UI Zensen Domei was concerned about possible competition between its enterprise unions and community unions established by regional councils over organizing of non-regular workers (Suzuki 2009b: 186–7).

under the control of upper-level organizations (Rengo's prefecture-level organizations and the national headquarters), the consolidated regional councils were given the functions of labour-counselling and labour dispute resolution, including the establishment of their own community unions. Regional councils were also expected to assume new functions including offering counselling services on livelihood issues to workers and residents, making policy proposals to municipal governments, and forming networks with NGOs and other resident movement organizations. To finance the increased cost of running regional councils, Rengo decided in 2008 to increase per capita assessments paid by affiliate unions by ¥10 (from ¥50 to ¥60). According to one observer, Rengo managed to gain the consent of the reluctant affiliated unions on the per capita increase by emphasizing a more effective role that the strengthened regional councils could play during election campaigns (Suzuki 2009b: 186–9; Rengo Soken 2010; Yoshioka 2009: 188).

In this way, Rengo assigned greater financial resources to its regional councils so that they would perform SMU-oriented activities. If the regional councils actively organize non-regular and other precariously-employed workers into community unions, help workers and residents solve livelihood issues and serve as network nodes between labour and social movements in their respective regions, the sphere of social movement unionism, still at the margins of the institutionalized labour movement, may be expanded. Although innovative activities of some 'progressive' regional councils are reported (see Rengo Soken 2010), it remains to be seen how widely new activism at the regional level will spread among the 300 councils.

Conclusion

This chapter examined the limits and the possibilities of social movement unionism in Japan in the context of industrial relations institutions. Previous studies of social movement unionism tended to treat industrial relations institutions as restraining the growth of SMU and therefore as an obstacle to overcome. While such characterizations of institutions may not be off the mark, they tended to overlook how such differences identified in cross-national comparisons of industrial relations institutions have influenced the development of social movement unionism in different countries. The chapter showed that the industrial relations institutions in Japan are dominated by cooperative enterprise unions and that these institutional features are related to the growth of social movement unionism in two senses. First, mainstream enterprise unions are embedded in the existing industrial relations institutions, despite the institutionally weak position of organized labour as a whole, and therefore are not receptive to the idea of revitalizing the labour movement based on SMU-oriented strategies. Second, although community unions developed as a counterweight to the conservative dominant unions, they have developed only at the institutional margins. Their impact on the labour movement as a whole is limited by the hostile attitudes of mainstream unions toward community unions, as well as by their own organizational and resource-related problems.

Taking advantage of an OISR survey of community unions, this chapter also examined the extent to which community unions sought broad goals, formed alliances with social movement organizations, and involved the rank and file. Community unions had characteristics of social movement unionism in terms of seeking broad goals and having relatively active rank-and-file involvement, and they were less active in forming alliances with social movement and community organizations. They were active, however, in forming networks with other community unions and in forming personal networks among union activists, activists of social movements, and experts such as lawyers and academics. Unlike coalitions between organizations, these personal networks are fluid and lack solid organizational structures but sometimes exert strong influence as in the case of the *Hakenmura* movement.

This chapter draws a rather pessimistic picture of the future development of social movement unionism in Japan, although pointing out two possible scenarios of partial labour movement revitalization. My pessimistic picture is largely due to an assessment of the dominant part of industrial relations institutions, i.e., labour-management relations at the enterprise level. They remain as stable as ever, despite economic and social changes surrounding the IR institutions. Enterprise unions continue to commit themselves to labour-management cooperation based on the idea of the 'politics of productivity' and are unreceptive to arguments such as those made by the Rengo Assessment Committee. Institutionalized enterprise-based industrial relations, however, are not totally impervious to the changes in their social and economic environments, including the development of community unions at the institutional margins. Enterprise unions have their own serious problems. Cooperation with management in workforce reductions through voluntary retirement schemes and loaning of employees to other companies has led to a steady decline in the membership and to a shrinking financial base. Excessively cooperative policies have also widened the social distance between union leaders and rank-and-file members, with the latter becoming increasingly indifferent to union activities. Whether impending enterprise union crises, coupled with criticisms made by union activists and observers, will bring about efforts for union revitalization from within and/or lead to a wider acceptance of social movement unionism inside the institutional mainstream is a subject of future research.

References

Azuma, Y. (2010). 'Nihon ni okeru Atarashii Rodo Undo' (The New Labor Movement in Japan). In M. Ishii, A. Hyodo, T. Onimaru (eds), *Gendai Rodomondai Bunseki*. Kyoto: Horitsu Bunkasha.

Baccaro, L., Hamann, K., Turner, L. (2003). 'The Politics of Labor Movement Revitalization: The Need for a Revitalized Perspective', *European Journal of Industrial Relations*, 9 (1), 119–33.

Bronfenbrenner, K., Friedman, S., Hurd, R.W., Oswarld, R.A., Seeber, R.L. (eds) (1998). *Organizing to Win: New Research on Union Strategies*. Ithaca, NY: ILR Press.

Chun, J.J. (2009). *Organizing at the Margins: The Symbolic Politics of Labor in South Korean and the United States*. Ithaca, NY: Cornell University Press.

Clawson, D. (2003). *The Next Upsurge: Labor and the New Social Movements*. Ithaca, NY: ILR Press.

Cornfield, D.B., McCammon, H.J. (eds) (2003). *Labor Revitalization: Global Perspectives and New Initiatives.* New York: JAI Press.

Doko, T. (2010). 'Godo Rosoga Tekisuru Hoteki Kadai' (Legal Disputes Concerning Regional General Unions), *Nihon Rodo Kenkyu Zasshi*, 604, 75–83.

Endo, K. (2009). 'Toshikoshi Hakenmurano Daiseiko' (Big Achievement of Hibiya Tent Village for the Jobless), *Keizai Ronshu* (Meiji University), 56 (3–4), 97–109.

Fairbrother, P., Yates, C.A.B. (eds) (2003). *Trade Unions in Renewal: A Comparative Study.* London: Continuum.

Fantasia, R., Kim, V. (2004). *Hard Work: Remaking the American Labor Movement.* Berkeley: University of California Press.

Frege, C.M., Kelly, J. (2003). 'Union Revitalization Strategies in Comparative Perspective', *European Journal of Industrial Relations*, 9 (1), 7–24.

Gordon, A. (1998). *Wages of Affluence: Labor and Management in Postwar Japan.* Cambridge, Mass: Harvard University Press.

Gray, K. (2008). *Korean Workers and Neoliberal Globalization.* London: Routledge.

Imai, J. (2011). *The Transformation of Japanese Employment Relations: Reform Without Labor.* New York: Palgrave Macmillan.

Inagami, T. (ed) (1995). *Seijuku Shakai no Nakano Kigyobetu Kumiai* (Enterprise Unions in Mature Society). Tokyo: Nihon Rodo Kenkyu Kiko.

Inagami, T., Whittaker, H.D. (2005). *The New Community Firm: Employment, Governance and Management Reform in Japan.* Cambridge: Cambridge University Press.

JUCF. (2002). *Zenkoku Komyuniti Yunion Rengokai Setsuritu Taikai Giansho* (Policy Proposals submitted to the Funding Convention of the JUCF), Tokyo: JUCF.

Kinoshita, T. (2007). *Kakusa Shakai ni Idomu Yunion* (Community Unions Challenging an Unequal Society). Tokyo: Kadensha.

Koido, Y. et al. (2005). 'UI Zensen Domei ga Jinzaihaken Shinpojiumu (Ge)' (A symposium on dispatched workers hosted by UI Zensen Domei: Part Two), *Workers' Radar* (May, 2005), 18–28.

Kotani, S. (2001). 'Tokyo Kanrishoku Yunion Kumiaiin no Ishiki Henyo' (Changes in Consciousness of Members of Tokyo Kanrishoku Union), *Rodo Shaigaku Kenkyu*, 12, 147–78.

Kotani, S. (1999). 'Josei no Atarashii Rodo Undo' (The New Labour Movement of Women), *Rodo Shakaigaku Kenkyu*, 1, 3–25.

Kumar, P., Schenk, C. (eds) (2006). *Path to Union Renewal: Canadian Experiences.* Peterborough: Broadview Press.

Lopez, S. (2004). *Reorganizing the Rust Belt: An Inside Study of the American Labor Movement.* Berkeley: University of California Press.

Martin, A. (2008). 'The Institutional Logic of Union Organizing and the Effectiveness of Social Movement Repertoires', *American Journal of Sociology*, 113 (4), 1067–103.

Milkman, R. (2006). *L.A. Story: Immigrant Workers and the Future of the U.S. Labor Movement*. New York: Russell Sage Foundation.

Milkman, R., Voss, K. (eds) (2004). *Rebuilding Labor: Organizing and Organizers in the New Union Movement*. Ithaca, NY: ILR Press.

Moody, K. (2007). *US Labor In Trouble and Transition: The Future of Reform from Above, The Promise of Revival from Below*. London: Verso.

Mori, T. (2003). 'Shokuba no Roshi Kankei no Kozo' (The Structure of Workplace-Level Industrial Relations). In K. Saguchi, S. Hashimoto (eds), *Jinjiromu Kanri no Shiteki Bunseki*. Kyoto: Minerva Shobo.

Oh, H. (2010). 'Godo Roso no Genjo to Sonzai Igi' (Organization, Activities and Significance of Regional General Unions in Japan), *Nihon Rodo Kenkyu Zasshi*, 604, 47–65.

Oh, H. (2004). 'Pato Taima no Soshikika to Iken Hanei Shisutemu' (Organizing Part-Time Workers and the System of Reflecting Their Opinions in Union Policies), *Nihon Rodo Kenkyu Zasshi*, 527, 31–47.

OISR (Ohara Institute for Social Research) (2010). 'Kojin Kamei Kumiai no Katsudo ni Kansuru Anketo Chosakekka Hokoku' (The Report on Results of the Survey on Individually-Affiliated Unions' Activities), Working Paper No. 41, Tokyo: Ohara Institute for Social Research, Hosei University.

Rengo. (2003). 'Rengo Hyoka Iinnkai Saishu Hokoku' (The Final Report of the Rengo Assessment Committee), Tokyo: Rengo.

Rengo Soken (Research Institute For Advancement of Living Standards). (2010). 'Chiiki Kyogikai no Soshiki to Katsudo no Genjo Chosa Hokokusho' (Report on the Current State of Organizations and Activities of Regional Councils), Available at: http://rengo-soken.or.jp/report_db/pub/search.php.

Shinoda, T. (2009). 'Which Side Are You On?: Hakenmura and the Working Poor as a Tipping Point in Japanese Labor Politics', *The Asia Pacific Journal: Japan Focus Website*. Available at: http://www.japanfocus.org/-Toru-SHINODA/3113.

Streck, W., Thelen, K. (2005). 'Introduction: Institutional Change in Advanced Political Economies'. In W. Streeck, K. Thelen (eds), *Beyond Continuity: Institutional Change in Advanced Political Economies*. New York: Oxford University Press.

Suzuki, A. (2009a). 'Nihon no Rodo Undo-Sai Kasseika no Kanosei to Rodoundo Shidosha no Gensetsu Bunseki' (The Labor Movement in Japan: An Examination of its Possible Revitalization Based on a Discourse Analysis of Union Leaders). In T. Shinkawa, T. Shinoda (eds), *Rodo to Fukushi Kokkano Kanosei: Rodoundo Saisei no Kokusai Hikaku*. Kyoto: Minerva Shobo.

Suzuki, A. (2009b). 'Rengo Seisaku no Tenkaino Bunseki-Seiji, Keizai, Soshiki Mondai o Meguru Tairitsujiku no Shikakukara' (Analysis of Rengo's Policies: Focusing on Internal Conflicts Over Political, Economic, and Organizational Issues). In

M. Ishida, H. Gankoji (eds), *Koza Gendai no Shakai Seisaku Rodo Shijo, Roshi Kankei, Rodoho*. Tokyo: Akashi Shoten.

Suzuki, A. (2008). 'Community Unions in Japan: Similarities and Differences of Region-based Labour Movements between Japan and Other Industrialized Countries', *Economic and Industrial Democracy*, 29 (4), 492–520.

Suzuki, A. (2005). 'Shakai Undoteki Rodoundo toha Nanika' (What is Social Movement Unionism? An Analysis of Its Concept and Conditions Based on Previous Research), *Ohara Shakaimondai Kenkyujo Zasshi*, 562/563, 1–16.

Takasu, H. (2010). 'Yunion Undo no Keisei to Genjo' (The Formation and the Current State of the [Community] Union Movement), *Nihon Rodo Nenkan*, 80, 40–68.

Tange, H. (2009). 'Konnichi no Wakingu Pua to Hiseiki Koyo Mondai' (The Working Poor and the Problems of Non-regular Employment at Present), *Nihon Rodo Nenkan*, 79, 39–69.

Turner, L. (2009). 'Institutions and Activism: Crisis and Opportunity for a German Labor Movement in Decline', *Industrial and Labor Relations Review*, 62 (3), 294–312.

Turner, L. (2003). 'Reviving the Labor Movement: A Comparative Perspective'. In D.B. Cornfield, H.J. McCammon (eds), *Labor Revitalization: Global Perspectives and New Initiatives*. Oxford: Elsevier Ltd.

Turner, L. (1991). *Democracy at Work: Changing World Markets and the Future of Labor Unions*. Ithaca, NY: Cornell University Press.

Turner, L., Katz, H.C., Hurd, R. (eds). (2001). *Rekindling the Movement: Labor's Quest for Relevance in the Twenty-First Century*. Ithaca, NY: ILR Press.

Voss, K. (2010). 'Democratic Dilemmas: Union Democracy and Union Renewal', *Transfer: European Review of Labour and Research*, 16 (3), 369–82.

Voss, K., Sherman, R. (2000). 'Breaking the Iron Law of Oligarchy: Union Revitalization in the American Labor Movement', *American Journal of Sociology*, 106 (2), 202–49.

Weathers, C. (2010). 'The Rising Voice of Japan's Community Unions'. In H. Vinken et al. (eds), *Civic Engagement in Contemporary Japan: Established and Emerging Perspectives*. New York: Springer Science Business Media.

Webster, E., Lambert, R., Bezuidenhout, A. (2008). *Grounding Globalization: Labour in the Age of Insecurity*. Hoboken, NJ: Wiley-Blackwell.

Yoshioka, K. (2009). 'Naze Shudanteki "Rodo Undo" ha Seiritsu Shinainoka' (Why Is It Difficult to Establish Collective Labor Movements?), *Gendai no Riron*, 20, 182–90.

Yuasa, M. (2008). *Hanhinkon: 'Suberidai Shaki' Karno Dashutsu* (Against Poverty: An Escape from the 'Sliding Society'). Tokyo: Iwanami Shoten.

JOOHEE LEE

4 A Renewal of Solidarity or Continued Decline? The Korean Retail Workers' Struggles against Neoliberalism

Introduction

In Korea, despite successful industrial growth and an explosion in the expansion of the industrial labour force, the political capacities and aspirations of the working class have lagged behind those economic and demographic factors. While uneven development processes and frequent state intervention have held back working-class organization, the transition to democracy in the late 1980s changed the lay of the land. During the transition period the labour movement grew rapidly, and major steps towards the development of a democratic labour movement took place. Since then, Korea has earned a reputation for a solidaristic and militant labour movement.

Because of Korea's authoritarian legacy and its uneven industrialization process, however, the democratic, political labour movement's inability to sustain class-wide solidarity was predictable. The Korean working class has generally lacked the organizational power to carry out economy-wide collective action. Most trade unions are organized on an enterprise basis, and as a result, collective bargaining structures are decentralized at the enterprise-level. Only core workers in strategically important export-led enterprises possess sufficient structural and organizational power to win economic concessions from employers. The promise of stable employment and higher wages has successfully appealed to core workers' narrow interest in the profitability of their own firms. As a result, core workers have increasingly demanded their union leaders focus on winning concrete economic gains. The gap in inter-firm welfare has widened and dual-economy tendencies have been reinforced. These changes have weakened the class-wide solidarity of the working class. The financial crisis of 1997 further deepened the crisis of the labour movement by producing a large number of non-regular workers. Regular (core) workers in large enterprises were reluctant to protect non-regular workers' rights because they would be a buffer against labour market changes and employment adjustments. Consequently, a majority of enterprise unions have refused to accept non-regulars as trade union members.

Despite the structural and emotional barriers that have obstructed collective action among core and non-regular workers, some unions have demonstrated working class solidarity. The prolonged strike of E-land workers, which lasted more than 500 days, is a case in point. Two enterprise unions in the E-land Group, which brought together regular and non-regular workers, fought hard to protect employment security for non-regular workers.

Why did E-land unions choose solidarity with non-regular workers over the narrowly-defined interests of regular workers? Despite an abundance of research on the labour relations dimensions of increasing, non-regular employment arrangements in Korea (Lee and Lee 2003; Kang 2004; Eun 2007), union policies toward non-regular employment have been little analysed. This study explores *the specific conditions* under which unions, even under the inescapable pressures of labour flexibility imposed by the neoliberal state, can develop the capacity to intervene in the regulation of labour markets to prevent the persistent marginalization of a casual workforce. This study then asks whether such solidarity can revitalize South Korea labour movements.

Neoliberal Labour Reforms and the Employment 'Protection' Act for Non-regular Workers

The problem of non-regular work has come to prominence in Korea since the financial crisis of 1997. Measures of fiscal austerity drove many firms and financial institutions into bankruptcy and temporary closure, resulting in severe employment adjustments. For example, banks reduced their total workforce by around 30 per cent and substantially increased the percentage of fixed-term, temporary workers (Lee and Park 2007). As a result, the number of non-regular workers increased rapidly. According to a statistical survey of non-regular employment conducted by the National Statistics Office, non-regular workers represented about 35 per cent of wage workers in the 2000s. The Korea Labour and Society Institute (KLSI), an independent, pro-labour think tank, however, estimated that, during the same period, about 55 per cent of wage earners were non-regular workers (see Table 4.1).

Table 4.1 Non-regular Employment, 2001–2009

	National Statistics Office		KLSI	
	Number (thousands)	%	Number (thousands)	%
2001	364	26.8	737	55.7
2002	384	27.4	772	56.6
2003	461	32.6	784	55.4
2004	559	37.0	816	55.9
2005	548	36.6	840	56.1
2006	546	35.5	845	55.0
2007	570	35.9	861	54.2
2008	563	33.8	840	52.1
2009	575	34.9	841	52.3
2010	569	33.3	859	50.4

Note: Surveys were conducted in August, except in 2009 (March), *Supplementary Survey on Economically Active Population* by National Statistics Office.
Source: The Korea Labour Institute (2010, 2011), *KLI Labour Statistics* and the Korea Labour and Society Institute (KLSI).

The statistical interpretation of the supplementary survey differs because the KLSI includes long-term temporary workers who work more than a year at a workplace (Han, 2009). Considering the wages and working conditions of these workers, it seems proper to include them in the category of non-regular employment. Their conditions are similar to non-regular workers except that they have longer contracts.

The size of the non-regular workforce raises concerns among trade unionists because of the increasing wage and general welfare gap between non-regular and regular workers. Table 4.2 illustrates workers in non-regular employment arrangements earned on average less than regular workers, and the wage gap grew in firms with more than 300 workers.

Table 4.2 Wage Differentials Between Non-regular and Regular Workforce in 2008 (%)

		Hourly wage
Total		-12.9
Firm Size	Less than 100 workers	-6.6
	100–300	-24.5
	More than 300 workers	-30.5
Trade Union	Yes	-9.6
	No	-27.3
Gender	Male	-10.8
	Female	-16.1

Sources: *White Paper on Labour* (2010), Ministry of Employment and Labour, p. 536.

To reduce the ever-increasing number of non-regular workers, the Act on the Protection, etc. of Fixed-term and Part-time Employees (hereafter Non-regular Employment Protection Act) was passed in 2007. At first glance, the law seemed not to be particularly damaging to non-regular workers. Actually, it expands rights to non-regular workers by prohibiting discrimination against non-regular workers engaged in the *same or similar jobs*[1] and limits the employment period of temporary workers to a maximum

1 Article 8 of the Act states that an employer shall not discriminate against fixed-term or part-time workers on the grounds of their employment status. They are not to be

of two years. After two years, employers are required to rehire non-regular workers with two or more years of tenure as regular employees.[2]

The Non-regular Employment Protection Act, however, has produced unintended consequences detrimental to the welfare of non-regular workers.[3] After the enactment of the law, employers adjusted non-regular jobs so that they would appear different from those of regular workers. They also extensively utilized outsourcing and refused to re-hire non-regulars with more than two years of tenure. Even when employers decided to keep non-regular workers, they simply re-classified their jobs as semi-regular with wages and working conditions similar to non-regular employment. The Act therefore brought about extensive outsourcing and non-regular worker layoffs. As a result, the Korean labour market became further divided, and working-class solidarity was even more damaged. Ironically, E-land workers struck against the implementation of the law, with regular and non-regular workers firmly united in resisting these neoliberal labour market reforms.

Research Methods

The retail sector utilizes far more temporary and part-time workers than the manufacturing sector in Korea, thus providing an ideal setting to explore union responses to increases in non-regular workers. This study utilizes

---

treated differently than other workers without a fixed term contract who are engaged in the same or similar jobs in a business or workplace.

2 The actual wording of Article 4 of the Act is as follows: an employer may hire a fixed-term employee for a period not exceeding two years...if an employer hires a fixed-term employee for more than two years, the fixed-term employee shall be considered as a worker who has made a labour contract with no fixed term.

3 The current Lee administration and the ruling Grand National Party are planning to extend the employment period for non-regular workers from two years to a maximum of four years, despite strong opposition from labour. If this plan is enacted, the employment situation of non-regular workers is expected to deteriorate further.

quantitative and qualitative methods. The first stage of research involved analysing structural characteristics of the retail sector, based on official, government statistics. The next step analysed a survey of retail workers conducted from September to November 2007. A total of 1,434 regular and non-regular workers completed the survey. The population of the survey included large retail firms such as E-land and major department stores. This study focuses on 289 Homever worker responses and 356 responses from New Core workers. The survey, conducted by the trade unions at these two firms, was not from a random sample, and the results should be understood to represent the views of trade union members. Finally, I conducted in-depth interviews from October to December 2008 with union leaders and members and non-regular workers in E-land and other retail firms.

Employment Relations in the Korean Retail Sector

Korea opened its retail market to global competition by 1996, but global retailers, such as Wal-Mart and Carrefour, were unsuccessful in the country. They struggled to understand local Korean retailing, which requires much more refined services. Although these global retailers' efforts to enter the Korean market were for naught, a sector that was once dominated by small-scale shops was fundamentally transformed by the emergence of discount store chains owned by *chaebol* (Korean conglomerate) firms. The share of sales of the four largest discount superstores, including E-land stores, approaches 86.2 per cent and the share of the three largest department stores 77.7 per cent (Kim, 2007).

Despite such changes, Korean retail jobs remained lower paid than the average Korean job. Furthermore, about 76 per cent of these jobs were non-regular employment, far above the national average which was about 50 per cent in 2007 (KCTU, 2007). To make the situation worse, very few retailers added non-regular workers who had been on the job for more than two years to the permanent workforce. Instead, they laid-off or outsourced the non-regulars. Even when they granted non-regular workers permanent worker status, they did this only on the condition that these non-regular workers belong to separate job-groups where working conditions and wage rates were more similar to non-regular than regular jobs.

It is not surprising that retail workers are barely organized. Union density in the retail sector is just 3.6 per cent, while 11 per cent of the total workforce (non-regular workers: 3.4 per cent; regular workers: 17.4 per cent) are union members in Korea. Among retail workers, only 1.7 per cent of non-regular workers are union members, while 11.9 per cent of regular workers are organized (Kim 2007). Furthermore, enterprise unions, most of whose members are regular workers, generally do not pay attention to the wages and working conditions of non-regular workers (Interview with a Service Workers Federation union official, 10/10/08).

The survey conducted by the trade unions in 2007, however, demonstrates that low union density was not because of retail worker disinterest. According to Table 4.3, 72.9 per cent of non-member workers expressed a strong desire to join a union in their enterprise, and these percentages were much higher among discount store workers and in some small shops in shopping malls. Further analysis shows that female non-members wanted to join a union more than male non-members. About 78 per cent of female non-members responded positively to union membership as opposed to 56 per cent of male non-members. That wages and working conditions of female workers were worse than those of their male counterparts could partly explain such gender differences.

Table 4.3 Respondent Characteristics Regarding Union Membership

	Discount Stores	*Department Stores*	*Convenience Stores*	*Small Shops (Cosmetics)*	*Small Shops (Food)*	*Fast Food Restaurants*	*Total*
No union in the workplace	4.4.	14.8	100.0	1.6	8.5	10.6	17.1
Ineligible for union	2.7	12.1	0.0	4.9	11.9	45.9	6.9
Do not want to join union	0.3	2.7	0.0	2.7	23.7	9.4	2.5
Union Member	92.6	70.5	0.0	90.7	55.9	34.1	73.6
Total	100.0	100.0	100.0	100.0	100.0	100.0	100
Only non-members responded							
Want to join union	93.7	82.1	8.4	95.0	75.5	44.6	72.9

Note: Numbers are % responded positively, N=1432. The number of respondents differs across stores and shops.

The same survey also demonstrates that these non-members in general consider unions unnecessary. However, a majority of workers in discount stores responded that they did not join a trade union because they were afraid of disadvantages or opposition from management. Actually, it turned out that management in discount stores was heavily involved in obstructing trade union activities. Non-member workers were threatened with losing their jobs or facing other disadvantages in the workplace, which explains why union density is so low in the retail sector.

Table 4.4 Reasons for Not Joining Trade Unions

	Discount Stores	*Department Stores*	*Convenience Stores*	*Small Shops (Cosmetics)*	*Small Shops (Food)*	*Fast Food Restaurants*	*Total*
Union not necessary	11.7	28.1	51.8	33.3	41.2	34.9	36.2
Disadvantage to joining union	41.6	21.9	8.8	41.7	11.8	9.3	19.5
No one solicits union membership	6.5	15.6	18.2	0.0	0.0	14.0	12.9
Do not know how to join union	9.1	12.5	10.9	16.7	23.5	4.7	10.7
Not satisfied with union activity	11.7	12.5	3.6	0.0	5.9	11.6	7.5
Opposition from management	10.4	0.0	0.0	0.0	0.0	0.0	2.5
Discouraged by co-workers /friends	1.3	0.0	1.5	0.0	0.0	7.0	1.9
Total	100	100	100	100	100	100	100

Note: Numbers are % responded positively; N=378. The number of respondents differs across stores and shops.

As a result, the organizational drive to increase the number of union members in the retail sector made by the KCTU (Korean Confederation of Trade Unions) and the Federation of Private Service Workers' Union was unsuccessful. When employers simply refused to renew the contracts of those temporary workers who expressed interests in trade union activities, unions for non-regular workers could not be expected to survive. The struggle of E-Land workers naturally stood out under such circumstances.

Conditions of Solidarity: the Case of the E-Land Strike

A Korean trade unionist noted, 'E-Land is a Korean Wal-Mart'. Its founder, originally a textile retailer, Park Sung-soo, is a highly religious Christian, and the E-Land Group in general has long pushed strong, anti-union strategies. The E-Land Group became one of the country's largest retailers after purchasing the New Core discount chain in 2003 and 32 Carrefour discount stores, which became Homever in 2006. The strikes were led by the New Core enterprise union and the E-Land general union, composed mostly of workers at Homever. By 2007, there were about 3,000 regular and 3,000 non-regular workers at Homever workplaces (Table 4.5). New Core outlets employed 1,700 regular workers and 500 non-regular workers. Unlike other enterprise unions, both unions accepted non-regular worker members.

Table 4.5 The Number of E-Land Group Workers and Trade Union Members in 2007

Name	*Number of Stores*	*Number of Workers*			*Number of Trade Union Members*		
		Regular Workers	*Non-regular*	*Total*	*Regular Workers*	*Non-regular*	*Total*
Homever	33	3,000	3,000	6,000	550	600	1,150
2001 Outlet	11	800	500	1,300	50	–	50
New Core Outlet	16	1,700	500	2,200	1,350	150	1,500
Total	60	5,500	4,000	9,500	1,950	750	2,700

Source: Kim (2007), taken from Table 5–2–1.

Outsourcing and casualization of work at Homever (then Carrefour) began as early as 1996, when dispatched workers were allowed at the workplaces. Although there was some discrimination in employment towards non-regulars, it was less prominent than in other enterprises. The trade union at Carrefour, which embraced non-regular workers, prided itself on its progressive membership policies. Possibly due to the similarities between regular and non-regular workers and a lack of discriminatory practices, the Carrefour enterprise union decided to organize non-regular workers as well (interview with a Homever trade union official, 22/10/08) and forged a collective bargaining agreement with Carrefour management that secured employment of all non-regular workers who had been in company for at least 18 months. In return, regular workers restrained their wage demands. With this agreement, the Carrefour union was able to organized more non-regular workers. When the E-land Group bought the French discount chain, it inherited the collective bargaining agreement that gave job security to non-regular workers with 18 months of seniority.

Immediately before the Act of Employment Protection became law, E-land failed to renew about 800 contract and temporary workers, refusing them re-employment as regular workers. Furthermore, E-land planned to implement massive outsourcing to avoid newly enacted Non-regular Employment Protection Law restrictions. Ever since, trade union members of the E-land Group have protested vehemently against the firm's decision. A 17-month long labour dispute started on 1 July 2007, when union members staged sit-in strikes at a Homever outlet in Seoul. The strikes spread to other outlets, including New Core stores. Seoul Metropolitan Police Agency arrested striking workers, but the repressive police crack-down fuelled full-scale combat between labour and capital, attracting the participation of many civic organizations and progressive parties. The enterprise union at New Core stopped the strike after management agreed to hire 36 non-regular workers. But New Core management laid off 18 trade unionists and refused to stop outsourcing. The conflict at Homever came to an end on 12 November 2008, when E-land and Samsung Tesco, which took over E-land's Homever outlets and changed them into Home Plus in October 2008, reached an agreement with the new Home Plus trade union.

The strike of E-land workers demonstrated that it was possible for enterprise unions to organize non-regular workers and fight for their rights.

It was the characteristics of the moral economy[4] of the E-land unions that explains the solidarity strategy. A variety of factors can determine the moral economy. The following conditions forged strong solidarity between regular and non-regular workers in the prolonged strike at E-Land retail companies.

Socio-Economic Similarity of Regular and Non-regular Workers

As previously discussed, the retail sector employs a disproportionately large number of non-regular workers whose wages and working conditions are below the national average. The truth is, however, wages and working conditions of regular workers in this sector are not very different than those of non-regular workers. For example, according to the 2007 survey of retail workers, a typical non-regular worker at Homever earned 820,000 won, while a typical regular worker at the same workplace earned 950,000 won. In addition, a vast majority of regular and non-regular workers at Homever were women workers in their mid-forties. They worked in the same shops doing the same cashier jobs. Their educational qualifications were almost identical. 83.3 per cent of non-regular workers and 82.3 per cent of regular workers were high school graduates. About 10 per cent of non-regular and regular workers held college degrees. 'They (non-regular workers) were not very different from us (regular workers)', said a former worker at Homever who had been laid off due to her active participation in the strike (Interview, 31/10/08). This similarly implies that, at least at

4 By moral economy, Swenson (1989) implies that nonmaterial values of workers, such as pay equity, matter, and thus it becomes imperative for union leaders to control norms regarding pay structure in order to regulate worker discontent. Shaping the moral economy via pay equity, according to Swenson, is not an easy task due to a wage policy 'trilemma', by which he refers to a set of powerful market constraints that unions face as agents in the moral economy. It describes systematic trade-offs between levelling within a union or confederation, external levelling either by increasing total wage share or by compressing interunion wage differentials and employment growth. Since no pair of objectives can be pursued simultaneously without sacrificing the third, unions need to fluctuate constantly between these distributional policy fronts. This trilemma can also apply to sector- or enterprise-level union strategies.

Homever, non-regular worker employment was precarious not because non-regulars lacked qualifications to become regular workers but because of corporate cost-cutting strategies.

Shared characteristics made it easy for the Homever trade union to recruit non-regular workers. Usually, an enterprise union found it difficult to persuade non-regular workers to join a union composed primarily of regular workers. Because their employment security was not guaranteed, non-regular workers who wanted to join a union were more prone to management abuse, a situation the Homever union wanted to change. Although the wage gap between regular and non-regular workers was not large, there was a significant, private welfare gap. For example, non-regular workers received no paid bonuses, nor did they enjoy paid holidays. When the union corrected these discriminatory practices, some regular workers were displeased with their union's exceptional attention to non-regular workers. The union leadership, however, continued to encourage non-regular workers to put their trust in the union. Most enterprise unions, even when they decide to organize non-regulars, create separate units for them. The Homever union maintained the policy of one union for all workers and provided individualized counselling services to non-regular workers who experienced problems with co-workers or management. In return for employment security for non-regulars, regular workers agreed not to raise their wage rates. As a union official said, 'it (the trust) was not just given; the union worked hard for it' (Interview, 22/10/08).

Therefore, when Homever management claimed that the clause in the collective agreement covered only 170 workers who were unionized at the time, regular workers were ready to fight for non-regular workers who might lose their jobs. That their fellow non-regular workers were dismissed in violation of the contract made the Homever union furious which led to the strike.

Regular Workers' Employment Insecurity

The situation at another E-Land-affiliated firm, New Core, was not very different. At New Core, outsourcing was more drastically implemented than at Homever. As New Core management began outsourcing cashier jobs in March 2007, regular cashiers had to transfer to other workplaces and/or different jobs, such as sales. Management not only eliminated non-regular jobs, but also threatened regular worker employment security (Interview with a laid-off former trade unionist, 10/12/09). In addition, precisely because of the larger non-regular workforce, the New Core union had to worry about losing the disruptive power of strikes in cases where non-regular workers went unorganized. If non-regular workers could substitute for regular workers jobs during strikes, the union's bargaining power would be diminished, providing strong incentives to organize non-regular workers and prevent extensive outsourcing of jobs.

Some enterprise unions, however, have chosen to do otherwise. Those in department stores face less pressure from management to layoff non-regular workers because department stores put more emphasis on high quality services than on low labour costs. Large department stores opted to keep non-regular workers and made them semi-regular workers. Hyundai Department Store (hereafter HDS), one of the three largest department stores in Korea, was an exception. When E-Land workers went on strike in June 2007, labour and management at HDS agreed to outsource the jobs of 416 non-regular workers, not because regular workers at HDS were protected from employment insecurity, but on the contrary, according to a survey conducted in 2007, about 72 per cent of union members who were regular workers at HDS worried that their jobs were not fully protected from employment adjustments and layoffs. HDS was known for its higher wages and fringe benefits, and the HDS union opted to protect regular workers (Kim 2007).

Therefore, employment insecurity of regular workers at E-Land group was just a contextual condition which consolidated the solidarity of regular and non-regular workers further. In other cases, for example at HDS, a similar situation could lead to the opposite conclusion. Most enterprise unions pay attention to non-regular workers only to increase their bargaining leverage but gain few concessions from management that increase wages or improve working conditions for non-regular workers. Common backgrounds and similarity of workers with different employment statuses made it possible for E-Land unions to produce favourable collective action outcomes.

Sense of Injustice

It was a sense of injustice that fuelled the bonding of regular and non-regular workers at Homever and New Core stores. The sense of injustice was inflamed by the neoliberal labour policies that produced large numbers of non-regular workers and exploded when E-Land management made various attempts to take advantage of the flawed Non-regular Employment Protection Act. The Korean Human Rights Commission found that E-Land management forced non-regular workers to use other people's names after having worked for more than a year. Management also forced them to sign 'blank' contracts lacking contract periods, making transition into regular contract impossible. E-Land workers were protesting not just mass dismissals and large-scale outsourcing of core job functions, such as cashiers and sales assistants, but also the negative impact of the very law that was supposed to 'protect' non-regular workers. The passage of the law temporarily decreased the number of temporary workers with fixed-term contracts but increased the number of part-timers, temporary agency workers and the workers employed by subcontracted firms. In sum, the law increased non-regular workers in lower wage and more unstable sectors (Kwon 2009). Their sense of injustice made itself well felt in the press release 'Why Strike?' (10 June 2007), co-signed by the Korean Federation of Private Service Workers' Union, KCTU Seoul Regional Centre, Democratic Labour Party's Non-regular Work Movement Organization, Democratic Labour Party's Seoul Regional Office, National Conference for Non-regular Workers' Unions, Working Voice, New Core Union, and E-Land General Union.

> *Why Strike?*
>
> It is very simple. So many workers lost their jobs unfairly and unreasonably. The law, which was supposedly made to protect non-regular workers, is actually laying off millions of these workers. The Ministry of Labour is heavily biased toward management. We workers must do it ourselves, because no one else would help us to win our just demands...
>
> A majority of union members are married women. They do not know what strikes do or mean. However, they cannot tolerate it any longer. Our jobs and pride are more important than the money we have lost due to this strike...

> E-Land Group did not talk with us. Instead, it is just ruthlessly oppressing us. Using termination of employment contracts, merciless outsourcing and forced reassignment of job duties, E-Land management is cold-bloodedly laying off both regular and non-regular workers. It has also threatened new members and non-members of the union with disadvantages and dismissal...
>
> We are sorry about inconveniences that the strike has caused to our shoppers and consumers. But we also plead with you to help us fight this battle. We need to be humanely treated so that we can serve you better. Consumers are also workers, or their family members are. If we can solve non-regular work problems in this retail sector, you consumers will also be better off. Please help us!
>
> The 21st century for us workers has been the century of despair and hopelessness, where this monstrous 'neoliberalism' is destroying our lives. Now it must be changed. We retail workers will fight for you. We will be united to create a world where there are no more non-regular workers and no more employment adjustments...We will certainly win this battle.

One of the core demands of the press release was that the government must immediately repeal the Employment Protection Act for Non-regular Workers. It was why the E-Land strike garnered moral support from many labour and civic organizations. The Korean Confederation of Trade Unions (KCTU) launched 'Zero-Sales Struggles', to boycott E-Land discount stores. Most civic groups joined the KCTU, blaming the E-Land Group for evading corporate social responsibility. Among political parties, the Democratic Labour Party was most engaged in the strike. Its Seoul Regional Office organized a regional committee just to help E-Land workers, and the committee launched one-person protests and candlelight protests. About 1,600 party members participated in the 'Zero-Sales Struggles' (Kim 2007). Collaboration between labour and civic organizations was common in Korea during the democratic transition, but since then several social movement organizations have become critical of trade union movements centred on core workers. The E-Land strikes reminded many trade unionists and labour activists of political and democratic labour movements in the late-1980s, which were known for social movement unionism.

The Outcome of the Struggle

The outcome of the struggle, however, was by no means a clear-cut victory for non-regular workers and trade unions. Of 3,000 non-regular workers, only 512 of the workers, who had more than two years of seniority, became regular workers at Homever. There were workers with more than two years of seniority who did not become regular workers. Employment contracts of these non-regular workers were terminated. At New Core, management laid off 380 non-regular workers and outsourced 220 positions (Kwon 2009). At the same time, several union leaders had to resign officially and leave the firm. The reasons for the setbacks were numerous, but I want to focus on the two most damaging factors. First, as the strike went on, small business owners who rented shops in Homever and New Core stores withdrew support for the striking workers as their profits declined. E-Land management also pressured them to increased sales. Second, and more important, E-Land management was determined to destroy its militant unions by employing harsh union-busting campaigns. They filed huge compensation claims against E-Land workers for losses that were incurred during the strike, and the retailer adamantly refused to reinstate the union leaders.

Trade unionists at the E-Land Group, however, did not think that their sacrifices were in vain. 'The New Core struggle was the best any trade union could do to solve the non-regular employment problem', a trade unionist said (Interview, 22/10/08). 'Usually, the hardest fought ones were sacrificed...but because of their sacrifices, the other retailers now think twice before they begin outsourcing or dismissing non-regular workers'. Actually, the E-Land workers' struggle held back relentless outsourcing in the retail sector as a whole. Unintentionally, it was also successful in illustrating the social problems and suffering caused by the Employment Protection Act for Non-regular Workers. It was unfortunate that the struggle did not revive the tradition of social movement unionism in Korea.

The E-Land Case in Comparative Perspective

As shown in Table 4.6, the struggle of the regular worker unions at E-Land Group was an exceptional case of working-class solidarity. Wages and working conditions for regular workers in the retail sector were not very different from those of non-regulars, and because of the large size of the non-regular workforce at E-Land, the unions were strongly motivated to organize non-regular workers. According to a workplace panel study conducted in 2006, only 14.7 per cent of regular trade unions admitted non-regular workers (Bae et al. 2008). In many manufacturing firms, non-regular employees were mostly located in the in-house, subcontracted workforce, and regular workers and their trade unions seldom supported them. On the contrary, most regular employees were frequently in conflict with non-regular workers when they sought to become permanent workers. For those who expected more positive outcomes, the E-Land case was disappointing. Even when both regular and non-regular workers struggled together for the same goals, employer concessions did not come easily.

Trade unions in manufacturing firms have been indifferent and sometimes even antagonistic towards non-regular workers and do not want to be burdened with additional negotiations with employers who adamantly refuse to bargain with in-house, subcontracted workers. In addition, there exists a subtle emotional gap between regular and subcontracted workers that has divided them and obstructed collective action. Both regular and subcontracted workers typically perform the same job on the assembly line, but non-regular workers' wages and fringe benefits are far less generous than those of regular workers. According to a government survey, approximately 22 per cent of workers at large manufacturing firms were subcontracted workers in 2008 (*Korea Herald*, 21 November 2010). This situation finally prompted the Supreme Court to rule in 2010 that in-house subcontracting at Hyundai Motor Company (hereafter HMC) was an illegal dispatch of labour. The Court ruled that HMC must hire subcontracted workers as regular employees, but HMC refused to accept the ruling. As a result, approximately 500 non-regular workers at HMC conducted a sit-in strike in November 2010.

Table 4.6 Major Labour Disputes Due to Non-regular Employment, 2000–2009

Firm/Trade Union	*Year*	*Types of Non-regular Employment*	*Solidarity/Support of Regular Workers' Union*	*Alliances with Social Movement Organ-izations*	*Outcome*
E-Land	2007–2008	Temporary Employment	Strong	Yes	Resolved
New Core	2007–2008	Temporary Employment	Strong	Yes	Resolved
KTX	2005–2008	In-house Subcontracting	Weak	Yes	Not resolved
Kiryung Electronics	2005–2008	In-house Subcontracting	Discord/ Conflict	Yes	Not resolved
Koscom	2007–2008	In-house Subcontracting	Discord/ Conflict	Yes	Resolved
Plant Firms in Ulsan	2005	In-house Subcontracting	Discord/ Conflict	Yes	Not Resolved
Posco E&C	2004, 2006	In-house Subcontracting	Discord/ Conflict	Yes	Resolved
Hyundai Hysco	2005–2007	In-house Subcontracting	Nonexistent	Yes	Resolved
Hyundai Motor Company	2005–2007, 2010–	In-house Subcontracting	Weak	No	Not resolved
Kia Motors Corporation	2005–2007	In-house Subcontracting	Weak	No	Resolved
GM-Daewoo	2005	In-house Subcontracting	Discord/ Conflict	No	Not resolved
Kumho Tires	2004	In-house Subcontracting	Weak	No	Resolved

Hyundai Heavy Industries	2003–2004	In-house Subcontracting	Discord/ Conflict	No	Not resolved
Carrier South Korea	2000–2001	In-house Subcontracting	Discord/ Conflict	No	Not resolved
Cargo Truckers Association	2006, 2008	Independent Contractor	Strong	No	Resolved
Dump Truckers Association	2005, 2006	Independent Contractor	Strong	No	Resolved
Korean Healthcare Workers Trade Union	2003–2004	Independent Contractor	Strong	No	Resolved

Sources: Kim (2010) and author's own data

The E-Land case was the exception rather than the norm because even industrial unions, which were supposed to organize all workers within an industry, failed to forge solidarity with non-regular workers. The Korean Metal Workers Union (KMWU) was established in 2001 to challenge neoliberal reforms and protect members who had been threatened by mass layoffs arising from the late-1990s, Asian financial crisis. Despite the change of union structure into an industrial one, most rank-and-file members in large firms still preferred enterprise-level bargaining (KMWU 2007a). Non-regular workers in metal sector firms could not join the same local union but had to become members of a separate unit. These workers did almost identical work while receiving about half of a regular worker's wages (KMWU 2007b). Therefore, non-regular workers in the metal sector have not benefited from the KMWU.

The Korean Financial Industry Union (KFIU) was established in 2000 also in response to the financial crisis and subsequent structural adjustments in the finance sector. The KFIU was even less successful in recruiting non-regular workers who could not join the locals where only regular workers were members. A separate local union for non-regular workers has been dormant since its establishment in 2004. Sectoral bargaining in the financial sector paid little attention to the issues particular to non-regular workers.

The most important bargaining topic has been to set acceptable ratios for the non-regular workforce (KFIU, 2006) which was quite important for maintaining the employment security of regular workers.

The Korean Health and Medical Workers Union (KHMU), the first industrial union established after the financial crisis, developed an elaborate system of sectoral bargaining that was relatively successful in improving wages and working conditions for non-regular workers. Although the number of non-regular workers was small in their industrial union, regular worker members were willing to accept lower wage increases to aid non-regular workers. The KHMU, however, has also felt the demands of regular workers to secure their own employment security and employer resistance to sectoral bargaining.

Conclusions and the Future of Social Movement Unionism in Korea

The solidarity between regular and non-regular workers demonstrated by the E-Land strike does not signify a renewal of Korean trade union movements. Scholars of South Korean labour movements note that the 1980s was an era of union revitalization or social movement unionism. Turner (2005: 387) defines revitalization as, 'a broad social phenomenon that greatly expands workforce mobilization and democratic voice'. He continues, 'revitalized labor movements generate social pressure that can reform or transform political and economic institutions'. The democratic labour movement in this period was certainly one of the most important opposition forces outside the formal political arena.[5]

5 The working class has been a significant actor in South Korean politics not just during the transition period. Whenever the authoritarian governments' coercive apparatus/ methods for settling industrial disputes weakened, workers vehemently protested authoritarian rule and the ways in which the regime treated workers. For example,

Social movement unionism in Korea did not last long, however. The flexiblization of labour and the resultant division and conflict among workers severely restricted the power and solidarity of the labour movement. The Asian financial crisis greatly exacerbated dualism in the labour market, and caste-like employment statuses divided the working class. As a result, the trade union movement in South Korea, once known for strong solidarity, has increasingly oriented itself to the interests and outlook of regular workers. Both the traditional enterprise unions and newly emerging industrial unions have been unable to restore vitality to the labour movement. Alternative labour movements based on region or minority statuses have not been effective enough to counter aggressive neoliberal, labour market reforms. For example, the only women's union, the Korean Women's Trade Union (KWTU), was established in August 1999, and its members grew from 400 at its inception to 6,000. A majority of its members (4,500) were non-regular, school employees. Because its members were isolated in their workplaces, its major activities were focused on legal and institutional reforms such as improving minimum wages. Although the KWTU certainly possesses a symbolic status in the Korean labour movements, its capacity to bargain with employers is limited.

The E-Land workers' struggles incorporated innovative mobilizing strategies and collaboration with political parties and social movement groups, but these experiences were not extended to long-term coalition-building and/or internal organizational reform of the mainstream enterprise unions. As shown above, the E-Land struggles were highly indebted to the sacrifice of union leaders and structural conditions favourable to the development of solidarity between regular and non-regular workers. Not all workplaces have the benefit of such conditions. Moreover, major trade union federations such as the KCTU were not very effective in transforming such struggles into sustained political action. Although the struggles

workers played a leading role in protesting socioeconomic injustice when the Rhee regime collapsed from uncontrolled corruption in 1960. The sudden collapse of the *Yushin* regime after President Park's assassination also provoked a militant response from workers.

generated publicity, Homever and New Core were just discount stores in the retail sector; their influence on Korea's labour market was limited. The owners also have frequently changed, thereby limiting the continuity of employment relations practices. These characteristics are quite different from Wal-Mart, the world's largest retailer and private employer.

What then are the possibilities for South Korea's labour movements to develop social movement unionism and revitalize themselves in the near future? To answer the question, it is necessary to review recent changes in the institutional framework of industrial relations. The January 2010 labour law revisions are a case in point. Starting in July 2011, the revised law permits multiple unions in a single workplace, which may facilitate the formation of secondary unions of previously unorganized, non-regular workers. The same law, however, may also strengthen regular worker-only, enterprise unionism because the law restricts unions that organize less than ten per cent of union members from bargaining. Non-regular workers are unlikely to organize more than ten per cent of all trade union members in a workplace.

While the institutional changes may constrain the radical reorganization of trade union movements, the ever deteriorating lives of non-regular workers offer the conditions for a major revitalization. The E-Land struggle is worthy of scholarly attention not because it was a successful case of union revitalization but because it reveals conditions critical for working class solidarity and shows the possibilities for bringing about small yet real changes to neoliberal labour market policies.

References

Bae, K., Yun, J., Cho, H., Lee, J. (2008). *The Korean Trade Union Movements After 1987*. Seoul: KLI (in Korean).

Eun, S. (2007). *Non-regular Workers and the Changes in the Korean Industrial Relations System (1)*. Seoul: KLI (in Korean).

Han, K. (2009). 'Ten-year-old War of Words on Non-Standard Worker Act, Is It to Conclude in September?', *Korea Labour Review*, 5 (27), 7–11 (in Korean).

Kang, H. (2004). 'A Case Study on the Exclusion of Non-regular Workers in the Workplace: A Study of Contract Company Workers', *Journal of Labour Studies*, 10 (1), 33–56 (in Korean).

Kim, J. (2010). 'Major Struggles of Non-regular Workers', *Labour Society*, Korea Labour and Society Institute (in Korean).

Kim, J. (2007). 'Labour Market Structure of Retail Sector and Trade Union Responses', *How to Respond to the Non-regular Employment Protection Act* (Research Report). Seoul: KCTU (in Korean).

KLI. (2010). *KLI Labour Statistics.* Seoul: KLI (in Korean).

Korean Confederation of Trade Unions (KCTU). (2007). *How to Respond to the Non-regular Employment Protection Act* (Research Report). KCTU (in Korean).

Korean Financial Industry Union (KFIU). (2006). *Collection of Collective Agreements.* KFIU (in Korean).

Korean Metal Workers Union (KMWU). (2007a). 'Organizational Reform Plan' (Unpublished Document). KMWU (in Korean).

Korean Metal Workers Union (KMWU). (2007b). 'A Survey on Non-regular Workers in the Metal Sector', *Research Report.* KMWU (in Korean).

Kwon, H. (2009). 'Temp-to-Perm Transition?: Recent Legislation on Fixed-term Employment and Firm's Choice'. In M.S. Jun (ed.), *Labour Issues in Korea 2009.* Seoul: KLI.

Lee, J., Lee, S. (2003). *Non-regular Labour Relations.* Seoul: KLI (in Korean).

Lee, J., Park, F. (2007). 'Globalization and the Changing Structure of Employment Relations in the Korean Banking Industry'. In R. Blanpain (ed), *Bulletin of Comparative Industrial Relations: Globalization and Employment Relations in Retail Banking, No. 63.* The Netherlands: Kluwer Law International BV.

Ministry of Employment and Labour. (2010). *White Paper on Labour* (in Korean).

Swenson, P. (1989). *Fair Shares: Unions, Pay, and Politics in Sweden and West Germany.* Ithaca, NY: Cornell University Press.

Tripartite Commission. (2004). 'Job Creation Social Pact' (Tripartite Commission).

Turner, L. (2005). 'From Transformation to Revitalization: A New Research Agenda for a Contested Global Economy', *Work and Occupations*, 32(4), 383–99.

PART TWO

Social Movement Unionism from a Cross-national Perspective

NOBUYUKI YAMADA

5 The Diversity of Social Movement Unionism: Towards a Cross-National, Comparative Framework

Introduction

There is no doubt that the revitalization of the labour movement is a recent tendency in various types of societies, and social movement unionism (SMU) is usually juxtaposed with such revitalization. Its conceptual content, however, is not necessarily definite. In fact, diverse aspects of different national labour movements are included in its revitalization and incorporated within the meaning of SMU. This situation seems to indicate that the concept of SMU and the revitalization of the labour movement should be constructed as an inclusive framework in which those diverse aspects can be compared across nations or different societies.

This chapter defines social movement unionism as an inclusive and operational framework for cross-national comparative analysis and, using this framework, compares SMU in the United States and Japan. First, it notes *similar* specificities of SMU in the labour movement – for example, the transformation and replacement of subjects, the enlargement and remoulding of organizations, the renewal of tactics, the shift of industry, the change of directionality and the formation of policies.

The *similarity* of these specificities results from a common social background – globalization, social exclusion, and neoliberalism. Each of these specificities can become a component of a revitalized labour movement and, if so understood, SMU as such can be an operational concept. The type in which and the extent to which they may come out can vary in different societies, and such conceptualization may lead us to grasp the diversity of the revitalization of the labour movement.

In other words, the revitalized labour movement should not be conceived as a single type but should be seen in its diverse forms. In one society, specificities of SMU could appear dominant but in others less remarkable. In another society, a different situation could arise when its labour movement is revitalized.

Second, this chapter clarifies the *type* and *extent* of labour movement revitalization occurring in the United States and Japan. To be sure, both countries have experienced revitalizations in their labour movements, but the type and extent are somewhat different. This chapter analyses these differences in terms of several variables and moulds distinct types for the content and extent of revitalization.

The Concept and Social Origins of Social Movement Unionism

Social Differences between Countries

First, we need to define the conceptual content of social movement unionism and specify its social origins. As already mentioned, SMU has diverse aspects and its conceptual content is not fixed (von Holdt 2002). Furthermore, analysts of labour movements in various regions of the world commonly refer to revitalization as a singular concept, although the historical traditions and present day configurations of those labour movements vary greatly. On the one hand, the labour movements in some newly-industrialized countries or regions – for example, South Korea, Brazil, South Africa – are often considered as examples of SMU (Scipes 1992; Seidman 1994; Chun 2006). It is often the case that the labour movements in such countries fully developed alongside industrialization in a relatively short period and that these labour movements developed in the context of authoritarian political regimes.[1]

1 Among these countries Brazil might be exceptional because it had already begun industrialization in the nineteenth century and has had a long labour movement

On the other hand, labour movements in advanced countries – for example, the United States, the United Kingdom and Japan – are also addressed as examples of SMU or revitalization (Cornfield and McCammon, eds, 2003; Clawson 2003; Fantasia and Voss 2004). These countries have in common long labour movement traditions in democratic political regimes and are also 'post-industrial'. The rise of the post-industrial society or the occurrence of 'post-industrialization' in the early 1970s has usually been discussed in advanced societies from a national perspective. It should not be forgotten, however, that such a post-industrial process entailed the transnationalization of capital or the increase of foreign direct investment. In other words, the decline of manufacturing with post-industrialization can be regarded from a global perspective as the relocation of production to developing countries. This may mean that manufacturing did not vanish but moved to developing countries. In addition, the cause of the decline of the labour movement in advanced societies might be the cause of its rise, not revitalization, in newly-industrialized countries. Therefore, they have experienced the rise, institutionalization and decline of the labour movement or class struggle, which have accompanied post-industrialization.

Labour movements in advanced and newly-industrialized countries have many differences in their historical and social backgrounds.[2]

tradition. Similar to other countries, however, its labour movement experienced authoritarian repression until recently. In experiencing authoritarian regimes, these labour movements were likely to build solidarity with other social forces and address other societal issues in addition to labour problems (Koo 2001; Seidman 1994). In other words, the labour movements in various regions were forced to take on the characteristics of 'social movements' from their inception. Thus, the labour movement in this region may be different from that in advanced societies because the latter may now be recovering such a nature after having lost it.

2 These differences can also be thought to be derived from the function of these countries or regions in global capitalism and, related to it, their class relations. From the perspective of world-system theory, class relations and social movements are determined by the positions in which they are located: the core, semiperiphery, or periphery (Arrighi, Hopkins and Wallerstein 1989). For example, manufacturing is most concentrated globally in the semiperiphery, where newly-industrialized countries are supposed to be situated. Therefore, because the labour movement can conventionally mobilize in manufacturing, it is most active in this region in the world-system. In

Even though superficial phenomena such as contentious movement styles and orientations for societal change are similar, these labour movements are difficult to categorize into the same concept, if their backgrounds are different. Therefore, this chapter will confine its subject to the cases of revitalization in advanced societies.[3]

Social Origins

What are the social origins of social movement unionism? As a social phenomenon, it has existed for the past two decades, and its origins can be found in social trends of this period. In retrospect, it can be seen that advanced societies have similar social trends related to each other – globalization, neoliberalism, and social exclusion. These trends have caused the labour movement to decline in many advanced societies for years.

Globalization has promoted the transnationalization of capital and labour. The drastic relocation of production and huge inflows of migrant labour are putting pressure on the labour movement in advanced societies. The ideology of neoliberalism has legitimatized harsh competition in market economies and endorsed deregulation, which has often denied workers protection. Deregulation of market relations has also given rise to the social exclusion of the weak, who are also disproportionately female and people of colour. In a word, revitalization should be the resulting reaction of labour's decline as a movement in advanced societies.

---

other words, even if development could be 'compressed' in this region, the labour movement might currently be established or *institutionalized* rather than *revitalized* in these countries.

3 It should be noted that labour movements in advanced countries do not necessarily have similar historical backgrounds even though the positions of advanced countries are similar in global capitalism (Yamada 1996). In short, both differences – one is derived from locations in the world-system and the other based on national traditions – must be taken into account in a comparative analysis of the revitalization of the labour movement in various countries. In this chapter, only the latter difference is addressed. In addition, each national tradition can be constructed through the logic of national capitalist development and contingency.

How do we define SMU? Based on the above discussion, we define it as a labour movement that pursues the transformation of industrial relations into labour-advantageous ones and, through this, the formation of institutions for societal change in advanced societies. In this sense, SMU can be understood as a phenomenon of the revitalization of the labour movement. In other words, a revitalized labour movement is not necessarily the equivalent of social movement unionism because revitalization does not necessarily include the formation of institutions for societal change. For example, in theory, business unions may be *revitalized* and transform industrial relations into labour-advantageous relations to raise wages and improve working conditions. As noted later, among the six variables related to the revitalization of the labour movement, the variables of *directionality* and *policy* are particularly crucial in SMU.

What Kinds of Situations Can We Call 'Revitalization'?

What kinds of situations can we describe as the 'revitalization of the labour movement'? For a cross-national comparative analysis, there needs to be an operational framework by which we can arbitrarily define to what extent the revitalization of the labour movement is present or occurs. The analysis in this chapter, however, is not necessarily quantitative.

The Subject

In defining social movement unionism, we have to confirm that the labour movement involves collective action by workers and that the transformation of industrial relations into labour-advantageous ones can only be achieved by workers. Revitalization is primarily predicated on the subjectivity of the worker. Given that workers as subjects revitalize the labour movement, the shift of the subject needs to precede the innovation of the labour movement.

This shift of subjects entails double processes – one is the *transformation* of the subject and the other the *replacement* of the subject. Workers are not all the same but are divided by various ascriptions – gender, race, ethnicity and so forth – and achievements such as wages, skills, credentials and the like.[4] Therefore, on the one hand, the shift of subject should mean the *transformation* of workers who cause the decline of the labour movement, that is, the self-conscious alternation of their actions. In this case, the primary actors of the labour movement will be the same. On the other hand, such a shift also means the *replacement* of workers, especially 'corrupt' leaders, who deteriorated the labour movement with ones who can activate it.

Organization

Given that the labour movement is a collective action, it necessarily needs organizations consisting of workers. If a force of labour is based on the number of mobilized workers, organizations of workers are required to enlarge themselves to strengthen the labour movement. Therefore, the revitalization of the labour movement requires the *enlargement* of organizations.

Nevertheless, revitalization also demands the *remoulding* of organizations. This is not only likely to include transforming existing organizations, that is, trade unions, but also creating new types of labour organizations. Furthermore, remoulding trade unions should mean that they try to renew their internal relationships – for example, the renewal of internal organizations, the shift of consciousness amongst leaders, the replacement of leaders, changing relationships between leaders and the rank-and-file and the like. Of course, these shifts cannot only be related to external relationships with employers but also other organizations such as unions and various pro-labour organizations. Put another way, they are also related to *tactics* and *directionality*.

4 These ascriptions are very likely to determine the extent of achievements that people with particular ascriptions can execute. In short, ascriptions and achievements are not independent but intertwined.

What does creating new types of labour organizations mean? For over a century trade unions have been thought of as primary organizations for workers, created for the purpose of bargaining. There is no reason, however, that they should be the only organization of this type. In fact, in the past, labour organizations such as *factory committees* existed in several European countries where they handled workers' grievances and tried to improve working conditions in factories. Therefore, revitalization is likely to demand other types of organizations. Furthermore, not only new types of organizations but also the relationships, that is, *networks*, of these organizations including existing unions will be crucial.

Tactics

To enlarge organizations through mobilizing more workers, adequate tactics are needed. If SMU faces difficulties in attaining its supposed goals, it has to think of new tactics. When existing institutions are more antagonistic to labour in the society, SMU will face even more difficulties in pursuing its aims and will be forced to devise new tactics. On the other hand, in societies where existing institutions are more pro-labour, it is more likely not to change its tactics in organizing.[5]

Industry

Related to tactics, SMU might be required to shift its target industries. For example, if it has not attempted to organize growing industries, it has to pursue organizing in those industries. Nevertheless, the target industries for SMU are not necessarily growing industries. It may also be the case that SMU has to aim at organizing old industries. In short, the industries to organize will depend on specific national situations.

5 As mentioned, this would mean that the multiplicity of national development forms, which can often be derived from *contingent* institutional differences, can affect the mode of SMU in the society.

Directionality

SMU is required to set up and/or alter directionality, or a strategic focus, to achieve its aims. While tactics are limited to a conventional *site* for organizing, directionality, or strategy, is related to a long-term perspective for organizing, and from such a perspective a new directionality or strategy is likely to pursue new sites for organizing. What kinds of sites must be taken into account?

On the one hand, given that the labour movement has had the point of production or specific shops as its main site, other sites could be demanded for new activities for revitalization because revitalization needs to address various needs and resolve diverse grievances. Taking into consideration that workers are not only producers but also live in specific localities, SMU should also be active in workers' residential areas. It requires *localism* or a *local orientation*. Of course, local problems cannot always be resolved in a specific locality. In that case, efforts would be made to solve these problems at a higher, national, level.

On the other hand, *transnationalism* or a *global orientation* is required, if globalization is one of the social backgrounds for SMU. Because globalization is accompanied by the transnationalization of capital and labour, SMU should resolve various problems arising from such transnationalization, if it seeks societal and institutional innovations. For example, because transnational corporations persistently reproduce hierarchical differences among workers in advanced and developing countries, the labour movement, in aiming for revitalization, will not only have to aim at increasing wages and improving working conditions for its membership, but also, to build solidarity, have to overcome the conflicts between different groups of workers that arise from those hierarchical differences.

Policy

If SMU seeks institutional change in a specific society, it will also have to participate in forming policies for the innovation of institutions to improve workers' lives. It must take political actions at various levels –local, national and global.

Conventionally, trade unions have articulated their political interests by supporting particular parties. Furthermore, in some countries, trade unions have more directly participated at various levels in policymaking through corporatism.[6] In addition, if organizations for workers are not limited to trade unions, more diverse activities for forming policies can be conceived for revitalization.

The Index and Extent of Revitalization

Above, we defined variables to examine the revitalization of the labour movement or the emergence of SMU. In the following, we define the index and extent of revitalization for each variable – subject, organization, tactics, industry, directionality and policy. It should be noted that each variable has its sub-category or sub-variable. Therefore, for each variable, a sub-category or sub-variable can be measured in scope and scale (see Table 5.1). For example, for tactics, their *singularity* or *conventionality* is in question. Furthermore, it should be noted that the extent of revitalization can be estimated in its scope, i.e., the variety of sites in which revitalization emerges, and scale, i.e., the extent of activities themselves through which revitalization emerges. As for scope, whether revitalization is *im-partial* or *partial* is in question; regarding scale, whether it is *large* or *small* will be measured.[7]

6 Generally speaking, corporatism, meaning the regulation regime of interests based on a compromise between capital and labour, is supposed to be established at three levels – macro, meso, and micro levels. The macro level means the national level, at which corporatism is built upon compromises of a large employer association and a huge trade union mediated by the state; the meso level occurs at the local or regional level; and the micro level means the corporation level, where corporatism can be related to corporate governance. Micro-level corporatism has been common in Japan since the 1960s, but the macro-level form has scarcely appeared in either the United States or Japan. For the concept of corporatism, see Yamada (1998: chap. 4).

7 The difference between scale and scope in this chapter is related to the ideas of the economy of scale and the economy of scope. While the former refers to the efficiency

For example, while revitalization in a country can emerge *im-partially* in the whole society, in another country it will realize itself *partially* in a specific industry. In the same way, while revitalization in a country can occur on a *large* scale in a specific industry, in another country it may realize itself on a *small* scale in industry as a whole.

Table 5.1 The Diversity of Social Movement Unionism

Variable	Sub-variable	Index	United States	Japan
Subject	transformation	new leadership	partial, but large in particular unions	partial and very small
	replacement	marginal workers	partial, but large in the service industry	partial and small
Organization	enlargement	union density	partial, but large in particular unions	partial, but large in specific industry
	remoulding	internal change and new organizations	partial, but large in particular sectors and organizations	partial and small
Tactics	renewal	singularity	more singular	almost conventional
Industry	shift	manufacturing	rare organizing	partial and small organizing
		the service industry	primary site for organizing	primary site for organizing

of production of similar goods, that is, mass production, the latter refers to the efficiency of production of various goods, that is, flexible specialization.

Directionality	change	localism	partial, but large in the low-wage service industry	im-partial, but small
		transnationalism	partial and small	partial and very small
Policy	formation	supporting parties	im-partial at the national level, but not necessarily effective	partial, but effective at the national level
		direct participation	im-partial, large and effective at the local level	partial and very small

I *The Subject*

First, what about the *subject?* Its *transformation* and/or *replacement* are/is required to revitalize the labour movement. How can we measure transformation, or what indices can we adopt to measure whether or not the subjects of the labour movement have transformed themselves? Given that revitalization requires new activism, the transformation of that subject means that its actions, which have not been carried out for years, are now seriously pursued. Therefore, whether or not such activism is present, and if present, to what extent, may be one of the indices of revitalization.

Next, how can we measure the *replacement* of a subject? By replacement we mean that workers who were marginalized in society and/or the labour movement have now become the main actors in the labour movement. Whether or not such workers have become primary actors, and if so, to what extent, may also be an index of revitalization.

II *Organization*

For organization, its *enlargement* and/or *remoulding* are/is required for revitalization. The enlargement of organization can be relatively easily measured as the increase in union density nationally or within any industry. Its remoulding is related to the transformation of the subject. This is because a transformative subject can also remould its organization. Therefore, whether or not the remoulding of an organization, examples of which are referred to above, is internally and/or externally present, and, if present, to what extent, can also be an index for revitalization.

III Tactics

How should tactics be categorized? Whether or not singular versus conventional tactics – those that challenge orthodox ways of organizing and acting as opposed to those that conform to existing institutions of industrial relations – are implemented, and to what extent, must be examined.

IV Industry

Industries can be divided into the old, i.e., manufacturing, and the new, i.e., the service sector. What must be examined in manufacturing, which is an existing site of activism, is whether new activism is present, and if present, to what extent. In a new site of activism – the service industry – the same must be examined and its extent measured.

V Directionality

Revitalization also involves directionality, the pursuit of other sites of activism. Therefore, examining whether or not *local* and/or *global* directionality are/is pursued clarifies the existence and extent of revitalization.

VI Policy

A final index to consider: policy, whether unions or other workers' organizations take advantage of political channels at various levels – supporting parties, direct participation, and so on – to realize interests and form policies must be examined. Furthermore, the extent to which those policies are effective is estimated.[8]

Given that revitalization is understood as a complex of various aspects of each variable in the labour movement, how do we estimate the extent of revitalization? Which aspects of each variable are most representative and significant for each variable? Furthermore, in so doing, we are likely to find that the most significant or representative aspects for each variable are varied in every country. Therefore, we also have to specify these aspects in each country.

In addition, if significant aspects are different, a single estimation standard cannot be specified. Therefore, it is difficult to implement quantitative analysis on the basis of the same standard in every country. For that reason, we will not analyse the index and extent of revitalization and compare them between countries quantitatively but will show the relative extent – *im-partial* or *partial* in scope and *large* or *small* in scale – of the emergence of significant aspects for each country.[9]

Representative Examples in the United States and Japan

Next, we will illustrate and compare representative examples of social movement unionism in the United States and Japan and estimate the extent of revitalization.

8 It should be noted that each variable and its sub-variables are deductively constructed and can be applied to each country. The order of variables and sub-variables, as described in this chapter, does not reflect the relative importance of variables and sub-variables.

9 The extent of revitalization measured in scope and scale are also the recent outcomes of revitalization, however *partial* and *small* they are. In other words, the revitalization of the labour movement is making progress in various countries and has not finished yet.

Subject –Its Transformation and Replacement

First of all, what about the subject? Its *transformation* and *replacement* must be examined as sub-variables. In the United States, we can confirm that the transformation of the subject has taken place at least for some union leaders. Since the latter half of the 1990s, some union leaders have reflected on past practices and altered them. John Sweeney, who won a contested election for the presidency of the American Federation of Labor-Congress of Industrial Organization (AFL-CIO) in 1995, was one such leader.[10] Under his leadership, the Federation shifted its policy on immigrants and came to organize them. Transformations have not necessarily occurred in most unions or in all industries but have taken place primarily in the service sector. Therefore, their scope should be regarded as *partial*, and their scale *small* in the whole of industry but *large* at least in the service industry.

Nevertheless, we can confirm that the replacement of the subject has taken place in many parts of the labour movement. For example, immigrant workers have been increasingly organized (Milkman, ed., 2000; Milkman 2006; Milkman et al., eds, 2010). Therefore, the primary actors of the labour movement, who were previously Anglo workers with various benefits, have been replaced with immigrant workers. Such replacement, however, has not necessarily happened in most unions in all the industries. As is well known, immigrant workers are mainly employed in the low-wage service industry. Therefore, such situations are *partial* in scope, but *large* in scale in the service industry.

What about the situation in Japan? The *transformation* of subject has scarcely happened in Japan. Certainly, most national federations – the Japanese Trade Union Confederation (JTUC), the National Confederation of Trade Unions (NCTU), and so on – have pursued new activities over

10 For many decades, no election had been held for president of the AFL-CIO because there was never more than one candidate. The election of John Sweeney from the New Voice group may mean the transformation of a part of the subject (i.e., national leadership).

the past decade.[11] Unlike the situation in the United States, however, these activities have not necessarily been implemented under new leadership but, instead, have occurred under the same conventional leadership. Therefore, the transformation of subject for leaders in Japan is *partial* in scope and *very small* in scale, unlike in the United States.

Some *replacement* of subject in Japan did occur, however. This is because marginal and underemployed workers, such as part-time workers, temporary workers, young workers, and foreign workers, have been organized in various new types of unions. Unfortunately, such organizing is *partial* in scope and *small* in scale because the primary trade unions are still enterprise-based and only organize employees in particular enterprises.

Organization – Its Enlargement and Remoulding

Several unions have been growing through organizing and mergers in the United States. For example, the Service Employees International Union (SEIU) has aggressively sought to organize immigrant workers – new subjects – and consolidate other trade unions for the past two decades.[12] Such *enlargement* of labour organizations, however, is still limited to several nation-wide unions mostly affiliated with the Change To Win (CTW) federation.[13] In unions such as SEIU, locals are not necessarily serious about organizing workers (Voss and Sherman 2000). Therefore, such enlargement is *partial* in scope but *large* in scale.

11 For example, as we will examine later, most national federations have begun to establish regional organizations over the past decade.

12 Criticism is often heard that SEIU seeks to enlarge its membership through consolidating other unions into its own membership. Recently, it was involved in a dispute with the Hotel Employee Restaurant Employee International Union (HERE) regarding which union had jurisdiction over which workers. For the style of SEIU, see Moody (2007). He describes SEIU-style unionism as 'corporate unionism' rather than social movement unionism.

13 The CTW, which split from the AFL-CIO in 2005, consists of six national/international unions including SEIU and HERE.

What about the *remoulding* of organization in the United States? If the enlargement of organization is a new activity for labour organizations, and has not been pursued until recently, it is likely to entail remoulding of the organizations. This is because enlargement is often required to mobilize the resources of organizations more efficiently and to restructure the organization itself. For example, international unions in the United States have strong leadership in local unions and have directed their activities so that local unions can employ new organizers. SEIU has established new departments such as the Latino caucus for addressing immigrant issues. Under the leadership of various international unions, many local unions have employed not only bi-lingual staff to organize immigrants but also activists from other social movements (Voss and Sherman 2000).

In addition, new types of labour organizations have emerged over the past decade in the United States, namely worker centres and labour non-governmental organizations (NGOs). In order to organize immigrants, worker centres, in many cases, have established themselves in specific ethnic communities (Fine 2006). Labour NGOs also exist in particular communities and often cooperate with various organizations such as unions and community groups to address and resolve workers' community issues. They primarily carry out three activities: first, organizing workers; second, conducting research on issues affecting communities; and third, making suggestions and carrying out campaigns for policy creation (Dean and Reynolds 2009). These new organizations are a part of the revitalization of the labour movement, and their emergence can also be regarded as a *remoulding* of labour organizations. In the United States, the scope of remoulding has occurred *partially*, but only in some sectors and organizations; its scale has been *large*.[14]

What is the situation in Japan? The most remarkable case of enlargement is the increase in membership of UI Zensen Domei (Japanese Federation of Textile, Chemical, Food, Commercial, Service, and General Workers' Unions) through union-shop agreements with employers of

14 Because this chapter primarily addresses a theoretical or conceptual issue, it, if necessary, only refers to concrete cases.

newly-organized firms. It increased its membership to 1,093,329, the largest membership in Japan, as of September 2010.[15] Furthermore, several enterprise-based unions in the service industry have tried to organize part-time workers.[16] In addition, many community-based unions and other unions with individually-affiliated membership were established as early as the 1980s, and these unions have also contributed to the increase in national union density.[17]

These developments, however, are still limited to a few industrial federations, and unions with individually-affiliated membership, even if their numbers are increasing, have limited power and resources.[18] Therefore, enlargement has happened *partially* in scope and, for specific industries, is *large* in scale in Japan.

To what extent has the remoulding of organization made progress? A few industrial federations and enterprise-based unions have tried to organize new members including part-time workers. Nevertheless, these activities have been implemented by conventional leadership and have occurred mainly in enterprise-based organizations. This means that remoulding has made little progress.

Certainly, a few national confederations are seeking to establish various regional organizations – *Chiiki Yunion* [regional union] in the JTUC and *Rokaru Yunion* [local union] in the NCTU – and these organizations are often not enterprise-based but have individually-affiliated membership. Many new types of unions have only a small membership and few resources, and so they have, at most, limited influence. As a result, the remoulding of organizations is *partial* in scope and *small* in scale.

15 http://www.uizensen.or.jp/about/index.html, accessed on November 29, 2010.

16 It is to be noted that enterprise-based unions, which are the primary style of unionization in Japan, do not usually organize part-time workers because they organize only full-time employees in the enterprise. Enterprise-based unions are only predicated on their membership of full-time workers in their companies. Unions in some restaurant companies, however, have tried to organize part-time workers.

17 In Japan, national union density increased, if only slightly, in 2009 after a long decline.

18 In fact, various unions with individually-affiliated membership have faced problems maintaining their membership because workers who joined such unions are likely to leave after resolving their issues.

Tactics – How Singular Are They?

US unions that are experiencing remoulding tend to have adopted new tactics in their daily activities. For example, they have implemented corporate campaigns[19] and won union recognition through card-check procedures.[20] These activities are different from those of conventional organizations and can make the movement more successful. Therefore, the singularity of tactics has been *partial* in scope and, in specific organizations, *large* in scale.

In Japan, unfortunately, new tactics have not been necessarily executed. New types of unions and new departments of conventional unions still utilize conventional tactics. This is partly because the existing institutions are more pro-labour than those in the United States and so labour organizations in Japan do not need to think of new tactics. One of the largest institutional differences in industrial relations between the two countries is the ease with which union recognition can be obtained. In Japan, only two employees are necessary to form a trade union and request collective bargaining with their employer, even if this union cannot gain the majority of employees. As a result, the primary *tactics* of unions are still the same as in previous periods, even if these unions are seeking new *strategies*.

19 The corporate campaign is a new style of union campaigning that targets not a worker's specific employer but those who use the worker's labour. Best known is SEIU's Justice for Janitors Campaign, which demanded raises and support for union recognition not from the janitorial service companies that employ building service workers but from the firms that actually use the services.

20 Union recognition through card check is also a familiar alternative to conventional union methods. A card check campaign involves seeking union recognition from employers by gathering signatures from over half a bargaining unit employees. It avoids the procedural requirements of National Labor Relations Board (NLRB) elections.

Industry – Old One or New One?

In the United States, enthusiastic organizing is being pursued in the service industry including the public sector, for example, public universities employing immigrant workers for various low-wage jobs. Above all, the low-wage service industry, in which immigrant workers are working on a large scale, has become a primary site for organizing. In contrast, organizing is not so enthusiastically sought in manufacturing. This is because business unionism, in which existing members' interests are more important than organizing new members, is still dominant in manufacturing.[21] The new and growing service industry is a main site for revitalization.

Similarly, in Japan, enthusiastic organizing appears to be sought in a growing industry – the service industry. As we have already mentioned, UI Zensen Domei is very active in organizing new members. If revitalization can be characterized by organizing more workers, increasing the number of new members, regardless of how membership is boosted, can be seen as a part of revitalization and the emergence of SMU. As in the United States, the service industry is a new and major site for revitalization.

Various new types of unions are trying to organize marginal workers in the service sector. But these unions, as previously mentioned, have few resources and little power. Consequently, they cannot contribute much to the increase of union density in Japan.

Directionality – Local or Global?

In the United States, local unions affiliated with unions such as SEIU and HERE are extending their activities from particular workplaces to workers' communities and are trying to win public support for workers (Chun 2006).

21 Basically, the reason why business unionism is still dominant in manufacturing can be derived from the risk of organizing – it is not evident whether organizing will be successful and how efficient it will be. Furthermore, resources for organizing are limited. In contrast, unions in the service industry have to organize immigrant workers, given that now many service sector workers are immigrants.

Worker centres and some labour NGOs based in particular communities focus not only on workplace issues but also on local political matters and issues affecting workers' everyday lives. In the San Francisco Bay Area, the Chinese Progressive Association (CPA), a worker centre situated in San Francisco's Chinatown that organizes Chinese restaurant workers, led a unique anti-sweatshop movement in 2008.[22] This anti-sweatshop movement was initiated as a research activity on the working conditions of restaurants in association with some local unions and research institutes. Restaurant workers, many of whom are immigrants who have recently come in the United States from China and are affiliated with this worker centre, gathered research data through personal interviews. Their research disclosed inferior working conditions in San Francisco's Chinatown restaurants; in a word, many of the restaurants were sweatshops, characterized by extremely low wages, physically demanding work, poor safety and *pre-modern (pre-capitalist)* relationships between employers and workers. For example, many newly-employed workers failed to earn any wages for at least the first month of service. This situation meant that many restaurant workers were not actually *workers in capitalism* because they received no wages for their labour.

The surveyors had their consciousness raised because, aware of their situations, they organized their colleagues through interviews and protested employers' hindrance of their research activities. This anti-sweatshop movement had the involvement of various organizations such as local unions and research institutes. In short, it created a forum in which various organizations could construct solidarity.

The success of this movement means that small worker centres can take initiative and contribute to building solidarity despite a paucity of resources and a general inability to have a large influence in the labour movement. In addition, given the inclusion of academic scholars in the movement, it can be regarded as a type of 'new social movement' (NSM), in which the new middle class is a major actor. NSMs, similar to SMU, offer the potential to overcome the rigidity of the conventional labour movement.

22 Data from the Chinese Progressive Association restaurant workers campaign were gathered during fieldwork from 2007 to 2011.

Of course, these *local-oriented* activities are *partially* carried out among all industries and organizations although they are *largely* pursued in the low-wage service industry. Nevertheless, neither unions that actively engage in *local-oriented* activities nor other labour-related organizations are consistent in executing *global-oriented* activities such as building solidarity with workers in other countries.[23] While some NGOs, which are often affiliated with unions such as HERE, are seeking to address sweatshop[24] problems,[25] this is still *partial* in scope and *small* in scale.

In Japan there has been local directionality in the labour movement for decades. As is well known, *Godoroso* (regional general unions or region-based amalgamated unions, see Takasu in this volume) have organized workers employed in small and medium-sized enterprises [*Chusho Kigyo*], or SMEs, in different localities since the 1960s.[26] Furthermore, Chikuro (the Regional Union Council) of Sohyo (Japan Council of Trade Unions, JCTU)[27] was established to organize workers and support a political party (Japan Socialist Party) in particular regions. In addition, as mentioned previously, the JTUC and the NCTU have recently established regional organizations and tried to organize marginal workers.

23 For various attempts and strategies to construct *global unions* against global capital, see Bronfenbrenner (2007).

24 Definitions of a sweatshop avoid definitive criteria, but they usually agree upon production facilities with low wages and inferior working conditions and harken back to images of the nineteenth century.

25 College student campaigns against sweatshops are well known in the United States. Many colleges and universities sell logo-emblazoned apparel and clothing that are often manufactured in sweatshops located in developing countries. The United Students Against Sweatshops (USAS), which is affiliated with HERE, has demanded that universities and their contracted manufacturers establish a code of conduct forbidding sweatshops. It has forced manufacturers to publish the location of their factories and monitors their activities. For the USAS, see Featherstone and USAS (2002).

26 If unions of SMEs are enterprise-based, it is difficult for them to engage in usual union activities such as collective bargaining because employers can easily prevent employees from joining unions or from engaging in union activities through *personalistic* control. Therefore, *Godoroso* have been trying to organize workers across enterprises in particular regions. Regarding *Godoroso* and their difficulties, see Hamamura (2004).

27 The JCTU dissolved itself into the JTUC in 1989, and then Chikuro was also basically abolished.

While these regional organizations are the offspring of conventional federations, other community-based unions, most notably the National Network of Community Unions, have emerged and built a national network among themselves (Community Union National Network ed. 1993). These unions are based on individually-affiliated membership and have devoted resources to organizing marginal workers through one-on-one counselling, which takes various forms from advice about labour law to help with loan problems. This private counselling is often conducted via the telephone.[28]

In this way, local directionality, or strategy, has prevailed *im-partially* in most conventional national federations and new, independent community-based unions, although these new organizations, above all independent community-based unions, have few resources and little power. Therefore, in Japan, such directionality is pursued *im-partially* in scope but is still *small* in scale because conventional federations remain enterprise-based and workplace-centred.

Cases of global directionality have been few, although most conventional federations have articulated a desire for international solidarity for years. That simple articulation has not been sufficient for revitalization, however. Among the new types of unions, there are a very small number of unions that seek to construct solidarity with foreign workers working with Japanese transnational corporations. For example, there is a union that supports labour disputes for workers in the Toyota subsidiary in the Philippines and has forged solidarity with workers there (Tono and Kaneko 2008). These activities are still very limited, though. Therefore, global directionality is *partial* in scope and *very small* in scale in Japan.

Policy – Forming New Institutions?

In both countries, as is usual in other countries, trade unions, particularly national confederations, have consistently supported particular political parties. In the United States, most trade unions and other labour-related

28 On this point, see OISR (2010).

organizations have conventionally supported the Democratic Party. Certainly, Barack Obama won his presidency partly because of the election support of labour-related organizations, and he has attempted to legislate or implement various progressive policies, for example, health insurance, immigration and industrial relations reform.[29]

Influencing policy through the electoral channels remains a conventional strategy and is predicated on the existing political regime. Institutional reforms have not made progress under the Obama presidency, and as a result, at the national-level policy, the influence of SMU is *limited* in the United States.

Nevertheless, at the local level, various institutional reforms have been realized (Dean and Reynolds 2009);[30] for example, an increase in campaigns for a 'living wage'[31] have been waged in various municipalities (Luce 2007); the movement for community benefits agreements[32] has emerged in some localities to regulate development plans by corporations (Gross, LeRoy and Janis-Aparicio 2005; Dean and Reynolds 2009; also see Luce in this volume); the clean port movement[33] has been succeeding in changing the

29 For example, insurance reform aims at institutionalizing affordable, national health insurance; immigration reform aims at the legalization of illegal immigrants; industrial relations reform aims at liberalizing the creation of unions for employees, that is, the Employee Free Choice Act.

30 These institutional reforms cannot necessarily be regarded as corporatism at the meso level because the relationships between capital and labour are not compromise-based but still antagonistic, and capital, above all, cannot necessarily fulfil its interests through forming new institutions. Therefore, these reforms are won by contentious movements involving coalitions of various organizations.

31 The living wage is a 'livable' wage with which working households can afford decent lives and is higher than the minimum wage. Living wage campaigns are typically undertaken at the municipal level and target low-wage employees in companies that have contracts with city agencies or work for firms that have received tax-payer funded subsidies.

32 Community benefits agreements (CBAs) are made between pro-labour community-based organizations and municipalities. They prohibit corporations from making development plans to exclude working people affected by gentrification.

33 This movement aims at re-regulating employment relations in the transportation industry at ports and improving the situation of truck drivers who suffer from low

status of truck drivers from independent contractors to workers and has brought stricter environmental regulations to some port areas (EBASE 2007; Bonacich and Wilson 2008; Yamada 2010). Therefore, at least at the local level, the movement for institutional change and policy forming is *im-partial* in scope and *large* in scale.

In Japan, trade unions have also conventionally supported political parties through election campaigns. For example, the JCTU had strong ties with the Japan Socialist Party. The relationship between the two was referred to as a 'bloc'. These relationships, even if weaker than before, are still present.[34] Revitalization, however, has been initiated and realized through the activities of NGOs. In December 2008, labour NGOs, in cooperation with trade unions, implemented support activities for dismissed temporary workers. This campaign attracted public notice and influenced the reform of temporary worker regulations.[35] At the *national* level, institutional reforms, even if *partially* achieved in specific areas, have led to progress. Nevertheless, at the *local* level, unlike in the United States, labour-related organizations have little influence on institutional change. New types of unions, community-based unions, have constructed nation-

---

income and long working hours. Given that truck drivers with low incomes have to purchase and maintain their trucks in the existing system, they can afford purchasing only old and air-polluting trucks. The re-regulation will establish an institution for the transportation industry to employ truck drivers as workers. An entity that purchases and maintains trucks can also resolve environmental problems around the port areas. The clean port movement is now growing in Los Angeles, Long Beach, and Oakland, California, and in Seattle, Washington and Newark, New Jersey and spreading nationwide.

34 Actually, the Japanese labour movement in the post-war era has continuously sought to address societal issues such as peace-keeping and environmental pollution through various channels. In this sense, it has oriented itself as a 'social movement'. The decline of the labour movement in Japan, however, has led to the decline in this characteristic. Given that social movement unionism is a new trend subsequent to the globalization-propelled decline of the labour movement, the Japanese labour movement in this period cannot be included in SMU.

35 In 2009, Japan had a change of government and the Japan Democratic Party took power. This campaign might have affected the election result and may influence the formation of policies under the Democratic Administration.

wide networks, but they can still only carry out day-to-day activities and can little afford to push the idea of new institutions and commit to campaigns for realizing them. Therefore, policy initiatives that advocate for new institutions through the labour movement can be taken up in specific areas. They are *partial* in scope but, at least at the *national* level, *large* in scale.

Discussion– Similarities and Differences

We have, to this point, examined to what extent each index of each variable for revitalization holds for the cases in the United States and Japan. Table 5.1 (see above) summarizes the discussion. As we have examined, the revitalization of the labour movement and the emergence of SMU are different in each country and encompass operational concepts. In the following we will compare revitalization in the two countries.

Similarities

First of all, the extent of overall or *im-partial* revitalization is *small* in both countries. That is, revitalization or the emergence of SMU is *partial* and/or *small*, for example, only in a particular industry or at a particular level. Second, organizing marginal workers is pursued in both countries even if the extent of replacement of the subject is very different. Third, the enlargement of organizations, that is, the increase of union density, which is the basis of revitalization, and thus the origin of the strength of labour, has been achieved through conventional trade unions in both countries even if it is *small* in scale. It should be noted, however, that the extent of the transformation of the subject is different between them – it is larger in the United States than in Japan.

Fourth, the remoulding of organization can be verified in both countries in that new types of organizations have certainly been created. Fifth, the service industry is a primary site for organizing in the two countries. This means that there has been little progress in organizing activities in manufacturing in both countries. Sixth, the labour movement in each country seeks global directionality only to a limited extent. Lastly, the formation of policy at the national level is likely to be pursued through the conventional method of supporting political parties.

Differences

Of course, there are many differences in revitalization and social movement unionism in the two countries.[36] First, both the transformation and replacement of the subject have emerged in the United States to a larger extent than in Japan partly because conventional trade unions in the United States tend to organize more marginal workers, more enthusiastically, than occurs in Japan, and marginal workers such as immigrants are already recognized as pivotal for rank-and-file workers. Second, related to the extent of the transformation of the subject, the remoulding of organizations appears to have been achieved more extensively in the United States than in Japan. This is partly because trade union leaders themselves – for example in the AFL-CIO – have become aware of the need to change to a larger extent. Third, tactics are more conventional in Japan than in the United States because labour-related institutions are more pro-labour in Japan. Last but not least, activities related to policy formation or the construction of new institutions tend to be primarily carried out at the local level through the coalition of various organizations in the United States, while in Japan such activities tend to be done at the national level primarily by supporting political parties.

36 As previously noted, in a strict sense, the quantitative comparison of variables between the two countries is impossible because concrete phenomena corresponding to variables in each country are different. Therefore, based on the social effects of each phenomenon, comparison in this section can be made only tentatively.

These similarities and differences are partly derived from the common social background of the labour movements and national (institutional) diversity. Current societal trends such as globalization, social exclusion, and neoliberalism can create constraints and challenges for the labour movement. Furthermore, national diversity leads to institutional differences. Because employers have been antagonistic towards labour and the industrial relations system has been relatively anti-labour, SMU in the United States has to be more singular in various variables. On the other hand, the industrial relations system has been comparatively pro-labour in Japan. Therefore, social movement unionism in Japan tends to be more conventional in the several variables. Above all, the tradition of the enterprise-based union as a pivotal organization can also be a constraint for revitalization.

References

Arrighi, G., Hopkins, T.K., Wallerstein, I. (1989). *Antisystemic Movements*. London: Verso.

Bonacich, E., Wilson, J.B. (2008). *Getting the Goods: Ports, Labor, and the Logistics Revolution*. Ithaca, NY: Cornell University Press.

Bronfenbrenner, K. (ed.). (2007). *Global Unions: Challenging Transnational Capital through Cross-Border Campaigns*. Ithaca, NY: Cornell University Press.

Chun, J.J. (2006). 'The Symbolic Politics of Labor: Transforming Employment Relations in South Korea and the United States', Berkeley, PhD Dissertation. University of California, Berkeley.

Clawson, D. (2003). *The Next Upsurge: Labor and the New Social Movements*. Ithaca, NY: Cornell University Press.

Community Union National Network (ed.). (1993). *Yunion, Ningen, Netowaku: Komyuniti Yunion Sengen* (Unions, Human Beings, and Networks: the Manifesto of Community Unions). Tokyo: Daiichisyorin.

Cornfield, D.B., McCammon, H.J. (eds). (2003). *Labor Revitalization: Global Perspectives and New Initiatives*. Oxford: Elsevier Ltd.

Dean, A., Reynolds, D.B. (2009). *A New New Deal: How Regional Activism Will Reshape the American Labor Movement*. Ithaca, NY: Cornell University Press.

EBASE (East Bay Alliance for a Sustainable Economy). (2007). *Taking the Low Road: How Independent Contracting at the Port of Oakland Endangers Public Health, Truck Drivers, and Economic Growth*. Oakland, CA: EBASE.

Fantasia, R., Voss, K. (2004). *Hard Work: Remaking the American Labor Movement*. Berkeley: University of California Press.

Featherstone, L., United Students Against Sweatshops. (2002). *Students Against Sweatshops*. London, Verso.

Gross, J., LeRoy, G., Janis-Aparicio, M. (2005). *Community Benefits Agreements: Making Development Projects Accountable*. Los Angeles: Good Jobs First and California Partnership for Working Families.

Hamamura, A. (2004). 'Godoroso Kara Komyuniti Yunion He' (From Consolidated Unions to Community-Based Unions). In A. Hamamura, T. Nagamine (eds), *Kumiai Kino No Tayouka To Kanousei*. Tokyo: Hosei University Press.

Hamamura, A., Nagamine, T. (eds). (2004). *Kumiai Kino No Tayouka To Kanousei* (The Diversification and Possibility of Union Functions). Tokyo: Hosei University Press.

Koo, H. (2001). *Korean Workers: the Culture and Politics of Class Formation*. Ithaca, NY: Cornell University Press.

Luce, S. (2007). 'The U.S. Living Wage Movement: Building Coalitions from the Local Level in a Global Economy'. In L. Turner, D.B. Cornfield (eds), *Labor in the New Urban Battlegrounds: Local Solidarity in a Global Economy*. Ithaca, NY: Cornell University Press.

Milkman, R. (2006). *L.A. Story: Immigrant Workers and the Future of the U.S. Labor Movement*. New York: Russell Sage Foundation.

Milkman, R. (ed.). (2000). *Organizing Immigrants: The Challenge for Unions in Contemporary California*. Ithaca, NY: Cornell University Press.

Milkman, R., Bloom, J., Narro, V. (eds). (2010). *Working for Justice: the L.A. Model of Organizing and Advocacy*. Ithaca, NY: Cornell University Press.

Moody, K. (2007). *US Labor in Trouble and Transition: the Failure of Reform from Above, the Promise of Revival from Below*. London: Verso.

Scipes, K. (1992). 'Understanding the New Labor Movements in the "Third World": the Emergence of Social Movement Unionism', *Critical Sociology*, 19 (2), 81–101.

Seidman, G.W. (1994). *Manufacturing Militance: Workers' Movements in Brazil and South Africa, 1970–1985*. Berkeley: University of California Press.

OISR (Ohara Institute for Social Research). (2010). 'Kojin Kamei Kumiai No Katsudo Ni Kansuru Anketo Chosa Kekka Hokoku' (A Report on the Results of the Survey on Indiviually-Affiliated Unions' Activities). Working Paper, No. 41, Tokyo: Ohara Institute for Social Research, Hosei University.

Tono, H., Kaneko, F. (2008). *Toyota In Firipin: Gurobaru Jidai No Kokusai Rentai.* (Toyota in the Philippines: International Solidarity in the Age of Globalization). Tokyo: Shakai Hyoron Sya.

Turner, L., Cornfield, D.B. (eds). (2007). *Labor in the New Urban Battlegrounds: Local Solidarity in a Global Economy.* Ithaca, NY: Cornell University Press.

Von Holdt, K. (2002). 'Social Movement Unionism: the Case of South Africa', *Work, Employment and Society*, 16 (2), 283–304.

Voss, K., Sherman, R. (2000). 'Breaking the Iron Law of Oligarchy: Union Revitalization in the American Labor Movement', *American Journal of Sociology*, 106 (2), 303–49.

Yamada, N. (2010). 'NGO To Foramu-gata Roudo Undo: Sanfransisko Bei Eria No Jirei Kara' (Labor NGO and a Forum-Style Labor Movement: A Case in the San Francisco Bay Area), *Komazawa Journal of Sociology*, 42, 31–57.

Yamada, N. 1998. *Kaikyu, Kokka, Sekaishisutemu: Sangyo To Hendou No Makuro Shakaigaku* (Class, the State, and the World-System: Macrosociology of Industry and Social Change). Kyoto: Minerva Shobo.

Yamada, N. 1996. *Roushikannkei No Reikishi Shakaigaku: Tagenteki Shihonnsyugi Hattennron No Kokoromi* (Historical Sociology of Industrial Relations: An Attempt at a Theory of Multiple Capitalist Development). Kyoto: Minerva Shobo.

MINJIN LEE

6 Varieties of Community Unionism: A Comparison of Community Unionism in Japan and Korea[1]

Introduction

Community unionism has attracted the attention of researchers concerned with trade union revitalization (Symon and Crawshaw 2009). These researchers are in general agreement about causes of union decline and about how to revitalize trade unions: union revitalization cannot be achieved without challenging traditional unionism (Tufts 1998; Fine 2001; Wills 2001; Black 2005; Martinez and Perrett 2009; Symon and Crawshaw 2009). Economic globalization and neoliberal economic policies have brought about a decline in the economic sectors that traditionally had a strong union presence. That decline has been counterbalanced by a growth in sectors with weak union presence and an increase in non-regular and precariously employed workers. The power of trade unions has declined in terms of union density and representativeness. Moreover, traditional workplace-based organizing strategies are ill-suited to organizing the growing number of 'hard-to-organize' workers in neoliberal economies. These workers, such as those in the low-wage service sector, those without

1 This chapter is a translation of an article that originally appeared in Japanese in the *Journal of the Ohara Institute for Social Research* (No.640, February 2012). The editorial board of the journal kindly granted permission for the translation of this article into English and its publication as a chapter in this volume. The translation is by Akira Suzuki.

employment security and home-based workers employed by sub-contractors, are rarely attached to a workplace on a long-term basis. If union revitalization entails organizing these workers, efforts should be made outside traditional workplaces and industries. Community unionism is suited to revitalization efforts because its main organizing and mobilization targets are geographical communities rather than the labour force of traditional workplaces/industries (Symon and Crawshaw 2009).

Previous studies have examined cases of community unionism in the United States, the United Kingdom, Canada, Australia and Germany. These studies take community unionism to mean community-based labour groups[2] and/or coalitions between trade unions and community-based non-labour groups, and they point to cross-national diversity in the forms of community unionism (Symon and Crawshaw 2009). Some researchers also argue that 'there is no single model of community unionism' (Martinez and Perrett 2009: 694).

Have community unionism or community unions developed in Japan and Korea? In Japan, 'new-type unions' [*shingata kumiai*] (Stewart 2006) have developed since the first half of the 1980s. These unions, commonly called 'community unions' [*komyunitei yunion*], engage in activities quite distinct from those of mainstream enterprise unions by organizing workers regionally, recruiting members individually, and offering counselling

2 Previous studies give different examples of community-based labour groups. Jane Wills cites central labour councils in the United States (CLCs, city-, county- or region-based federations to which local unions of national and international unions voluntarily join) and Trade Union Councils in the UK (voluntary organizations of union branches at the local level) as examples of such groups. She regards Battersea and Wandsworth Trade Union Council (BWTUC) in Southwest London as a typical example of a community-based labour group (Wills 2001). Janice Fine and Cynthia J. Cranford et al. offer worker centres in the US and Canada as examples of community-based labour groups (Fine 2001, 2005; Cranford et al. 2004). Simon J. Black regards social movement organizations involved in labour issues, such as the Ontario Coalition Against Poverty (OCAP) and the National Mobilization Against Sweatshops (NMASS), as examples of community-based labour groups. These social movement organizations often have close relations with worker centres: for example, NMASS 'operates out of two worker centres in New York City' (Black 2005: 29).

services on labour issues (see Suzuki and Takasu this volume).[3] Although the membership of community unions is small (about 30,000 in total), community unions have the potential to revitalize the Japanese labour movement as a whole (Suzuki 2008). Observers have characterized community unions in Japan in various ways: 'Japanese-style general unions' (Makoto Kumazawa), 'a new type of region-based labour unions' (Hirosuke Kawanishi), 'a new trend in the Japanese labour movement' (Sachi Kotani), 'amalgamations of labour and social movements' (Ikuro Takagi) and 'labour unions adopting NGO-style activities' (Yusuke Fukui) (see Fukui 2003). Akira Suzuki points out, however, 'previous studies have not used the conceptual framework of community unionism [as discussed in case studies in North America and Europe] to examine Japanese community unions' (Suzuki 2008: 493). Suzuki argues that Japanese community unions have characteristics similar to worker centres in the United States and Canada, but also notes differences in activities between the two types of labour organizations in Japan and the United States, thus suggesting 'varieties in the forms of community unionism' (Suzuki 2008: 515).

In Korea, 'regional general unions' were established as early as 2000. Although these unions are not called 'community unions', they organize workers on a regional basis, regardless of their employment status.[4] The establishment of regional general unions was necessary for three reasons (Lee, Kang-Ik 2006). First, organizing strategies across occupations and industries needed to be adopted to organize an increasing number of non-regular workers affected by changes in industrial structures and the increasing flexibility of labour markets. Second, in the gradual transformation of union organizations from enterprise unionism to industrial unionism, some union officials and activists felt it necessary to establish unions that allowed individual-based affiliation and thus made themselves available to 'hard-to-organize' workers such as those in small firms. Third, some union

3 See Takagi (2000) for why region-based, individually-affiliated unions in Japan have come to be called 'community unions'.

4 One exception is Youth Community Union, which characterizes itself as a 'community union' of young people, http://cafe.daum.net/alabor.

officials and activists regarded regional general unions as potential coalition partners with community-based social movements. They expected union-community coalitions to take up workplace as well as livelihood issues such as quality of life issues in the region so that unions would engage in activities across firms.

Trade union laws provide regional unions with legal rights and protections. The National Council of Region- and Occupation-based General Unions was established with 21 regional general unions and a total membership of 5,000 in February 2006. As is the case in Japanese community unions, there has been no research examining regional general unions based on the framework of community unionism. Moreover, no previous studies have made cross-national comparisons of community unions in Japan and regional general unions in Korea.

This chapter will compare Japanese community unions and Korean regional general unions based on the conceptual framework of community unionism. The second section of the chapter builds a comparative framework based on previous studies of community unionism. The third section outlines research methods and briefly introduces six unions in Japan and Korea. The third section then applies the comparative framework to the six cases and shows their characteristics. The fourth section makes two types of comparison: first, between Japanese community unions and Korean regional general unions, on the one hand, and community unionism in other industrialized countries on the other, and, second, between community unionism in Japan and Korea. The section then explains reasons for differences in community unionism in Japan and Korea. In conclusion, the chapter summarizes my findings and discusses their contributions to cross-national studies of community unionism and their implications for future research.

Research on Community Unionism and a Comparative Framework

To understand the meaning of community unionism it is important to note the distinction made by Simon J. Black (2005) between 'community unionism as a process' and 'community unionism as an organizational model'. Black defines the former as 'the cooperation between a trade union and a community group for a common objective' and the latter as 'an autonomous community-based group' (Black 2005: 25–6).[5] He refers to the latter as 'community unions'.

Coalitions between Unions and Community Groups

Coalitions between trade unions and community groups or labour-community coalitions have been the subject of many studies.[6] Typical examples of such coalitions include living wage campaigns formed between trade unions (and/or their city-or county-level federations [central labour councils]) and community groups in many cities and counties in the United States. Through these campaigns, labour-community coalitions have pushed for the enactment of living wage ordinances, which require companies that

5 Black does not define 'an autonomous community-based group'. From the examples (OCAP and NMASS) that he examines in his article (Black 2005), autonomous community-based groups appear to be organizations of workers including worker centres characterized by community-based organizing and involvement in struggles for various worker demands.

6 Tattersall, in discussing 'labour-community coalitions', points out that the term 'community' has three meanings: (1) 'a surrogate for the phrase community organisation', (2) 'a group of people who have common interests or identities', and (3) 'place, as in a defined geographic area'. She argues that '[t]hese three alternative meanings of community allow us to understand community's multiple dynamics', and that 'in practice, community operates as the combination of each of these different meanings' (Tattersall 2007: 5).

sign service contracts with local governments to pay wages and sometimes benefits above legally mandated minimums (Luce 2007; see also Luce in this volume). In Britain, too, UNISON (a public-sector union) and the community group TELCO (the East London Communities Organization)[7] formed a coalition and engaged in a living wage campaign in East London (Wills 2004).

What is the purpose of coalitions between trade unions and community groups? With regard to living wage campaigns in the United States, 'labor and community groups were feeling under attack' because privatization and contracting out of public sector jobs resulted in an increase in low-wage jobs that were replacing better-paid jobs in the public sector. Unions formed coalitions for the purpose of raising the wages of workers holding low-wage jobs (Luce 2007: 22). Stephanie Luce identifies two types of trade unions that participate in labour-community coalitions: 'unions or central labor councils that participate in living wage coalitions to build new alliances or strengthen ties with community allies' and 'unions that become involved in living wage campaigns to advance specific goals, such as organizing workers or winning raises for workers they already represent' (Luce 2007: 25). For the first type of unions, coalition formation itself is the main motivation for participation. This particularly applies to central labour councils, because these city- and county-level federations have from the mid-1990s sought to build coalitions to increase the presence of organized labour in communities. CLC policies to form coalitions with community groups were a part of the Union Cities Program that started under the initiative of the AFL-CIO's New Voice Leadership (Wills and Simms 2004).

The second type of unions, regardless of their motivations, form coalitions with community groups to achieve the common goals of coalition partners. For example, the Canadian Union of Postal Workers (CUPW) formed a coalition with Rural Dignity (an organization of community groups) to prevent restructuring policies planned by Canada Post Corporation (CPC), such as 'closure of rural post offices' and 'franchising of

7 TELCO, established in 1995, is a federation of local organizations in East London.

postal offices to retail firms'. Both the CUPW and Rural Dignity regarded post offices as closely associated with 'community identity'. Their closures would represent the loss of rural community identities (Tufts 1998: 234–5). In Australia, the New South Wales Teachers Federation conducted 'campaigns for public education' in the 1990s against the restructuring of public schools and reductions in public education expenditures by forming coalitions with a group of radical principals and 'local organizations led by a locally-based parent, principal and teacher'. Coalition-building was promoted by a common concern with maintaining the quality of public education. Amanda Tattersall argues that the 'mutual interest connection' between trade unions and community groups is an important factor in coalition formation. She also points out that unions with 'broad' identities form coalitions with community groups to address issues beyond their immediate interests such as the human rights of workers and social justice (Tattersall 2007: 16–21, 129–30). For example, the US union, Service Employees International Union (SEIU), in its campaign organizing office building janitors, reframed the purpose of the campaign as an issue of social justice (Justice for Janitors). Based on the reframed purpose, SEIU formed coalitions with and received support from community groups.

Do labour-community coalitions contribute to recruiting members and to a stronger union voice? Steven Tufts, in his study of community unionism in Canada – at the CUPW (see above) and the Ontario District of the International Ladies' Garment Workers Union (ILGWU) – concludes that '[c]ommunity unionism is an effective collective bargaining strategy and tool for organizing workers in geographically isolated sectors of the economy' (Tufts 1998: 244). In other words, labour-community coalitions give unions an advantage in collective bargaining and provide an effective tool for organizing 'hard-to-organize' in-house workers. Moreover, some studies suggest that coalitions bring benefits to both trade unions and communities. Wills and Simms, in their discussion of community unionism in the United Kingdom, argue that labour-community coalitions developed from 'representational community unionism' to 'reciprocal community unionism'. In the former, 'unions were represented in local and national government and sought to act for the community'. In the latter, in contrast, unions seek to sustain 'relationships with community groups to help improve local life as well as fostering trade union growth' (Wills and Simms 2004: 64, 66). In other words, reciprocal community unionism not only improves the livelihood and welfare of people in the community but also increases union membership and influence in the community. Examples of the latter include labour-community coalitions in living wage campaigns in the United States, the coalition of UNISON and TELCO in the living wage campaign in East London, and collaboration between the Organizing Centre of the Battersea and Wandsworth Trade Union Council (the BWTUC) and community groups in South West London (Wills and Simms 2004).

The relationship between coalition partners varies from ad hoc to on-going. Amanda Tattersall (2006) classifies three types of relationships between unions and community groups. They are (1) 'ad hoc relationships' that 'occur around an event'; (2) 'simple coalition relationships' whose relationships 'occur around any issue' and have 'more formal decision-making structures' in which 'actors participate instrumentally'; and (3) 'deeply engaged relationships' that 'occur around a mutual "broad social vision" with high level of rank and file consciousness and engagement' (Tattersall 2006, quoted by Symon and Crawshaw 2009: 146–7). This typology illustrates the diversity of labour-community coalitions.

Autonomous Community-based Labour Groups

Black (2005) calls autonomous, community-based labour groups 'community unions' and notes they have characteristics that set them apart from trade unions. First, their membership structures and organizing target are communities rather than workplaces. They seek to organize working people in a given community, regardless of their occupations or employment status. They organize those workers whom trade unions have failed to organize, including 'workers in the informal economy', 'workers in "flight" sectors such as the garment industry or call centers', and unemployed and underemployed workers. In other words, community unions make a broad definition of labour performed by workers and recognize the emotional and physical labour of health care workers, labour performed by homeless people who engage in trash pick-up and recycling, and labour performed by sex workers (Black 2005: 27–8). The National Mobilization Against Sweatshops (NMASS) in New York City, one of Black's examples of community unions, 'seeks to organize "injured workers, students, mother and care-givers working in the home, retirees, [and] unemployed persons"' (Black 2005: 30).

Second, community unions redefine and promote a sense of solidarity that 'goes beyond the workplace'. In this way, community unions can organize workers based on class interests regardless of their employment status and in turn strengthen the political power of working people (Black 2005: 27). Based on the broadened sense of solidarity, NMASS demanded 'a 40-hour workweek at a living wage' for all workers including the unemployed and care-givers who work at home (Black 2005: 30).

Third, while trade unions are mainly concerned with workplace-related matters, community unions are concerned with a whole range of issues affecting working people's lives. For example, the Ontario Coalition Against Poverty (OCAP) in Toronto not only gets involved in 'the struggle for decent work' but also addresses 'housing, and social assistance' issues. Targets of OCAP's campaigns are not only employers, but also government authorities such as social welfare and immigration bureaus and city councils, and landlords. Its recent campaign for reforming the social assistance system in the province of Ontario demanded payment of supplementary welfare benefits (which had gone only to those with special dietary needs) to all social assistance recipients. The campaign received support from a wide range of people in the progressive community of Toronto (Black 2005: 28–9).

And fourth, community unions take direct actions to pressure city councillors to pass legislation benefitting working people and push employers to grant wage and benefit increases. The repertoire of collective actions used by community unions includes lobbying, picketing, sit-ins, demonstrations, boycotts and 'letter writing campaigns' (Black 2005: 29–31).

Black regards community unions as a relatively new type of organization distinct from trade unions, which are formed on the basis of workplaces and/or places of employment. Jane Wills and other researchers, in contrast, think that 'local multi-union structures', such as Central Labour Councils (CLCs) in the United States and Trade Union Councils (TUCs) in the UK, have since the mid-1990s exemplified practices of community unionism as an organizational model. Wills argues that CLCs 'take a much broader approach to trade unionism'[8] because they operate with a 'geographically focused nature' and 'get resources from a wide range of organizations' including from charitable organizations and foundations (Wills 2001: 473).[9] Their 'broader approach to trade unionism' promotes region-based organizing and labour-community coalitions and builds networks of activists 'who can be called upon…to come and support local demonstrations' (Wills 2001: 473).

Some observers are sceptical about community unions (or community unionism as an organizational model) and argue that such unionism does not bring union members economic gains, which trade unions could have won through collective bargaining. In response, Black argues that, despite their limitations, community unions 'win economic concessions through lobbying, direct action, and other tactics'; the power of community unions 'is primarily political, not economic'. They have to continue building powerful labour-community coalitions to promote progressive legislation and social reform and 'win the hearts and minds of voters to add moral and political legitimacy to their campaigns' (Black 2005: 31).

This chapter so far has examined characteristics of community unionism based on Black's distinction between 'community unionism as a process', and 'community unionism as an organizational model'. The two types of community unionism, while conceptually distinct, in practice frequently share characteristics. For example, when community-based labour groups (Black's community unionism as an organizational model) form coalitions with non-labour community groups, the distinction between the two types is irrelevant. This chapter will refer to both labour-community coalitions and community-based labour groups as community unionism.

8 Not all CLCs take a broader approach to trade unionism. Fernando Gapasin and Howard Wial (1998), in their studies of central labour councils, make a distinction between progressive CLCs and conservative CLCs, and argue that the former type of CLCs function as an advocate of social reform and play an active role in promoting labour-community coalitions.

9 In addition to grants from AFL-CIO for special projects and affiliation fees from local unions, CLCs can 'seek additional funding from charitable, government and foundational sources'. Such additional sources of funding make CLCs 'semi-autonomous' organizations (Wills 2001).

Characteristics of Community Unionism in a Comparative Framework

This chapter proposes six characteristics by which community unions in Japan and regional general unions in Korea can be compared. The following six characteristics not only describe diverse forms of community unionism but also explain their differences cross-nationally:

1. The base of union organizing is communities rather than workplaces.
2. They seek to organize workers whom the existing unions have labelled 'hard-to-organize': informal sector, low-paid service sector, migrant, and in-house workers, as well as independent contractors, and unemployed and underemployed workers.
3. They address issues related to employment and working conditions as well as livelihood and community-related issues such as housing, healthcare and social welfare.
4. They seek to promote solidarity among workers regardless of workplace or employment status.
5. They build coalitions between trade unions and community groups.
6. They rely on demonstrations and other forms of direct action in addition to institutionalized dispute-resolution such as collective bargaining.

Research Methodology and Overviews of Cases

Author interviews with union officials/activists (conducted between September 2009 and June 2011)[10] and documents obtained from these unions form the basis of this chapter's analysis of three community unions in Japan and three regional general unions in Korea. I use pseudonyms for

10 The interview survey was a part of the research project 'Organizing Non-regular Workers and Labour Movement Revitalization: A Comparative Study of Japan and Korea' funded by Grant-in-Aid for Scientific Research (2009–2011). The author would like to thank those union officials and activists who agreed to be interviewed.

the community unions in Japan: the MU Union, Union MI, and N Union. Each union's origins differ. MU Union was established with the support of a regional labour council of Sohyo (the leftist, national confederation that dissolved in 1989 when it joined the newly established confederation, Rengo, see Suzuki in this volume). Union MI was established as a general union (*ippan roso*, a union consisting of SME-based locals, see Takasu in this volume) but later converted into a community union by admitting members on an individual basis. Labour-issue counselling activities of city council members affiliated with the Japan Socialist Party (JSP) led to the establishment of N Union. Union MI and N Union are formally affiliated with the Japan Community Union Federation (JCUF [*Zenkoku Yunion*]), while the MU union is affiliated with JCUF as 'an observer'.

The three regional general unions in Korea have the pseudonyms of B General Union, CH Regional Union, and KN General Union. Trade union activists established all three, which are affiliated with the National Council of Region- and Occupation-based General Unions and belong to the Korean Confederation of Trade Unions (KCTU) through their respective province-level regional councils.

An overview of the six cases follows.

Amagasaki Regional Council [*Amagasaki Chihyo*] (ARC) of Sohyo established the MU Union in May 1988. During the Spring Wage Offensive in 1988, ARC created the first hotlines on labour issues for part-time workers. The MU Union was established as an individually-affiliated union to represent part-time and other non-regular workers who were working and/or living in the Amagasaki area and contacted ARC through the hotlines. It initially consisted only of individually-affiliated members but established the first workplace local [*bunkai*] in 1994. It establishes workplace locals when more than two workers in the same workplace join the union, and there are currently 27 such locals. The membership of the union is about 450 members (as of February 2010), including some migrant workers. The union charges one per cent of members' monthly wages as membership fees. MU Union focuses on labour-issue counselling but also engages in collective bargaining and/or negotiations with employers on behalf of union members and supports members who have filed lawsuits against employers.

JSP-affiliated city council members established N Union in March 1988 to address labour-issue counselling activities for part-time workers. They felt it necessary to establish a union to represent those workers who had contacted them in negotiations with their respective employers. N Union accepts any workers on an individual basis who either live or work in Chiba Prefecture. As in the case of the MU Union, N Union has a policy of establishing workplace locals when more than two workers in the same workplace join the union; it currently has three workplace locals. N Union's main activities are labour-issue counselling and negotiating member disputes with employers. The membership of the union (as of February 2010) is about 150, and membership fees are ¥2,000 per month for those union members who are regular workers and ¥1,200 for members with non-regular status.

The establishment of Union MI was occasioned by a split of the MI General Union (affiliated with the Rengo NUGW [*Zenkoku Ippan*]) in 1995.[11] Those activists and locals oriented toward community unions [*komyunitei yunion*] established Union MI. The newly established community union started labour-issue counselling and accepted individually-affiliated members. At the time of its founding, Union MI had 17 workplace locals (the total membership of these locals was 500). In subsequent years, individually-affiliated members increased, and the number of workplace locals decreased to 10. Union membership as of March 2011 is somewhere between 500 and 600. Union MI's activities mainly consist of labour-issue counselling and negotiations on behalf of members to resolve disputes with employers. The union supports members who have filed lawsuits against employers and actively organizes migrant workers. The union charges each member ¥2,000 per month as a membership fee, and those who belong to workplace locals pay one per cent of monthly wages as an additional fee.

In Korea, B General Union, established in April 2000, was the nation's first regional general union. Union activists involved in the establishment of B General Union envisioned a union open to non-regular and unemployed workers, seeing general unions in Japan as a model. It organizes

11 For details of NUGW, see Takasu in this volume.

regular and non-regular workers in small-sized firms in various industries/occupations in Busan and neighbouring areas. The union organizes workers mainly on the basis of workplace (there are 37 workplace locals); the number of individually-affiliated members is limited. The union mainly bargains over wage issues, but also offers labour-issue counselling services. The membership of B General Union is about 600 (as of September 2009), and membership fees are 2 per cent of monthly wages.

CH Regional Union was established in May 2001. Several union activists in the Chungnam region, inspired by the establishment of B General Union a year earlier, established CH Regional Union to organize workers across firms. Since there is a major automobile factory in the Chungnam region, a large proportion of union members work in manufacturing, particularly auto-related, industries. The union mainly organizes in the workplace (there are 30 workplace locals), and the number of individually-affiliated members is very small. As in the case of B General Union, CH Regional Union directs its resources mainly to collective bargaining, but the union also provides labour-issue counselling services. The membership of CH Regional Union is about 1,200 (as of September 2010), and membership fees are 2 per cent of monthly wages.

KN General Union was formed in January 2005 by the merger of two general unions in neighbouring areas, Jinju General Union and Gyeongnam General Union. The former union was established in 2001 by leaders inspired by the formation of B General Union. The latter was established in 2002, covering the Masan-Changwon region. KN General Union mainly organizes workers in Gyeongsangnam-do, and 70–80 per cent of union members work directly or indirectly for local governments. Union membership is about 2,000 (as of June 2011). The union mainly organizes in their workplaces (there are 50 workplace locals), but there are 20–30 individually-affiliated members. Membership fees are 1.3 per cent of total wages.

Analysis of the Six Unions' Activities

Community Unions in Japan

THE BASE OF UNION ORGANIZING

Three community unions organize workers on the basis of regions. The MU Union organizes workers in Amagasaki City (where the union is based) as well as workers in Sanda City (the city north of Amagasaki) and in Shiga Prefecture. N Union and Union MI organize workers in Chiba Prefecture and Mie Prefecture, respectively. Community unions developed by organizing workers on an individual basis by offering labour-issue counselling, but they also organize workers on the basis of workplaces. The MU Union and N Union started as individually-affiliated unions, but established workplace locals when more than two workers in the same workplace joined the unions. Most workplace locals consist of a few members, ten members at most. In many cases, a workplace local forms when an aggrieved worker who became a member of community union through labour-issue counselling organizes other workers in the same workplace with similar grievances. In contrast to the MU Union and N Union, Union MI started as a union of workplace locals but increased individually-affiliated members through labour-issue counselling.

ORGANIZING TARGETS

The three community unions organize regular workers, part-time and temporary workers, dispatched workers and workers dismissed from various industries and occupations. The MU Union and Union MI also organize migrant workers.

ADDRESSING BROAD ISSUES

The three community unions are concerned not only with protecting members' employment and working conditions but also with improving regional working conditions in general. For example, the MU Union was involved in a labour dispute over the working conditions of members whose jobs the city of Amagasaki had outsourced. Its newsletter argued that improving members' wages and working conditions would directly lead to higher wages for non-unionized, non-regular workers in the region (*MU Union Newsletter*, No.201, 1 July 2009). In line with this belief, it campaigned for a living wage ordinance for workers employed by subcontractors doing business with the city government. According to the union, a living wage ordinance should function as a safety-net providing workers covered by the ordinance with a decent standard of living. Furthermore, paying a reasonable wage should prevent the quality of (outsourced) public-services from suffering (*MU Union Newsletter*, No.208, 1 January 2010).

Union MI considers wage increases and improving members' working conditions its primary goals but recognizes the importance of improving conditions for the unorganized. In addition, it regards occupational health and safety as a concern for workers in general. The union has demanded from public authorities in Mie Prefecture that the minimum hourly wage be raised to ¥1,000 because a decent livelihood at the legal minimum wage was impossible. The union also staged a campaign demanding that jobs at subsidiaries and related companies of AEON (a major retail store chain) should pay the minimum hourly wages of ¥1,000. In addition, Union MI embraced community issues, for example, a struggle against the construction of a new ward at a local hospital that would decrease the living space of hospitalized patients and worsen their quality of life.

BUILDING A SENSE OF SOLIDARITY AND CLASS CONSCIOUSNESS ACROSS FIRMS

The three community unions are involved in various projects to build solidarity across firms. The MU Union offers members working in different workplaces the opportunity to get to know each other and develop friendships through an annual 'Workers' School'. It has a 'Building Friendship' [*fureai*] local where individually-affiliated members can meet, and it holds 'study meetings for the youth' where young union members in different workplaces can meet. Along with two other community unions in Hyogo Prefecture it formed in 1998 a prefecture-level federation of community unions called Hyogo Union. Currently six community unions are affiliated with Hyogo Union, share information on their activities, and coordinate joint protest actions and support for members involved in litigation against employers.

Union MI holds 'Yunion Juku' (a seminar on labour issues) every month to promote working class consciousness among members. The union also holds a meeting every three months where members exchange stories of labour disputes and resolutions. In addition, the union sets up 'a joint mobilization day' once a month where members mobilize for their own or other union members' struggles. The events provide union members with opportunities to learn the power of solidarity.

Union MI has established an organizational structure of three 'local networks' of individually-affiliated members for quick, labour dispute mobilization. The networks cover the northern, central and southern regions of Mie Prefecture. Since 2000, Union MI also has taken the initiative to strengthen the movement of community unions in the Tokai Region by establishing a loose coalition of community unions.

N Union actively mobilizes members for protests and other JCUF-affiliated community union events. According to the union, those members who participate in the JCUF actions and learn from meeting with other community union members are more willing to get involved in supporting labour disputes of other community unions.

The MU Union regards its members as having a strong consciousness as workers because the union, unlike enterprise unions, connects workers across firms. N Union also thinks that its members have a high level of union consciousness. Union MI observes that its members have successfully resolved labour disputes through mutual-aid and have learned the importance of solidarity among members.

BUILDING COALITIONS BETWEEN UNIONS AND COMMUNITY GROUPS

In 1992, the MU Union joined in a movement for a referendum to disclose Amagasaki City Council member activities and dissolve the City Council.[12] The union joined a broad coalition of 148 organizations, 'the Joint Citizens' Conference for the Dissolution of City Council', which consisted of ARC, civic organizations and organizations affiliated with the JSP and Japan Communist Party (JCP). In 2007, the union joined 'the Conference to Realize a Living Wage Ordinance in Amagasaki' (established in March 2007)[13] and actively campaigned for a living wage ordinance in alliance with a group of city councillors who supported the legislation. A bill for a living wage ordinance was submitted to the City Council twice (December 2008 and May 2009), but it rejected the bill. Had the bill been passed, Amagasaki City would have become the first local government in Japan to legislate a living wage ordinance. Despite the defeat, MU Union expressed its willingness to continue the living wage campaign by expanding the membership of the Conference to Realize a Living Wage Ordinance in Amagasaki (*MU Union Newsletter*, No.201, 1 July 2009). The union also continued to hold seminars on living wage issues.

Besides its involvement in the political/policy issues of Amagasaki City, the MU Union occasionally cooperates with NGOs assisting migrant workers and their family members. It, however, has not developed a strong relationship with these NGOs, and their members seldom participate in MU Union meetings or protests.

Union MI is active in organizing migrant workers and works closely with the NGO 'Solidarity Network with Migrants in Japan' [*ijuren*] to resolve disputes over dismissals and violations of migrant worker rights.

12 The movement started when some city councillors were suspected of having misused public money.

13 The Conference to Realize a Living Wage Ordinance in Amagasaki consisted of the MU Union, Amagasaki City Government Workers' Union, the regional union federation that succeeded ARC, which was dissolved in 1993, a coalition of city councillors and a research institute on local governments.

Other Union MI coalition partners include an association of labour lawyers in the Tokai Region and a community group of teachers, civic movement activists, retirees and public-sector workers established in 2002.

DIRECT ACTION

Since the three community unions have the right to engage in collective bargaining with employers on behalf of their members, they try to resolve labour disputes through negotiations. When employers refuse to bargain or when collective bargaining comes to a deadlock, the unions have other means to resolve disputes, such as filing complaints with the labour board, initiating lawsuits against employers, and/or mobilizing union members into direct action. Specific tactics include distributing fliers, picketing in front of company buildings, holding protest meetings, or organizing letter-writing campaigns protesting insincere attitudes toward workers and/or their unions. Direct actions target not only employers but also client companies that hire dispatched/ contract workers and government authorities.

Petition campaigns are another direct action tactic. The MU Union organized a petition campaign for a living wage ordinance among citizens of Amagasaki City, and Union MI held a petition campaign demanding a minimum hourly wage of ¥1,000.

Regional General Unions in Korea

THE BASE OF UNION ORGANIZING

Although the three Korean regional general unions proclaim they will organize workers across the country,[14] they in fact organize in specific regions. B General Union, CH Regional Union, and KN General Union organize workers in Busan and its neighbouring areas, the Chungnam

14 The statutes of the unions state organizing targets are across the country so that the unions can organize workers of a company with a nation-wide chain of branches

region, and the Gyeongnam region, respectively. The three general unions formally accept individually-affiliated members,[15] but their number is limited. CH Regional Union adheres to a strict policy in accepting individually-affiliated members: the union does not accept those workers who regard the union as a kind of a service agency to resolve their individual grievances. The three unions are organized mainly on the basis of workplaces, but take positions in opposition to enterprise- or workplace-centred consciousness among union members. For example, B General Union, in line with its identity as a region-based unified organization, organizes shop-floor committees as the union's basic unit. The union reasons that if members concentrate on shop-floor-based activities, their enterprise consciousness will become weak. In the case of KN General Union, the union signatory for a collective bargaining agreement is its president rather than the leader of the local.

ORGANIZING TARGETS

The three unions organize regular and non-regular small firm workers in various industries and occupations. CH Regional Union targets mostly workers in small manufacturing firms that serve as subcontractors of the Chungnam region's single major automaker. The three unions also organize unemployed, dismissed and discouraged workers.

ADDRESSING BROAD ISSUES

The regional general unions are concerned not only with improving members' employment and working conditions but also the livelihood and welfare of local residents by reforming social institutions. The leadership of B General Union thought that because the union was region-based, it

(or with branches in other regions). B General Union in fact organized non-regular workers of the Boram Sangjo Company that had a nation-wide chain of branches.

15 The president of B General Union said in an interview that individual-affiliation was one of the advantages of general unions.

was important to be involved in community social institutions. Since 2001, a year after its founding, it has campaigned against mismanagement in companies that have contracted to perform public services outsourced by local governments. One of the leaders admits that the union has been more deeply involved in improving social institutions than in raising wages. For example, B General Union charged that ward authorities did not properly supervise the companies that signed outsourcing contracts. They charged night soil treatment companies that had contracts with ward authorities with overcharging residents for their services and understaffing treatment facilities. The union also accused a social welfare corporation of poorly managing facilities for the elderly and children and suspected that managers of the corporation embezzled donation money.

KN General Union was also involved in similar struggles. It exposed various misdeeds in a waste collection company that had a contract with a city government, including overcharging for garbage bags. The union publicized these wrongdoings and demanded proper supervision of the company. The leadership of KN General Union sees the union and community residents in a mutually-supportive relationship and supports activities to aid residents. For example, the union gives scholarships to students whose families cannot afford school tuition and encourages union members to volunteer to clean senior citizen centres and help farmers.

One of the missions of CH Regional Union is to create 'a community of work and life', and it has made efforts to become a place where its members can receive counselling services about livelihood issues. Unlike B General Union and KN General Union, CH Regional Union has not been involved in struggles for the reform of social institutions but has engaged in a campaign to eliminate sub-minimum wage work.

BUILDING A SENSE OF SOLIDARITY ACROSS FIRMS

B General Union stresses the unity of workers and sees labour education as an important means to promote solidarity among union members. Thus, the union makes it a point of demanding in collective bargaining that employers allow union members time-off for labour education (two hours per month) and provide a space for educational activities. Three to four times a year the union holds educational sessions, at which attendance is high, for newly-recruited union members. In addition, a high proportion of members attend union meetings held, on average, two or three times per month.

CH Regional Union originally held meetings of all members once a month (later, once every three months) so that union members in different firms could get to know each other. An increase in union members, however, has made holding such meetings difficult. Thus, the union has started to hold smaller meetings and events[16] to encourage exchange between members. Individually-affiliated members of CH Regional Union belong to the 'Equality Local,' which holds a meeting once a month at which members exchange information about current conditions and discuss regional union and local issues. The local also presents lectures about the economy and politics.

CH Regional Union mobilizes its membership to support members from other workplaces involved in labour disputes; more than 300 members have attended those actions. Since workplace locals are dispersed in the Chungnam region, it often charters buses to support those actions. The union holds labour education sessions for rank-and-file members and leaders every three months. The union makes it a point of demanding that employers allow union members time-off for labour education (one to two hours every three months).

The leadership of KN General Union tries to convey through labour education that although each workplace local has a small number of members and by itself lacks power, union members are backed by the union with unity of purpose and a membership of 2,000 committed members. The union provides new recruits with eight educational sessions in which it hopes to instil in members working class pride and a sense of solidarity. The union, like the two other unions, demands time-off for labour education in its collective bargaining agreements. The union also holds a monthly 'Day for Local Members'. The meeting gives union members in the same area, regardless of workplace, an opportunity to get together and discuss various issues including families and personal matters.

16 For example, the union holds sporting events, such as bowling, fishing, and mountain-climbing events, for union members and their families.

BUILDING COALITIONS BETWEEN UNIONS AND COMMUNITY GROUPS

To address the problems of subcontracting night soil treatment (see above), B General Union formed a coalition, 'the Committee of Residents to Eliminate Unfair Night Soil Treatment Practices', with community groups, trade unions, ward councillors of the Democratic Labour Party (DLP), and local residents in the region. The coalition requested a resident audit of the night soil treatment companies and demanded that ward authorities stop outsourcing the services. When ward authorities decided to cancel their contracts with the night soil treatment companies, B General Union demanded continued employment for the company workers. To press the ward authorities, the union's president and others staged a hunger strike, and the Busan Regional Council of the KCTU, Busan Minjung Yeondae (Busan People's Solidarity), and other civic organizations joined the struggle.

Another example of B General Union's coalition-building was its campaign against the closing of ticket offices in Busan train stations after the transportation corporation automated ticket sales and dismissed the non-regular employee ticket agents. The union also sought to build solidarity with social movements by forming a coalition called 'the Committee for the Continuation of Employment (of Ticket Agents)' with the Busan Regional Council of the KCTU, Busan People's Solidarity, and the DLP. According to B General Union, whenever it needs the solidarity of citizens for its struggle, the union forms a coalition with civic organizations and progressive political parties such as the DLP and the New Progressive Party (NPP).

CH Regional Union was involved in a struggle for the continued employment of cleaners who worked at one of the universities in the Chungnam region. When a new cleaning company replaced another company as the contractor for the university, the issue of continued employment of cleaners (some of whom were organized by CH Regional Union) came to the forefront. The union formed 'the Regional Committee for Countermeasures' with civic organizations and the NPP and mobilized community support for the cleaners. CH Regional Union, however, does not actively engage in coalition-building activities on its own because the Chungnam Regional Council of the KCTU serves as the main coalition partner representing the labour movement.

KN General Union, along with progressive members of the local assembly and social movement/civic organizations, engaged in a campaign to organize contract workers employed by local governments. The union also fought a coalition-based struggle against a sewage treatment company that had a contract with the Sacheon City Government. The new sewage treatment company replaced another company as the contractor of sewage treatment services and refused to rehire the unionized workers of the previous contractor (members of KN General Union). Instead, the company pressured these workers to quit the union. Under the umbrella of 'the Sacheon Committee for Countermeasures', the union, progressive political parties and Sacheon Jinbo Yeonhap (Sachen Progressive Federation) fought a coalition-based struggle for the employment of union members by the new contractor.

KN General Union does not form such committees when it can resolve labour disputes with the help of city councillors from progressive parties. It does, however, naturally engage in solidarity activities with social movement organizations in the region, such as Gyeongnam Jinbo Yeonhap (Gyeongnam Progressive Federation) and Minsaeng Minju Gyeongnam Hwei (Gyeongnam Congress for Welfare and Democracy).

DIRECT ACTION

Since the three regional general unions are legally recognized as trade unions, their main activities are to improve wages and working conditions of members through collective bargaining. The unions engage in negotiations and strikes to resolve serious issues such as dismissals of union members or workplace closures. They adopt various tactics from holding sit-ins in front of company buildings to instigating litigation against employers.

B General Union, as shown above, denounced the night soil treatment companies for their misconduct and demanded continued employment for workers after the ward authorities cancelled existing company contracts. During the campaign, it engaged in a variety of direct actions: it demanded a meeting with ward mayors, held protests in front of ward office buildings and mayors' residences, staged hunger strikes during sit-ins in front of ward office buildings, publicized the ward authorities' negligence in supervising contractors, and launched a signature collection campaign among local residents.

CH Regional Union, in its struggle for continued employment of university cleaners (mentioned above), demanded a meeting with the university's president and demonstrated at the university and the new cleaning contractor with a banner demanding continued employment and a guarantee of minimum wages for the cleaners.

KN General Union filed a lawsuit against the authorities of a national university when they refused to bargain over the cleaners' employment and insisted that they were not the cleaners' employer. When the court ruled that the Korean Government, rather than the university, employed the cleaners, the union started negotiations with the MEST (Ministry of Education, Science and Technology) and the MOJ (Ministry of Justice). In addition to negotiations with the central and local governments, KN General Union held protest meetings and sit-ins in front of the office building of the local government and appealed for citizen support by distributing fliers.

Comparative Analysis of Community Unionism in Japan and Korea

The previous section examined characteristics of community unionism in Japan and Korea based on the six characteristics of community unionism. The Japanese and Korean cases share four of six characteristics: the base of union organizing is a region rather than the workplace (first characteristic); the unions organize 'hard-to-organize' workers such as workers in small firms, non-regular, dismissed, and migrant workers (second); they seek to promote solidarity among workers regardless of workplace or employment status (fourth); in addition to collective bargaining, the unions engaged in direct actions (sixth).

As for the third characteristic (addressing a broad range of issues), this policy orientation is pronounced in two Korean unions (B General Union and KN General Union). The two Korean unions were committed to addressing the issues related to residents' livelihood and fought against contractors' misconduct (night soil treatment and waste collection). The Japanese unions (especially MU Union and Union MI) were also concerned with broader issues, but their concerns were limited mainly to the improvement of wage levels in their respective regions. Thus, Japanese community unions are less committed to the third characteristic than their Korean counterparts. This observation confirms Takagi's finding that few Japanese community unions are involved in livelihood issues in their communities (Takagi 2000).

The fifth characteristic (coalitions between unions and community groups) applies to all three Korean cases and two of the three Japanese cases. Moreover, although MU Union and Union MI in Japan have cooperated with community groups and NGOs, the two unions have weaker relationships with social movement organizations than the three Korean unions. The latter unions actively engage in region-based solidarity struggles with civic organizations and are closer to the community unionism model prevalent in other industrialized countries than the Japanese unions. If we apply Tattersall's classification of the three types of relationships between trade unions and community groups (Tattersall 2006, see above) to Japanese and Korean community unionism, all three Korean unions formed 'simple coalition relationships', i.e., issue-based coalitions with formal decision-making structures. MU Union in Japan also formed a simple coalition relationship in its campaign for a living wage ordinance. The relationships between MU Union and Union MI and NGOs concerned with assisting migrant workers[17] can be characterized as 'ad hoc relationships' that 'focus on one-off requests for support, participation in events' (Tattersall 2006: 590).

Suzuki (2008) argues that coalitions between Japanese community unions and community groups and social movement organizations are underdeveloped. He gives two reasons for the underdevelopment: (1) 'the relatively weak presence of community-based organizations capable of forming alliances with community unions' due to the relative underdevelopment

17 Suzuki points out that the cooperation between MU Union and NGOs concerned with assisting migrant workers takes place 'on an ad hoc basis' (Suzuki 2008: 511).

of civil society and (2) Japanese law allows for the liberal recognition of unions, which makes unions less reliant on community allies (Suzuki 2008: 513–14). Can these factors explain differences in the development of labour-community coalitions in Japan and Korea?

Korean procedures for recognizing trade unions are also liberal. While Korean unions are required to notify the public authority of their establishment,[18] they have the right to bargain collectively from the first day of their establishment. When the public authority issues certifications of establishment, unions are legally guaranteed their rights and status. Since the public authority returned the documents filed by Korean Government Employees Union (KGEU) and Youth Community Union and rejected the establishment of these unions, observers noted that the government had adopted a stricter union recognition procedure. These cases of rejection are exceptions rather than the rule, however. When the three regional general unions notified the public authority of their establishment, the authority accepted the filed documents and issued certifications of establishment.[19]

Suzuki's first explanation that labour-community coalitions are underdeveloped in Japan because civil society is weak does not apply to Korea. Korean civil society has developed on the basis of the democratization of Korean society since the mid-1980s (Lee, M. 2006). Since the announcement of the Declaration of Democracy in 1987, Korean society has seen

18 According to the Labour Union Act and Labour Relations Adjustment Act, a group of workers who establish a trade union are required to file a report of union establishment and union statutes with the public authority. The public authority, upon examination of the documents, issues a certification of establishment, requests further information, or returns the filed documents (i.e., rejection of union establishment) within three days. The authority seldom returns the filed documents, but there were two recent cases of union establishment rejections (Korean Government Employees Union and Youth Community Union). The public authority explained that they returned the filed documents to these two unions because the lists of union members included unemployed and dismissed workers.

19 When B General Union notified the public authority of its establishment, its statute did not include unemployed workers as qualified union members. After a certification of establishment was issued, the union revised the statute and accepted dismissed workers as qualified members (Jin 2007: 169).

not only an upsurge in the labour movement with the establishment of many independent unions but also the development of civil society organizations, which had the support of the middle class and demanded policy and institutional reforms. Many of these organizations participated in and influenced the decision-making process of public policies during the Kim Young-Sam and Kim Dae-Jung administrations. Many citizens also supported the activities of these civil society organizations, especially their roles in institutional reforms and as watch-dogs of the government.

Two features to be noted about social movements in Korean civil society: civil society organizations address broad and diverse agendas,[20] and they are active in developing relationships of solidarity among themselves. Eun Soo-Mi has observed that although solidarity between labour and civil society had weakened in the years between 1991 and 2001, the Korean labour movement still had a tendency to mobilize resources through coalition-building with civic movement organizations (Eun 2005). This tendency has become pronounced with the onslaught of neoliberal globalization since the late 1990s because coalition-building came to be seen as a means to prevent the power of the labour and social movements from declining. In 2003, Korean People's Solidarity was established as a permanent organization for joint actions by 37 organizations including trade unions and farmer and civic organizations. In 2007, the Korea Alliances of Progressive Movements (KAPM) was established as a federation of 22 organizations of trade unions, farmers, students, religious believers, and citizens in the progressive camp. And in 2008, about 400 trade unions, civic organizations, and opposition/progressive parties formed Minsaeng Minju Kukmin Hwei (National Congress for Welfare and Democracy). The KCTU played an active role in the establishments of these labour-civil society coalitions. These coalitions also established regional organizations to promote coalition-building and joint actions at the regional level. These bodies extended their activities to regions other than Seoul to counter the tendency for civil society organizations to be concentrated in the capital city.

20 Cho (2000) calls Korean civil society movements 'comprehensive civil society movements'.

In interviews with the author, leaders of B General Union and KN General Union listed regional organizations such as Busan People's Solidarity, Gyeongnam Progressive Federation, Sacheon Jinbo Yeonhap (Sacheon Progressive Federation), and Minsaeng Minju Gyeongnam Hwei (Gyeongnam Congress for Welfare and Democracy) as partners. The coalition-building of regional general unions was made easier by their affiliation with the regional councils of the KCTU,[21] which served as the regional hubs for labour-community coalitions.

Based on the above analysis, I argue that liberal union recognition procedures and union collective bargaining rights apply to both Japan and Korea and cannot explain the degree to which labour-community coalitions have developed in the two countries. A more plausible explanation for the development/under-development of labour-community coalitions is the degree of development of civil society in the two countries. An active Korean civil society brought about robust relationships of solidarity between trade unions and civil society organizations.

If we take a closer look at the nature of labour-community coalitions in Korea, we notice that regional general unions do not join such coalitions automatically, but their involvement in coalitions is selective. For example, the president of KN General Union reports that the union does not get involved in coalitions with community groups, if the union judges that it can resolve an issue by itself. The president of B General Union similarly remarks: 'Coalitions between labour unions and civil society organizations contribute to the improvement of social problems, but may weaken the presence of labour unions. So we sometimes take actions by ourselves.' In other words, the regional general unions form coalitions with community groups when they judge that they need the support of groups that play an important role in the formation of public opinion in regional communities.

21 The three regional general unions are not only affiliated with province-level regional councils of the KCTU but also share the same office buildings with KCTU councils. The regional general unions and KCTU regional councils consult closely on labour issues and in resolving labour disputes. This contrasts with the case of community unions in Japan. They are unaffiliated with regional federations of national union organizations, such as the Japanese Trade Union Confederation (JTUC or Rengo).

We also need to note the common characteristic of community unions in Japan and regional general unions in Korea which distinguishes them from community-based labour organizations in the United States, Canada and the United Kingdom. Region-based unions in Japan and Korea are trade unions with the right to bargain collectively; in the latter three countries, employers have no legal obligation to bargain with community-based labour organizations. As a result, bringing economic benefits to workers by negotiating with employers is especially difficult.

In summary, community unionism in Japan and that in Korea have a common characteristic of 'community unionism with labour union functions'. The difference between them is that community unionism in Korea has shown a greater concern with livelihood issues in the community and more actively builds coalitions with community groups than its Japanese counterpart.

Conclusion

This chapter examines new types of trade unions, community unions and regional general unions, in the Japanese and Korean labour movement and finds these new trade unions have put community unionism into practice. Community unionism in Japan and Korea, unlike its counterparts in North America and Britain, incorporates trade union functions. Despite this common feature, an important difference is the greater degree of labour-community coalition development in Korea. The diversity of community unionism reflects the different degree to which civil society and the relationship of solidarity between the labour movement and civil society organizations have developed in the two countries. It can be argued that the community unionism in Korea is closer to community unionism in other industrialized countries than it is in Japan. The Korean regional general unions we examine in this chapter go further in establishing 'resident trade unions' that serve both residents and workers. This new type of unionism will reconstitute its organization from workplace-based locals to units based on administrative districts of local governments such as wards or counties. In my example,

KN General Union is oriented to this type of unionism.[22] It remains to be seen how the transformation of regional general unions into 'resident trade unions' will affect relationships between labour and community.

This discussion of a union movement oriented to community-based activities and organizing (i.e., community unionism) has developed in the process of searching for a new model of unionism that overcomes the stagnation of labour movements under the impact of neoliberal globalization and organizes and represents 'hard-to-organize' workers. Previous studies were mainly concerned with cases of community unionism in industrialized countries other than Japan and Korea. Thus, 'samples' of community unionism covered by previous studies was not large enough to discuss diverse forms of community unionism. It is hoped that this chapter, through an examination of community unionism in Korea and a cross-national comparison of Japan and Korea, will make a contribution to discussions about cross-national diversity in community unionism.

The findings of this chapter have some limitations because they reflect the cases of only six unions in two countries. To make the findings generalizable, further studies should examine other community unions in Japan and regional general unions in Korea from the analytical framework of community unionism.

References

Black, S.J. (2005). 'Community Unionism A Strategy for Organizing in the New Economy', *New Labor Forum*, 14 (3), 24–32.

Cho, H. (2000). 'Civic Action for Global Democracy: a Response to Neo-liberal Globalization', *Inter-Asia Cultural Studies*, 1 (1), 163–7.

22 Besides KN General Union, S General Union (the author conducted an interview with this union) is also oriented to 'resident labour unionism'. The union aims to establish a union in which union members and residents engage in activities together. To realize this goal, the union is planning to reorganize its organization based on wards and assign full-time activists to ward-based units.

Cranford, C.J., Gellatly, M., Lado, D., Vosko, L.F. (2004). 'Workers' Centres and Community Unionism: Organizing for Fair Employment in Toronto'. Paper Presented at the International Colloquium on Union Renewal, Montreal, November 18th-20th. Available at http://www.crimt.org/2eSite_renouveau?Abstract?Cranford_e.

Eun, S.(2005). 'The Possibility of Social Movement Unionism in the Korean Labour Movement', *Studies on Labour Policies* (Korea Labour Institute), 5 (1), 43–73 (in Korean).

Fine, J. (2005). 'Worker Centers Organizing Communities at the Edge of the Dream', *Briefing Paper*, Economic Policy Institute, September.

Fine, J.(2001). 'Building Community Unions: In Stamford, Connecticut, Organizers Are Putting the Movement Back in Labor', *Nation*, 1 January.

Fukui, Y. (2003). 'NPO-type Labour Unions – from the Perspective of Japanese Small Local Unions'. In SHAKAI-SEISAKU GAKKAI (Society for the Study of Social Policy (ed.), *The Changing Employment*. Kyoto: Horitsu Bunkasha (in Japanese).

Gapasin, F., Wial, H. (1998). 'The Role of Central Labor Councils in Union Organizing in the 1990s'. In K. Bronfenbrenner et al. (eds), *Organizing to Win: New Research on Union Strategies*. Ithaca, NY: ILR Press.

Jin, S. (2007). 'Factors Influencing the Effectiveness of Contingent Workers' Unions: Focusing on Bargaining Power Hypotheses'. PhD Dissertation, Department of Business Administration, Graduate School of Korea University (in Korean).

Lee, K-I. (2006). 'Factors for the Development of an Organizing Model as a Strategy of Labor Unions: Based on Cases of Regional General Unions', *Social Science Research* (Social Science Research Institute, Kangwon National University), 45 (2), 1–21 (in Korean).

Lee, K. (2009). 'Mass Production of Non-Regular Workers and Their Responses to Illegal Labour Acts', *Reflection and Prospect* (Busan Democratic Movement Memorial Association, Democratic Society Research Institute), 229–57 (in Korean).

Lee, M. (2006). 'Korea: the Impact of Globalization on Korean Civil Society and Search for Asianism'. In *Sociological Studies on Citizens' Consciousness and Activities in Globalizing Societies* (Report of Grant-in-Aid for Scientific Research [research project headed by Kokichi Shoji]) (in Japanese).

Luce, S. (2007). 'The U.S. Living Wage Movement Building: Coalitions from the Local Level in a Global Economy'. In L. Turner, D.B. Cornfield (eds), *Labor in the New Urban Battlegrounds: Local Solidarity in a Global Economy*. Ithaca, NY: Cornell University Press.

Lucio, M.M., Perrett, R. (2009). 'Meanings and Dilemmas in Community Unionism: Trade Union Community Initiatives and Black and Minority Ethnic Groups in the UK', *Work, Employment and Society*, 23 (4), 693–710.

MU Union News Letter No. 199–No. 208 (from 1 May 2009 to 1 February 2010) (in Japanese).

Nagamine, T. (2003). 'The Twenty-Year History of Community Unions: Their Current State and Issues'. In A. Hamamura, T. Nagamine (eds), *Diversities and Possibilities of Trade Union Functions*. Tokyo: Hosei Daigaku Shuppankyoku (in Japanese).

Stewart, P. (2006). 'Marginal Movements and Minority Struggles? The Case of the Japanese Minority Social and Labour Movements', *The Sociological Review*, 54 (4), 753–73.

Suzuki, A. (2008). 'Community Unions in Japan: Similarities and Differences of Region-based Labour Movements between Japan and Other Industrialized Countries', *Economic and Industrial Democracy*, 29 (4), 492–520.

Symon, G., Crawshaw, J. (2009). 'Urban Labour, Voice and Legitimacy: Economic Development and the Emergence of Community Unionism', *Industrial Relations Journal*, 40 (2), 140–55.

Takagi, I. (2000). 'Organization and Activities of Community-based Unions'. In SHAKAI-SEISAKU GAKKAI (Society for the Study of Social Policy) (ed.), *State and Region in Social Policy*. Tokyo: Ochanomizu Shobo (in Japanese).

Tattersall, A. (2007). 'A Little Help From Our Friends: Exploring and Understanding Labor-community Coalition Formation', Revised and Resubmitted to *Labor Studies Journal*, September 2007, pp. 2–36. Available at: http://powerincoalition.com/wp-content/uploads/2010/01/Tattersall-A-little-help-from-our-friends-LSJ.pdf.

Tattersall, A. (2006). 'Powerful Community Relationships and Union Renewal in Australia', *Relations Industrielles/Industrial Relations*, 61 (4), 589–614.

Tufts, S. (1998). 'Community Unionism in Canada and Labor's (Re)Organization of Space', *Antipode*, 30 (3), 227–50.

Wills, J. (2004). 'Organizing the Low Paid: East London's Living Wage Campaign as a Vehicle for Change'. In G. Healy, E. Heery, P. Taylor, W. Brown (eds), *The Future of Worker Representation*. New York: Palgrave Macmillan.

Wills, J. (2001). 'Community Unionism and Trade Union Renewal in the UK: Moving Beyond the Fragments at Last?', *Transactions of the Institute of British Geographers*, NS 26, 465–83.

Wills, J., Simms, M. (2004). 'Building Reciprocal Community Unionism in the UK', *Capital & Class*, 82, 59–84.

PART THREE

Meso-level Mediating Factors Explaining the Diversities of Social Movement Unionism

STEPHANIE LUCE

7 Labour and Community Coalitions: Challenges for Growth

Introduction

Trade unions have worked with community groups throughout their history in the United States, but scholars have noted that coalition work increased in the mid- to late 1980s amidst a wave of plant closings, attacks from politicians, and a rapid drop in union density. In the 1990 book *Building Bridges: The Emerging Grassroots Coalition of Labor and Community*, Jeremy Brecher and Tim Costello note the emergence of 'the first fruits of a new social alliance which is unheralded at the national level – and virtually unreported in the national media – because it is being built at the grassroots' (p. 9). The national organization Jobs with Justice (JwJ) was founded in 1987 by labour activists hoping to build a more social movement oriented labour movement and tighter connections between unions and community organizations. In the Midwest and Northeast coalitions formed to fight plant closings, which were destroying communities (Brecher and Costello 1990).

Since the early 1990s, the labour-community coalition model has flourished. JwJ has chapters in more than 40 cities. The official labour movement has also come on board with efforts to revitalize Central Labour Councils by integrating their work with community organizations. Since 1994, labour-community coalitions have won living wage ordinances in over 125 cities and counties across the United States. Some of these coalitions have gone on to other issues, fighting to win paid sick leave, health care reform and tax reform. A new wave of campaigns developed to advocate for Community Benefits Agreements (CBA), which push for higher standards for economic development projects.

Some unions and labour organizations have seen the potential of coalitions with communities as a way to build social movement unionism and rebuild labour's power. For some, this comes as recognition of labour's weakness and the need to develop allies and influence public opinion. Others are pulled into coalitions through the work of individual leaders or organizers who come from a community organizing background (Rose 2000; Sherman and Voss 2000; Nissen 2004; Tattersall 2010).

The situation has changed quite a bit since Brecher and Costello wrote their book. Today, there is national attention on labour-community coalitions, and the national media have even focused on some of their work.[1] While there has been some excellent work that chronicles the successes of these coalitions (Pastor Jr., Benner and Matsuoka 2009; Tattersall 2010), there has been less analysis of the limitations and challenges coalitions face in trying to build larger movements and deeper power. Despite more than 20 years of organizing, union density has not turned around. The labour movement has not been able to win many of its demands on the federal level, even when the presidency and both Houses were controlled by the Democratic Party. Nationally, public opinion of unions is close to a historic low. In 2009, for the first time since data were collected, Gallup polls showed that less than half of Americans approved of unions (Saad 2009). Approval rose to 52 per cent in 2011, but this is far below approval rates in the post-WWII era (Jones 2011).

This chapter will examine some of the common challenges that labour-community coalitions have faced in working and staying together, as well as some of the reasons why unions have not always found this an easy avenue to revitalization. The chapter will primarily rely on four case studies. Three of these are regional labour-community coalitions, and one is a project within a national union. I begin with an overview of coalitions in the United States as well as discussion on how to evaluate their success. I then provide details on the four case studies and some of the common themes of challenges they face. I will argue that activists have placed too much value on the formation of coalitions for the sake of coalition-building

1 ACORN, a major player in many labour-community coalitions, was targeted by conservative forces as one of the main parties responsible for the housing crisis due to its successful efforts to fight racism in credit markets.

and have not paid enough attention to the longer-term visions of what such coalitions might build. Labour-community coalitions need to look beyond the coalition model, if they want to overcome some of the challenges preventing labour movement revitalization.

Labour-Community Coalitions: An Overview

Labour-community coalitions are neither new nor unique to the United States. In the last several decades, however, there has been a steady growth in the number of such coalitions and in the level of co-ordination between them, which coincides and intertwines with a growth in organizations advocating for economic justice at the local level (Pastor Jr., Benner and Matsuoka 2009). The coalitions exist primarily on the local level and bring together trade unions and labour councils with other unions, community organizations, student groups, faith-based organizations, environmental groups and independent activists.

Tattersall and Reynolds (2007) examine labour-community coalitions in the United States and Australia and develop a theoretical framework to describe different types of coalitions as well as the common elements that underlie their formation. These common elements include 'the nature of common concern, the structure of organizational relationships, organizational capacity and commitment, and the scale of coalition activity'. Dean and Reynolds (2009) further categorize labour coalitions into labour-community alliances, labour-minority-immigrant alliances and labour-interfaith alliances.

Coalitions of these types have existed in over 100 US cities and counties over the past decade. Some prioritize union struggles (such as strike support), while others work on environmental justice, transportation, health care or housing. Many began as a single-issue campaign, such as a living wage ordinance. Some were able to sustain themselves and move into other kinds of campaigns, such as Community Benefits Agreements or paid sick-day ordinances. Some of the coalitions that have been anchored by Central Labour Councils and were active in the Union Cities program are actively trying to rebuild.

Other coalitions have been anchored by 'think and act tanks' – labour- and foundation-funded organizations that conduct research and aid organizing efforts. These are meant to be an improvement on 'think tanks' that just produce research reports or organizations that undertake campaigns but do not engage in strategic research. The idea of the think and act tank is to employ researchers and policy analysts to study the city, local industries and employers and opportunities for organizing. That research is informed by political work on the ground. The research then is meant to assist union organizing efforts and policy campaigns. They also employ full-time organizers who work to help run these campaigns, such as a community benefits agreement. Some of these think and act tanks, such as the Los Angeles Alliance for a New Economy or the Connecticut Center for a New Economy, were started by the Hotel and Restaurant Employees union. SEIU has supported others, such as the Front Range Economic Strategy Center (FRESC). Some of the coalitions are part of national networks, such as the Partnership for Working Families and Building Partnerships USA.

The coalitions have achieved a considerable number of victories, including over 140 living wage ordinances in cities, counties and on university campuses. Some coalitions have played an active role in local elections; others have assisted union organizing. The coalitions have won over two dozen Community Benefits Agreements: agreements regarding economic development projects, which usually include within a development things such as a living wage but also card check/neutrality for construction and sometimes for the retail workers; low-income housing; environmental provisions; jobs for local residents; child care facilities; and green space for public use. Groups have won greater access to public transportation and affordable housing.

Despite the successes, not all coalitions stay together. Tattersall and Reynolds (2007) argue that there are four ideal type coalitions, starting with ad hoc coalitions and moving to simple coalitions, then mutual interest coalitions and finally deep coalitions. Some groups may begin at one level and progress while others are more static or disintegrate. Nissen (2004) examines some of the traditional ways unions have pursued 'vanguardist' type coalition work and failed to move beyond ad hoc coalitions. These unions want to control the coalitions and engage in them only in a unidirectional manner. According to Dean and Reynolds (2009), only a minority of the coalitions have been able to move to the level of deep coalition.

Unions enter into coalitions with allies for a variety of reasons. The ad hoc coalitions that Tattersall and Reynolds (2007) describe are created primarily out of the need to win a particular struggle or campaign. Many unions have learned that they may need to bring in allies to win, particularly in industries where workers have little leverage on the job, but unions hoping to see their coalition work build their capacity and, ideally, the labour movement, need to invest in more advanced forms of coalition building.

The most direct measure of union revitalization would be an increase in the number of union members in a local, the creation of new locals, and an increase in union density in a workplace, industry or region. Given the tremendous decline in national union power, success may simply be the ability to maintain membership at current levels or to slow the pace of union decline more than it would otherwise.

Table 7.1 provides a list of cities that have had active labour-community coalitions in the past two decades. We provide union density for those cities and the total density in their states for select years starting with 1990.[2] Cities with coalitions are listed below with state totals beneath each city. We calculate the percentage point change in density from 1990 to 2009, as well as from 2000 to 2009. Most regions show a drop in union density, but a few cities had a slower decline than others. The data show mixed results. Declines in density for some cities with labour-community coalitions were less steep than in their states but not uniformly. For 1990 to 2009, in four cities the pattern was different. In Baltimore and Cleveland, union density declined less than in their respective states, Maryland and Ohio. In Boston and San Jose, union density increased, while it declined in Massachusetts and California.

2 The data are from the Current Population Survey and have a few weaknesses: data are provided for metropolitan regions and not the city proper, definitions of metropolitan areas change over time in some cases, and the CPS sample is not drawn for the purposes of measuring union density.

There was not as much coalition activity in the 1990s as in the current decade, and it may be that coalition work in the 1990s did not bear fruit right away. For 2000 to 2009, we see that only two of the nine cities profiled had significantly better changes in union density rates than their states: Cleveland and San Jose. Other cities had either the same rate of change as the state, or worse.

Table 7.1 Union Density for Cities with Labour-Community Coalitions

Region	1990	1995	2000	2005	2009	Percentage change 1990–2009	Percentage change 2000–2009
Baltimore	13.7	14.1	15.4	14.8	13.2	-0.5	-2.2
Maryland	14.5	14.9	14.6	13.3	12.6	-1.9	-2
Boston	15.8	15.6	13.7	12.6	15.9	0.1	2.2
Massachusetts	17.6	16.2	14.3	13.9	16.6	-1	2.3
Cleveland	20.9	19.5	15.9	16.1	16	-4.9	0.1
Ohio	21	18.5	17.3	16	14.2	-6.8	-3.1
Denver	11.7	11.4	9.6	8.9	7.7	-4	-1.9
Colorado	10.5	9.9	9	8.3	7	-3.5	-2
Los Angeles	17.8	14.5	15.2	14.9	15	-2.8	-0.2
California	18.4	17.7	16	16.5	17.2	-1.2	1.2
Miami	11	6.6	6.5	5.5	5.7	-5.3	-0.8
Florida	8.1	7.3	6.8	5.4	5.8	-2.3	-1
Milwaukee	24.5	21.5	22	15.3	14	-10.5	-8
Wisconsin	20.6	17.7	17.6	16.1	15.2	-5.4	-2.4
New Haven	21.3	19.4	20.7	17.5	17.2	-4.1	-3.5
Connecticut	17.7	20.2	16.3	15.9	17.3	-0.4	1
San Jose	11.7	13.1	11.2	14.3	13.4	1.7	2.2
California	18.4	17.7	16	16.5	17.2	-1.2	1.2

Source: Current Population Survey data, as compiled by Barry T. Hirsch and David A. Macpherson, available at unionstats.com.

We did the same analysis for comparable cities within these states and found similar, mixed results, which suggest that a cursory examination of labour-community coalitions and changes in union density provides no magic answer to why union membership is shrinking or a magic bullet for how to revitalize unions.

From the union perspective, it is also difficult to measure the outcome of labour-community work. Some unions that have been active in coalitions seem to be growing more (or declining less) than unions that are not as involved; however, because national unions have been merging and restructuring, it becomes difficult to separate out whether union membership growth is due to a real increase in unionized workers versus a merger or raiding members from another union. Therefore, membership data by union do not necessarily support the argument that labour-community coalitions are a clear strategy for growth.

This raises at least two key questions:

1. Are there other measures we should examine for positive impacts from labour-community coalition work, such as increases in political power, higher average wages, increases in worker-friendly legislation, etc.?
2. What factors might be keeping coalition work from translating into greater gains for unions?

Other research suggests answers to the first question. Clawson (2003) argues that it is likely that union density may increase quickly rather than incrementally. We may first need to create the conditions for union growth – such as changing public opinion about unions, creating allies, building political power, changing laws, or reducing the power of employers and their coalitions. The 'Building Regional Power'[3] research project evaluates

3 This project was launched in 2003 by the AFL-CIO and the United Association for Labor Education. The Regional Power Building Network is a group of scholars who have been working to document case studies of cities where labour councils have been attempting to transform their relations with community groups, assist unions in new organizing, and build greater political power. The case studies have been published in various journals and books. See Reynolds (2004).

labour-community coalitions on the basis of various criteria including: electing pro-labour candidates to office at the local level, holding politicians accountable to promises made, shifting the public debate on labour and community issues, leadership development, and winning concrete legislative victories (Reynolds 2004).

Based on these measures, it is possible to find some examples of success in many of the labour-community coalitions. It seems clear, however, that after more than 20 years the gains that coalitions have won have not yet translated into larger-scale advances for the labour movement. Therefore, this chapter will focus on the second question: what might be keeping coalition work from greater success?

Case Studies

This chapter is based primarily on case studies of labour-community coalitions in Cleveland, Denver and New Haven; and a national effort by the National Education Association to launch living wage campaigns for education support professionals (ESPs). As part of the Building Regional Power project, I worked with colleagues to interview key participants in labour-community coalitions in these cities. Mark Nelson and I conducted interviews with union and community organization staff, Denver Area Labor Federation (DALF) leadership, national and state AFL-CIO staff, and a journalist, in late 2003 and early 2004. We then did similar interviews in Cleveland in 2005. In 2007, I worked with Louise Simmons to interview labour and community coalition participants in New Haven. In all, we conducted approximately 40 interviews. In each case, interviews were supplemented with reviews of local media, campaign materials, city council records, and other studies (Simmons and Luce 2009).

Each of the three regional cases is an example of a city where labour-community coalitions have been active and achieved some gains. Denver activists revitalized a local Jobs with Justice chapter in the mid-1990s and launched a living wage campaign in 1996. In 1998, some of these leaders decided to take control of their local labour council and push it in a more activist, social movement direction. Leslie Moody, former organizer with Jobs with Justice, became the new president of the Denver Area Labor Federation. DALF undertook major electoral work, attempting to build labour power at the municipal level but also worked with other labour and community groups to influence politics at the state level. DALF, along with SEIU, also helped found the Front Range Economic Strategy Center, a think and do tank that has conducted research on the local economy and tied that into campaigns to unionize workers and win a Community Benefits Agreement for redevelopment of the Gates Rubber plant – a 52-acre brownfield site in south central Denver.

In Cleveland, a similar story emerged. Labour activists built a strong Jobs with Justice chapter, then took over the leadership of the local labour council. John Ryan of the CWA became president and provided support for a range of activities in Cleveland, including living wage campaigns and the creation of the regional think tank Policy Matters Ohio. Labour and community activists also worked together on electoral work, including city, state and federal voter turnout. The city is also home to the United Labor Agency (ULA). ULA was founded in 1970 to provide services to union members, such as strike support, but also day-care, services for senior citizens and assistance in job training and placement. ULA is supported through the Labor Council and United Way. More recently, ULA has been working to expand beyond service-provision and into a vehicle for organizing. Over the past few years, it has worked with labour and community groups on voter registration and turnout efforts. It has also built programs to provide pre-apprenticeships in the building trades for city residents and created a local hiring hall.

The New Haven case is dominated by the story of Yale University. Yale is the largest, and by far the wealthiest, employer in the city. Yale employees have been engaged in efforts to unionize for many years, with success in some areas (clerical workers and building services), but not in others (graduate teaching and research assistants, and health care employees at Yale-New Haven Hospital). The New Haven Labor Council, unions, community and faith groups worked together on a living wage campaign and on various strike support efforts in the 1990s and 2000s. In 1999, the Connecticut Center for a New Economy was formed to combine strategic research and organizing. The Center helped launch the Community Organizing for Responsible Development (CORD) to organize about issues of economic development in the city. CORD's first major campaign was an effort to win a CBA regarding Yale-New Haven Hospitals plan to build a new cancer ward. The expansion would take place in the heart of a low-income community and result in possible serious traffic and environmental problems. In addition, 1199 SEIU had been trying to organize a union for hospital workers for over ten years, but had faced repeated resistance and interference from the hospital administrators. CORD organized to win a comprehensive CBA, which included health care for low-income residents, job training and hiring, and an agreement from Yale-New Haven Hospital that it would be neutral regarding the effort to organize hospital workers.

In addition to these three regional case studies, I have conducted research on the living wage effort by the National Education Association (NEA). The NEA is the largest union in the United States, with 3.2 million members. The NEA began in 1857 as a professional association, and for many years was not considered a trade union. In 1966 the NEA joined forces to work in partnership with the American Teachers Association.[4] It is not a member of a labour federation but has worked closely with the AFL-CIO and Change to Win in recent years. The NEA represented primarily K-12 teachers, but over time, has come to represent others in the education field, including university professors and staff, substitute teachers, and education support professionals. ESPs include para-educators who work in schools to provide teaching assistance, including for students with special needs. Para-educators are often part-time jobs with low wages and few or no benefits, unless unionized. The NEA organized ESPs in Ithaca, New York, where workers gained a 50 per cent wage increase. In 2002, after seeing how successful the Ithaca campaign had been it decided to launch a national living wage effort for ESPs. These campaigns look a bit

4 This was initially the National Association of Colored Teachers, founded in 1904 as an association for Black Teachers.

different from traditional living wage campaigns that target city governments. The NEA living wage campaigns try to build labour-community coalitions to support collective bargaining and/or legislative demands for higher wages for ESPs. To date, the NEA has supported local campaigns in dozens of states.

In all four cases, labour and community leaders have been able to work together to achieve victories. In all cases, the coalitions have created new relationships, and have been associated with the formation of new organizations. In each case, however, the coalitions have faced challenges that have held their work back or weakened their achievements. This includes internal and external challenges.

Internal Challenges

Labour-community coalitions face a number of internal challenges which have at times impeded their ability to win further gains or strengthen the coalition. Two of these major challenges are building real solidarity, and structural issues.

Building real solidarity

Most labour-community coalitions are able to form through a shared value or goal. For example, many polls show that the population is heavily in favour of higher minimum wages or living wages: some polls show that support as high as 80 to 90 per cent. This makes the living wage a good concept on which to build a broad coalition. Unionists can support a higher minimum wage as it can reduce the union-non-union wage gap, making it less attractive for employers to employ non-union labour. Community groups might support the idea of higher wages for members who are living on the edge of poverty. Small businesses might see a higher minimum wage as a good business strategy, as it could help stabilize their workforce and bring more money into the local economy. While the living wage might be a good issue on which to build initial coalitions, it could also lead to the trap of the 'least common denominator'. Coalitions are sometimes stuck working only on the issues that everyone agrees on and avoiding controversial demands.

One place where this reality of least common denominator politics could be seen was in San Francisco. In 2003, an alliance of labour and community groups secured a measure on the city ballot to establish a citywide living wage rate of $8.50 an hour, to be indexed annually with the cost of living and covering all businesses in the city with 10 or more employees. The ballot measure had wide support in the city; in fact, one poll showed that support for the measure would have been higher, if the living wage rate had been set at $10 an hour. On Election Day, the measure passed easily. However, on that same day, voters also passed Proposition M, extending penalties for panhandling. This suggests that some living wage supporters may only want to support 'the deserving poor'.

Steve Cagan, a former organizer for Cleveland Jobs with Justice gives another example of the challenges of this kind of politics. He notes that in the first five years of Cleveland JwJ steering committee meetings there was only one disagreement. Cagan thinks this was a sign that people were holding back and not sharing their true opinions. This made the meetings fun, and the group was able to work on some projects but was not pushed to go deeper and engage one another in areas where they disagreed. After the living wage ordinance was passed, the organization floundered a bit, lacking clarity about what to do next. Cagan eventually left the staff of JwJ. The organization hired a new organizer but JWJ struggled to find a new campaign that brought as much energy and activity as the living wage. Cagan believes this was in part because the coalition members never really addressed the deeper political issues between them.

In Denver, there was the opposite dynamic. The local labour movement was plagued by in-fighting. Many leaders were not on good terms with one another, and this made it difficult to build strong alliances. There were divisions within the labour council and, later, divisions between the labour council and Jobs with Justice. From the outside, it was difficult to assess which problems were due to serious political differences, which were due to fights over turf and resources and which were due to personalities. In any case, it appeared that the historical pattern of in-fighting was difficult to break, even with leadership turnover.

Although the past can be a yoke, it may also be necessary to directly confront historical divisions. In particular, many building trades unions, and sometimes labour councils, were party to practices that excluded people of colour from membership and jobs. In some communities, African Americans remain distrustful of trade unions that for many years had kept them from jobs. In Cleveland, several interviewees noted that while building local coalitions was a positive step, but to do so, it was necessary for union leaders to engage in a public discussion of and perhaps a public apology for the past. One interviewee suggested that coalition work was limited because white labour leaders 'don't really understand the politics within the black community, including the history of a deep nationalist tendency and focus on electoralism' (Luce and Nelson 2005). The interviewee was highlighting the ways in which some African American activists had focused energy on winning elected offices and had enjoyed relative success in some cities, including the election of black mayors in cities like Detroit, Atlanta, and Chicago, as well as success in other positions and entry into the Democratic Party more generally. This success has created a particular political space for some African Americans who believe there is a continued need to organize in the arena of electoral politics. Others, including many white labour activists, might not agree that electoral politics is a priority, and might not even see all of these black officials as allies. Our interviewee believes that it is not possible to form deep coalitions among these black and white activists without an historical examination of racism and the reasons for the political priorities of different groups.

Due in part to history but also due to the different needs of organizations involved, it can be difficult to trust your coalition partners. Community Benefits Agreement campaigns are built on the idea that CBAs will include something for everyone in the coalition. However, there is the temptation for one partner to cut a deal and leave the rest of the coalition behind. For example, early on in the development process, the building trades in New Haven were able to negotiate that construction on the hospital extension be done by union workers at prevailing wages, and they did not participate in the CBA campaign. Some partners in the Denver CBA campaign were always nervous that the building trades might take unilateral action and pull out of the coalition.

It isn't just that any one coalition partner might be tempted to stray. As Gwen Mills, an organizer with the Connecticut Center for a New Economy (CCNE) notes, employers and opponents use the same kind of union-busting tactics on the coalition as they do in a union drive. This includes 'divide and conquer' tactics designed specifically to break the coalition. The Yale-New Haven hospital leadership targeted community leaders and tried to persuade them to support the expansion. This worked in at least one case, with a pastor taking money from the hospital to build a church and leaving the coalition. Mills suggests that coalitions must do inoculation campaigns early on: educating coalition members about the kind of opposition they would see and preparing them for the employers' tactics – just as unions do when organizing a workplace.

This same divide and conquer tactic was employed in Chicago in a 'Big Box' living wage campaign. A large coalition of unions and community groups proposed a city ordinance that would require large retailers to pay a minimum wage of $10. Wal-Mart and Target strongly opposed the ordinance and worked hard to defeat it. Similar to New Haven, they targeted prominent African-American leaders (such as former Atlanta mayor Andrew Young) to oppose the ordinance and argue that Wal-Mart could offer jobs to black workers. Dorian Warren (2005) notes that all public polling data showed that African-Americans in Chicago favoured the Big Box ordinance, at a rate higher than other races. Wal-Mart, Mayor Daley and opponents, however, effectively split the coalition and managed to frame the issue as unions versus black workers. They succeeded in part because of the history of discrimination unions practiced against black workers in the city.

A final challenge for building internal solidarity is the in-fighting that occurs among the coalition partners. In particular, over the past decade trade unions have been embroiled in a series of internal battles; the split between the AFL-CIO and Change to Win; divisions within SEIU; divisions within UNITE HERE; divisions within the building trades. These internal battles do not have to have negative implications for labour-community coalitions.

In fact, in some places strong local coalitions were able to keep in-fighting to a minimum. For example, after Change to Win unions left the AFL-CIO, some local affiliates continued to stay active in the Cleveland AFL-CIO, and others soon signed Solidarity Charters to stay connected.

Still, the battles divert precious time and energy away from other work. And while the AFL-CIO and Change to Win split did not appear to do major damage to most local coalitions, the recent internal fights related to the split of UNITE HERE were more serious, as HERE was a founder of a number of local groups, such as the Los Angeles Alliance for a New Economy (LAANE), CCNE in Connecticut, and the East Bay Alliance for a Sustainable Economy in California.

The disagreements can involve individual locals as well as federations. In all three cities, activists complained about 'rogue unions' that wanted to operate on their own, separate from the labour council or coalitions. In Denver, the Carpenters have often pursued their own agenda, and the UFCW has at times threatened to disaffiliate from DALF. In Cleveland the UAW never participated in the Labor Council. In New Haven the building trades generally operate on their own.

In some communities, the NEA may not have a tradition of working closely with local unions, as they are not part of a national federation. Debbie Minnick is the former president of ESP/Ithaca (NEA), who is now on staff at the national NEA working on living wage campaigns. She reports that in parts of the country there are NEA members who themselves do not identify as union members because they live in conservative areas that are generally anti-union. Minnick says, 'Within our own organizations – there are some members – in certain regions of the country – if you even use the word "union" instead of association they freak out. They say, "I don't want any part of a union"'.

Structural Issues

Labour-community coalitions have other internal challenges that in part derive from the nature of coalitions. The first of these is that coalitions are usually built by leadership-to-leadership connections. Typically those in charge of running a group must develop relationships with other leaders, and the basis for coalition work is established. It is necessary to have leaders on board to give legitimacy and authority to a coalition. The danger is that the coalitions may not go much deeper than the leaders. This can be a weakness when a particular leader leaves and there is not enough depth to keep the coalition going. It can also be an issue when particular individuals are dynamic leaders who are seen as the key to the coalition.

For example, many interviewees in Cleveland mentioned the role of John Ryan, Cleveland Labor Council president, in developing the strong coalition in that city. Ryan was respected by most unionists but also seen as someone who could build bridges to community groups and faith-based organizations. One activist said that he joined the living wage coalition just for a chance 'to be in the same room as John Ryan'. Ryan's leadership was valuable, but when he stepped down from his position in 2006 to work on a Congressional race, there was not a natural choice to fill his position as an anchor to the coalition. One interviewee said that when talented organizers emerged in Cleveland they were often promoted to work for their union at the national level but rarely would a successful organizer move to Cleveland.

Leader-driven efforts can also be problematic, if a leader operates as a roadblock to moving a campaign forward. Many labour leaders may want to avoid confrontational type campaigns, believing that they have good relations with the mayor, or city council, or some employers. Debbie Minnick of the NEA says that there are presidents of NEA locals that represent ESPs who claim that they have a good relationship with the school superintendent. Minnick responds, 'If your relationship is so good, why are the ESP wages so low?'

Having leader-driven coalitions can also mean a smaller role for rank-and-file members of unions and community groups. Some of the coalitions we studied had been on-going for some time, and deep relationships had been built between organization leaders. Member to member ties, however, were not necessarily deep. Rank-and-file involvement is crucial to provide power to the coalition, but, unfortunately, according to Reynolds and Kern (2001), 'Most labor organizations, however, have little or no structure in place to turn out their rank-and-file members for living-wage events such as rallies and marches, direct actions, grass-roots lobbying, door-knocking, flyer distribution, and public hearings'.

It isn't just that it is difficult to involve rank-and-file members. In some cases, leaders or staff want to keep them out. According to former NEA organizer Ellen David Friedman, some business agents in the NEA saw the active participation of ESPs as a threat. David Friedman notes, 'For the business agents in our midst…uh oh! It encourages the low wage para-educators to get uppity!'[5] When rank-and-file workers get active they may push leaders to take the campaign in a different direction. They may even begin to push for more leadership roles within their union or organization. A union staff member noted that some union leaders see their rank-and-file members as a potential threat to their job.

Nissen (2004) also argues that many rank-and-file union members are not interested in labour-community coalitions but rather are used to thinking of their union only for servicing needs and bargaining contracts. Donna Iverson, a leader of the NEA living wage campaign in Burlington, Vermont, remarked that getting consistent participation from NEA members was one of the biggest challenges of the campaign: 'Whenever we tried to recruit Burlington para-educators to help us in the fight, about six new people would show up for one meeting and maybe one school board meeting and then drop out. So other than the core group, there was constant turnover'. Debbie Minnick adds that this was a challenge living wage organizers had to address. First, members are not used to thinking that they are worth the higher wage. They may feel that they are in their jobs to serve the needs of the students and therefore are reluctant to put their own needs forward. Second, the members are used to thinking that changes are up to the leaders. They are not used to seeing that they have a role to play in union activity. Minnick counters that by putting time and energy into educating members, the campaign was able to overcome these potential obstacles.

5 Bruce Nissen (2004) notes that in an early South Florida labour-community coalition, 'organized labor's official presence in coalition meetings was almost entirely through one individual, the secretary-treasurer of the central labor council'. Nissen states that while this person was committed to helping the coalition win its campaign for a living wage, he made no effort to involve other labour people in any way and kept labour's involvement strictly 'top-down'.

Keeping rank-and-file members involved and active in the coalition can also be challenging because of structural differences in the types of organizations involved. Some organizations, such as some unions and community groups, are built as member-organizations and meant to be run by and for the members. Others, such as churches, do not necessarily have a democratic structure for member involvement. Still others, such as some NGOs, don't have members at all.

This lack of equivalent organizational structures relates to a final challenge for coalition work: the power and resource imbalance between organizations. Coalitions are often stronger for their diversity as the participating groups bring very different strengths to the table. For example, in Denver the building trades had experience negotiating with developers and city officials; Jobs with Justice brought a history of engaging in more confrontational style politics; and groups like 9-to-5 and Rights for All People provided connections with communities often ignored by segments of the labour movement (women and immigrants). Yet, the diversity means groups have different weaknesses as well. It also means there can be a large difference in resources. One union may have 1,500 members while a campus anti-sweatshop group has 10. Another union may be able to offer office space, staff time and financial contributions while the women's shelter has very few resources to spare. Does each partner get one vote, no matter how many members they represent? Does every organization's voice get heard, even if they have little to give the coalition? Usually coalitions aspire to be representative and fair, but in practice larger partners have greater voice, as they have implicit power in their ability to leave the group and take their resources with them. Certain strengths are more valued than others. At the end of the day, the ability of the building trades to negotiate carries more weight than the ability of Rights for All People to bring immigrant workers to the coalition.

Some NEA activists believe that ESPs, because they have no leverage on their own, can only win higher wages with community support. Emma Mulvaney-Stanak, a living wage activist in Vermont who now works with the Vermont NEA, believes that because ESPs are low-wage, often part-time workers and not usually active in the union, they have no power on the job. In this sense, they did not have much to bring to the table in the living wage coalition. In the end, Mulvaney-Stanak thinks the campaign helped build the Living Wage Coalition more than it helped revitalize the union.

In New Haven, some environmentalists felt their demands were not highlighted in the CBA. Campaign leaders respond that environmentalists joined the effort after it was underway and after extensive community outreach was done to develop campaign demands. Here, the tension was whether to adjust campaign demands that had been developed through a community process. This is another structural challenge for coalitions: how do you add in new partners, maintain democratic practices, and keep campaigns moving forward?

External Challenges

While the internal challenges of coalition building can be daunting, they are perhaps easier to overcome than external challenges, which are numerous.

Economic constraints

There is little consensus within the economics discipline about the path for successful economic development. While many theories exist, Ha-joon Chang (2008) argues that almost no country has experienced major economic growth without significant government intervention, including investment in research and development, subsidies for infant industries, provision of infrastructure, protectionism, war and espionage. While Chang is focused on countries, the implications are relevant at the municipal level. It is unlikely that cities can do much to promote economic development without active participation in the local economy. City governments, however, are fairly restricted in their ability to intervene. For this reason, local coalitions and local governments are often at the mercy of larger economic forces.

In this context, local coalitions have less power to make demands on employers and cities. I do not assert that they have no power; however, it is limited by the strength or weaknesses of the local economy. For example, in cities with high unemployment and low growth, workers can be forced to choose between a bad job and no job. With very weak safety nets for the unemployed, choosing 'no job' is a serious and risky decision. Even cities with stronger economies may face the 'threat effect': large employers threatening to leave a city or not come at all if the city passes regulations such as living wage ordinances or a CBA.

Debbie Minnick says that the most difficult living wage campaigns the NEA engages in are in rural areas, where unemployment rates are very high and wages are low for most workers. In this context, teachers' wages may be the highest in the region. This makes it hard to argue that educators deserve a living wage, when few others earn a living wage or even have a job, but a local teachers union has little leverage to influence their own wages, let alone the town's economy.

Emma Mulvaney-Stanak was the staff member for the Livable Wage Campaign in Vermont when the NEA approached her about extending living wage work to ESPs. She says that the initial campaign was successful, but the current economic recession puts real limits on what local governments can afford to pay workers. Limited budgets are exacerbated by the cost of health insurance, which has been going up quickly. Between local government budget crises and health insurance costs, the living wage rate is now beyond what the school district can afford.

Economic constraints have sometimes meant that coalitions can have success in small campaigns but not larger ones. Chicago and New York passed living wage ordinances that cover city contractors. These do not affect a large number of workers, particularly relative to the city labour force. In both cities, measures that would require large private sector employers to pay a living wage were defeated. Most coalitions have not yet found a way to organize locally on a larger scale. The few cities with citywide minimum wage laws – San Francisco, Santa Fe, Albuquerque and Washington, DC – are the exception.

Similarly, public sector workers at the local level are often paid through monies coming from a county or state. If a state is suffering a budget crisis it will be difficult to get the money for higher wages at the local level, a serious problem in the current moment when states across the country are in financial hardship. State legislatures could easily fill the budget gap by closing corporate tax loopholes or increasing taxes on the wealthy, but few coalitions, and even fewer politicians seem willing to push for this option. In fact, many politicians have blamed public sector workers for the budget crisis.

The state and governance

The second external challenge relates to the nature of the state and governance. Municipal governments are constrained in their ability to govern based on their state home rule laws. Some states restrict the ability of local governments to set taxes and establish zoning regulations. Some federal laws also restrict local capacity. The *Employee Retirement Income Security Act* of 1974 (ERISA) pre-empts localities from establishing health care mandates that would interfere with ERISA plans. The National Labor Relations Act (NLRA) greatly restricts cities from getting involved in union issues at the local level, such as passing ordinances that require employers to sign card-check or neutrality agreements in the area of labour relations.[6] Living wage advocates faced this obstacle early on when they considered adding in health insurance requirements to living wage ordinances. CBAs are an attempt to circumvent some of these restrictions. CBAs are agreements between coalitions and developers, and not municipal ordinances. They utilize city government power to hold up developments but they are different from ordinances.

6 There are some exceptions in both cases. San Francisco passed a citywide health care mandate in 2006; employers challenged that it was not allowed under ERISA. The case was in the courts for a while. In 2008, the 9th Circuit upheld the law. In the case of the NLRA pre-emption, some courts have upheld the right of the cities to mandate employers to engage in peaceful labour relations when doing work for the city, on the basis that labour disputes could cost the city money (see Sahu 2002).

Even though there is more latitude with CBAs, local coalitions are still fairly limited in their tool-kit. This is exacerbated by the competitiveness that pits cities against one another in trying to lure and retain businesses. Legal scholar Richard Schragger (2009) argues that capital mobility has had a significant impact on local governments. Because cities are geographically-fixed, they are 'inclined to give too much away in trying to attract mobile capital'. On the other hand, Schragger asserts that cities then try to extract as much as they can from businesses already located in the city. He sees corporate subsidies and tax breaks as examples of the former, while CBAs and living wage ordinances are examples of the latter.

In addition, cities may also lack the ability to monitor and enforce laws and agreements. Monitoring takes staff and resources, and cities have little to spare. As I have demonstrated in other work, a pervasive business ideology makes city officials reluctant to penalize powerful employers who don't follow laws (Luce and Nelson 2004).

Furthermore, while CBAs offer more leeway to coalitions by side-stepping the state, they also decrease the government's ability to enforce agreements. In New Haven, the Yale-New Haven hospital committed gross violations of the CBA union organizing compact. The CBA allowed the union to take their complaints to an arbitrator, who ruled that the hospital violated the agreement. Neither the arbitrator nor the city, however, had a mandate to enforce the agreement. Instead, the hospital violated the agreement with impunity, and workers still lack union representation.

Labour-community coalitions have had more success at the local level because this is where members have more power as voters and citizens. It is easier to gain direct access to elected officials and easier to hold those officials accountable to campaign promises. State-wide and federal campaigns are dominated by large financial contributions, and most community organizations cannot compete. Therefore, the nature of electoral politics poses another major challenge to the ability of coalitions to expand their reach. To impact state and federal politics they likely need more financial resources and access to politicians.

Two of the case study cities – Cleveland and Denver – are located in states with strong Republican Parties. Both states have alternated between 'red' and 'blue', meaning the state legislatures, governors, senators and

Congress members have switched between the Republican and Democratic Party. State and federal politics can dramatically affect local conditions. Coalitions in both cities have put considerable effort into electoral politics, including 'get out the vote' efforts for state and federal races. In Colorado, there have been numerous ballot initiatives aimed against the labour movement, such as 'right to work' laws and laws repealing the ability of public sector unions to use payroll deduction for dues collection. Both of these ballot measures were defeated but would have had significant impact on unions in the Denver area.

Yet, even New Haven, located in a fairly solid 'blue' (Democratic) state, feels the effects of state and federal politics. There is no guarantee that Democratic politicians will be favourable to labour-community coalitions. In fact, in November 2010, several Democratic governors were elected promising to get concessions from public sector unions. In this context, local coalitions have little room to manoeuvre. It is necessary to scale their efforts up to the state-wide level, at a minimum. Ideally, because states are played off against one another, coalitions would even work on a regional or national level to establish minimum standards.

A final challenge related to issues of governance is the increasing role of public-private partnerships (PPPs) in the realm of city management, economic development and service delivery. Public-private partnerships have increased dramatically in number over the past few decades as municipalities have contracted out work and privatized assets (Warner and Hefetz 2008). There is also an increasing number of PPPs that handle economic development for city governments. These PPPs take many forms, from ad hoc partnerships for a particular real estate development, to on-going organizations sanctioned by the city to help attract and retain business. The literature on the impact of PPPs records their mixed efficacy, but many scholars have raised concerns about the implications for democratic governance when authority over city resources and development is given, at least in part, to private interests (Mullin 2002). Analysts and activists have also questioned whether the public bears the majority of the costs and risks, while private interests accrue the benefits.

While some CBA campaigns target deals negotiated by PPPs, the continued growth of PPPs is a problem for labour-community coalitions.

The information on pending development projects and subsidies is difficult to obtain from PPPs. It is also hard to figure out financial details for development projects because PPPs combine private investor monies as well as city, state and federal funds. The people who run the PPPs are usually appointed by a mayor and have no democratic accountability.

There are PPPs in each of the three case study cities. In these cities, the coalitions have not faced much direct challenge from PPPs. In fact, in Denver, public agencies (such as the Denver Urban Renewal Authority) presented greater obstacles in their CBA campaign. However, the PPPs are usually tasked with guiding economic development overall, which means that the whole arena of job creation, so crucial to labour-community coalitions, is placed in the hands of authorities that have no accountability to the public and no shared goals for the types of jobs created. This connects governance with economic questions. In Denver, Cleveland and New Haven unemployment has been between 8 and 12 percent since 2008, and the cities have lost many good jobs. Michael Charney, a long-time activist in the Cleveland Teachers' Union, said this about the local labour movement, 'We have influence. But the reality is that we're helping to administer the decline of the city. There is no real control where it matters – no control over capital flight. It's Lowell, Massachusetts in the 1870s'.

Ideology

A final challenge for labour-community coalitions relates to ideology – or rather, the lack of a clear ideology behind many coalitions. Nissen (2004) found that one factor that influenced the formation of labour-community coalitions in Florida was the ideological outlook of coalition leaders. According to Nissen, 'The other characteristic of most but not all South-Florida bridge builders is that they have a broadly progressive "left" political ideology that views the world in terms of class struggle. Leaders with this perspective see organized labour as part of a larger social movement for social and economic justice, so coalitions seem to be natural'. Nissen notes, however, that even with a broader vision labour leaders are under pressure to deliver short-term results. This means there is little time or space to discuss long-term goals and broader alternative models.

In our case studies, there is little evidence of broader ideological vision within the coalitions. While many coalition leaders have a broad 'social movement unionism' perspective and engage in power analyses and strategic planning, there was no evidence of deeper theoretical debate taking place within the coalitions. More groups are recognizing the value of 'framing', as advocated by Lakoff (2004). Unions and community groups are hiring consultants to help them shape stories, metaphors and counter-narratives to get their ideas across and 'message' their campaigns. Yet this framing is often done in a shallow or short-term perspective – having better websites, commercials and social media messages.

To get beyond the challenges mentioned above, I argue that coalitions need to work through a theory that can set the foundation for an alternative 'counter-narrative'. This does not necessarily require theoretical unity among activists or organizations, which seems difficult to impossible to achieve. I argue that coalitions need to discuss and debate longer-term goals so they can better plan strategy and be explicit about differences.

The question is not whether to engage in reform struggles but how best to do that in a way that builds towards longer-term goals. Neoliberals spent decades developing a core of academic and political advocates of a theory promoting the expansion of markets and reduction of certain forms of government. There is not full consensus on all aspects of the theory or how it is applied in practice, but it has served as the foundation for movements ranging from school reform to foreign policy to financial deregulation. Labour-community coalitions in the United States do not have their own theory to counter neoliberalism or unite various struggles. In fact, the legacy of anti-communism, alongside sectarian left politics, on one hand, and anti-intellectual traditions, on the other, has left little space for informed, serious debate. Trade unions and community groups avoid this space altogether, whereas the right has put their ideological quest to expand free markets and attack the idea of socialism/communism at the very centre of their project.

Hahnel (2005) argues that to move to a more just system, we must first define the principles that underlie that system. For Hahnel, those principles are 'economic justice', defined as 'to each according to one's effort', and 'economic democracy', defined as voting proportional to the degree one is impacted by the decision at hand. From these principles, Hahnel (along with his co-author Michael Albert) calls for an alternative economic system. To deepen dialogue among partners, labour-community groups might start by discussing the principles that underlie their work and goals.

There are concrete examples of this dialogue, most of which are located within the arena of electoral politics. In South Africa, the Coalition of South African Trade Unions (COSATU) works in coalition with community groups around a variety of issues, including improving service delivery of public goods such as education and health care. COSATU prepares documents for public release 'in order to stimulate discussion within COSATU and the democratic movement' (COSATU no date). This document analyses the relationship of COSATU with the African National Congress and the state in general, class struggle, power relations, and long-term goals. Other examples are: the Workers' Party in Brazil, which formed specifically as a multi-tendency party and launched the first participatory budgeting, and several projects in Canada that have relied on deliberative democracy as a method to consider new forms of political representation in British Colombia and Ontario (Fung and Wright 2003; Warren and Pearse 2008). In all these examples, coalitions can discuss longer term goals for the economy and political structure. It seems unlikely that labour-community coalitions could overcome the challenges posed above without this kind of deeper theoretical engagement.

Conclusion

The number of active labour-community coalitions has blossomed in the past few decades, and while there is a growing body of work that evaluates some of their work and dynamics, more research is needed. Researchers should work to develop metrics for measuring success. Coalitions are varied and have many goals: passing legislation, winning wage increases, enforcing agreements, building alliances, influencing local political elections and increasing the strength of coalition partners. It is possible that coalitions may fail at some of these goals while succeeding at others.

While many of the coalitions are new, the concept of labour-community coalition is not. We would benefit from more historical and comparative analyses.[7] What did similar coalitions accomplish in the past? Did they face similar obstacles, and if so, were they able to overcome any of them? Is there anything particularly American about these kinds of coalitions and campaigns, or can we learn from experiences in other parts of the world?

Researchers and practitioners should also frame their analysis of labour-community coalitions in a broader framework. While these coalitions are usually an advance over politics that pits organizations against one another, we should interrogate their long-term goals. Are coalitions forced to pursue pragmatic, least-common-denominator campaigns only, or can they work toward long-term structural change? Is the coalition a means to an end, or an end-in-itself?

Perhaps after several decades of practice it is time to find ways to move beyond coalitions. To achieve deeper change and increased strength, coalitions may need to develop new organizations that are capable of addressing some of the internal and external challenges mentioned here. This might mean establishing political parties or national organizations that have greater capacity to affect large-scale reform. For example, a national organization might have the ability to influence federal and state politics

7 Tattersall and Reynolds (2007) provide a comparison of such coalitions in Australia and the United States.

in a way that could create more space for local coalitions to act. A national organization could push for coordinated action between communities that are pitted against one another in a race to the bottom.

To some extent, local coalitions have already begun to develop national organizations. The Partnership for Working Families, established in 2005, connects local coalitions in over a dozen cities, including Atlanta, Boston, Los Angeles, New Haven and San Jose. The Economic Policy Institute created the Economic Analysis and Research Network (EARN), a network of state and regional organizations that engage in research and advocacy on labour-related state and national issues. There are currently 57 EARN partners, in 43 states. Not all affiliates are labour-community coalitions, but most work with such coalitions in some capacity.

Ideally, these networks and national organizations will continue to build on the local successes of the labour-community coalitions. But to scale the victories to a greater degree, it seems necessary to explicitly discuss the challenges discussed in this chapter. That will require ideological debate about historic questions relating to the nature of the state and economy.

References

Brecher, J., Costello, T. (1990). *Building Bridges: The Emerging Grassroots Coalition of Labor and Community.* New York: Monthly Review.

Chang, H. (2008). *Bad Samaritans: The Myth of Free Trade and the Secret History of Capitalism.* London: Bloomsbury Press.

Clawson, D. (2003). *The Next Upsurge: Labor and the New Social Movements.* Ithaca, NY: Cornell University Press.

COSATU. No date. 'Advancing Social Transformation In the Era of Globalisation.' Available at http://www.cosatu.org.za/show.php?ID=2357&cat=National%20Congress#_Toc486920404. Accessed 10 June 2011.

Dean, A.B., Reynolds, D.B. (2009). *A New New Deal: How Regional Activism Will Reshape the American Labor Movement.* Ithaca, NY: ILR Press.

Fung, A., Wright E.O. (eds) (2003). *Deepening Democracy: Institutional Innovations in Empowered Participatory Governance.* London: Verso.

Hahnel, R. (2005). *Economic Justice and Economic Democracy.* New York: Routledge.
Jones, J. (2009). 'Approval of Labor Unions Holds Near Its Low, at 52%', Gallup, August 31.
Lakoff, G. (2004). *Don't Think of an Elephant!: Know Your Values and Frame the Debate.* White River Junction, VT: Chelsea Green.
Luce, S., Nelson, M. (2005). 'The Cleveland AFL-CIO', *Working Paper, Power Building Project.* Available at http://powerbuilding.wayne.edu/power/downloads/Cleveland.pdf
Luce, S., Nelson, M. (2004). 'Starting Down the Road to Power', *WorkingUSA*, 8 (2), 183–206.
Mullin, S.P. (2002). 'Public-Private Partnerships and State and Local Economic Development: Leveraging Private Investment', *Reviews of Economic Development Literature and Practice*, No.16 Washington, DC: US Economic Development Administration.
Nissen, B. (2004). 'The Effectiveness and Limits of Labor-Community Coalitions: Evidence from South Florida', *Labor Studies Journal*, 2 (1), 67–89.
Pastor, M.Jr., Benner, C., Matsuoka, M. (2009). *This Could Be the Start of Something Big: How Social Movements for Regional Equity Are Reshaping Metropolitan America.* Ithaca, NY: Cornell University Press.
Reynolds, D. (ed.) (2004). *Partnering for Change: Unions and Community Groups Build Coalitions for Economic Justice.* Armonk, NY: M.E. Sharpe.
Reynolds, D., Kern, J. (2001). 'Labor and the Living-wage Movement', *WorkingUSA*, 5 (3), 17–45.
Rose, F. (2000). *Coalitions Across the Class Divide: Lessons from the Labor, Peace, and Environmental Movements.* Ithaca, NY: Cornell University Press.
Saad, L. (2009). 'Labor Unions See Sharp Slide in U.S. Public Support', Gallup, September 3.
Sahu, S.J. (2001). 'Living Up to the Living Wage: A Primer on the Legal Issues Surrounding the Enactment and Enforcement of Living Wage Laws', *Guild Practitioner*, 59. 44.
Schragger, R. (2009). 'Mobile Capital, Local Economic Regulation, and the Democratic City', *Virginia Public Law and Legal Theory Research Paper Series* (University of Virginia School of Law), No. 2009–03.
Sherman, R., Voss, K. (2000). 'Organize or Die: Labor's New Tactics'. In R. Milkman (ed.), *Organizing Immigrants: The Challenge for Unions in Contemporary California.* Ithaca, NY: Cornell University Press.
Simmons, L., Luce, S. (2009). 'Community Benefits Agreements: Lessons from New Haven', *WorkingUSA*, 12 (1), 97–111.

Tattersall, A. (2010). *Power in Coalition: Strategies for Strong Unions and Social Change.* Ithaca, NY: Cornell University Press.

Tattersall, A., Reynolds, D. (2007). 'The Shifting Power of Labor-Community Coalitions: Identifying Common Elements of Powerful Coalitions in Australia and the U.S.', *WorkingUSA*, 10 (1), 77–102.

Warner, M.E., Hefetz, A. (2008). 'Managing Markets for Public Service: The Role of Mixed Public–Private Delivery of City Services', *Public Administration Review*, 68 (1), 155–66.

Warren, D. (2005). 'Wal-Mart Surrounded: Community Alliances and Labor Politics in Chicago', *New Labor Forum*, 14 (3), 17–23.

Warren, M.E., Pearse, H. (eds) (2008). *Designing Deliberative Democracy: The British Columbia Citizens' Assembly.* New York: Cambridge University Press.

CHARLES WEATHERS

8 Political Activism and Union Revival in Australia, the United States and Japan

Introduction

Unions in the United States, Australia and Japan suffered some of the democratic world's worst losses of membership and influence from the 1970s. In response, they stepped up not just new member recruitment but political action as well. The resulting political campaigns recently proved exceptionally successful when organized labour played important roles in bringing new governments to power in three consecutive years – in Australia, in 2007, in the United States, in 2008 and in Japan, in 2009.

Despite making major, possibly decisive, contributions to these victories, unionists quickly encountered major difficulties in influencing political partners. The problems included muddled political agendas (especially in Japan), strained relations with political partners (Australia) and unremitting hostility from business and conservatives (the United States). Moreover, all three union movements saw their political partners suffer stinging electoral setbacks in 2010, including an especially severe reversal in the United States.

This chapter depicts the changing dynamics of political action (primarily in the electoral realm) for American, Australian and Japanese unions. Three key points are made. First, the cases support the contention that grassroots activism is a necessary, though not always sufficient, condition for workers to benefit from union political activism. Second, the cases indicate that despite the seemingly increased effectiveness of organized labour political action, unions may still encounter great difficulty in having desired policies enacted, or even seriously considered. This reflects in large part the currently difficult environment for progressive policymaking and politicians in all three countries. Third, the cases point up major differences between US and Australian unions, on the one hand, and those in Japan on the other. Unions in the former two countries regard neoliberal policymaking and aggressive business practices as threats to their influence if not survival, and accordingly seek to apply social movement tactics to political action; in contrast, Japan's mainstream unions, embedded in the policymaking institutions of both corporations and government, continue to conduct political action in form but fail to engage in actual activism.

The following section outlines an explanation of union political action in an era of neoliberal policymaking. Subsequent sections describe recent union political action in the United States, Australia and Japan, respectively, making comparative points about efforts (or lack thereof) to mobilize grassroots support. The conclusion sums up the findings, pointing up weaknesses in Japanese unions' approach to political action.

Revitalization and Political Action

Political action is a vital component of union activity. As Lowell Turner and Richard Hurd (2001) emphasize, unions cannot function effectively without support from politicians who share their concerns. Conversely, even sympathetic politicians may decline to support labour-friendly agendas in the absence of support – and sometimes pressure – from unions and progressive social movements. Two well-known instances are the failure of America's Democrats to enact labour reform legislation in either 1978 or 1994 despite controlling the White House and both houses of Congress. Unions could not gain the commitment of Democratic politicians to even modest reform because, as Turner and Hurd point out, they 'lacked the will or capacity to mobilize large-scale support' (2001: 11).

Despite their importance, however, union-party partnerships have become increasingly difficult to maintain over the past thirty years. Not only has declining influence made unions less desirable partners, but leftist politicians have come under pressure to support much of the neoliberal agenda to create jobs or strengthen international competitiveness. Consequently, they have deliberately distanced themselves from unions in Canada, Britain and other countries (Glyn 2001; Savage 2010; Panitch and Leys 2001; see also Luce in this volume). With traditional allies becoming more distant, unions have diversified their political strategies. One way to deal with a more difficult environment has been to engage new political partners (Upchurch, Graham, and Mathers 2009). However, this approach risks fragmenting organized labour and further diluting its influence.

Under pressure from neoliberal politicians and the growing legion of hostile employers, unions may have few realistic alternatives to working with major left-leaning parties. Consequently, some union movements have applied stronger pressure on allied politicians and partners to support the labour/union agenda. This chapter's cases show that American and Australian unions have adopted multiple approaches, seeking new social partners and adopting social movement-type practices to political action, while also in some respects strengthening their ties to the Democratic Party and the Australian Labor Party, respectively.

In contrast, mainstream Japanese unions have not made serious efforts to ally with social movements in either organizing or political campaigns. This reflects in part lack of opportunity, since Japanese social movements tend to be weak (Suzuki in this volume). But in the context of political action, it also reflects the unions' non-confrontational, technocratic orientation. Strongly committed to cooperative labour-management relations, unions have avoided challenging managers over issues like wages and representation of women, seeking instead to improve worker welfare through policymaking participation. As a result, unions enjoy insider status within both corporate and policymaking realms, reducing their motivation to 'innovate' or develop new strategies for revival (Baccaro, Hamann, and Turner 2003; Yamada in this volume). However, critics allege that they do little to represent marginal workers or women (e.g., Endo in this volume).

Despite insider status, Japanese unions have experienced steady weakening of their positions. Major corporations have retrenched and begun replacing core workforces (the main source of union membership) with non-regular workers, and conservative prime ministers from the mid-1990s began to exclude unions from meaningful policymaking participation (Miura 2008; Nakakita 2009: 17–19). Nevertheless, as we shall see, Japanese unions have failed to adjust their basic political strategies.

The United States

The AFL-CIO long remained passive about electoral politics (as well as declining union membership), even as it became clear that Democratic politicians were reluctant to support many policies desired by unions. This situation changed in part because of an emergent political danger. In 1994, the Republican Party unexpectedly gained control of the House of Representatives for the first time in 40 years; the sudden threat that Republicans might introduce new anti-union legislation helped spur reformers to seize control of the AFL-CIO the following year. The new leaders quickly reversed the basic stance of the AFL-CIO, until then possibly the democratic world's most conservative federation, and turned it into a vanguard of liberal policymaking. New member organization and political action became pillars of the new activist strategy, and health care reform and stronger rights for immigrant workers soon became core political demands.

The new approach to politics was both more strategic and more aggressive (Francia 2006: 31–9). Before 1995, the AFL-CIO and its unions usually distributed money to Democratic politicians with little regard to either politicians' financial needs or actual policies. The new strategy called for concentrating resources on strategic contests and encouraging (or pressuring) politicians to actively support the organized labour agenda. Unions have sometimes opposed Democratic politicians judged insufficiently supportive of union-backed policies (and, on occasion, supported Republican candidates; Meyerson 20 October 2002). 'We are doing things differently', said senior official Richard Trumka (and AFL-CIO president from 2010), so that politicians who ignore labour concerns will 'ultimately pay a price' (Francia 2006: 6).

As a result of the new emphasis on political activism, the AFL-CIO quickly developed into possibly the most effective organization in American politics. In addition, some AFL-CIO members, including the Steelworkers (USW) and UNITE-HERE, have established cutting-edge political operations. Besides contributing ever larger sums of money, unions bolstered their ability to mobilize volunteers for political campaigns. They also shifted emphasis toward promoting member education and getting out the vote. The new practices have put strong emphasis on direct, preferably face-to-face, contact with voters. Union household voters constituted 23 per cent of the 1996 turnout (while accounting for just 16 per cent of persons eligible to vote), up from 19 per cent in 1992, and rising to 26 per cent (15 per cent of eligible voters) in 2000. Post-election polls have verified that union voters strongly support Democratic candidates.

The more determined and better conceived campaigns helped bring policymaking successes, such as blocking Republican attempts to weaken union protections. Apart from helping to raise the minimum wage in 1996, however, the successes tended to be negative (obstructing free trade treaties) rather than positive measures to help workers or improve labour laws. Worse, George W. Bush's election victory in 2000 ended hopes for significant progressive policy reforms. Subsequently, unions intensified their political efforts. They spent an estimated $70 million encouraging members to vote and to support union-sponsored candidates in the 2004 and 2006 elections, more than double the spending on the previous two elections. Education campaigns (for union members) seemed to become more effective. 74 per cent of AFL-CIO-affiliated union members voted for the congressional candidate endorsed by their unions in 2006, up from 70 per cent in 2004 and 68 per cent in 2002, according to the polling firm Peter D. Hart.[1]

1 Cited in *Wall Street Journal* (8 November 2008). A shift in the social composition of members, away from more conservative blue-collar workers, might explain part of the shift.

The 2006–2008 Election Cycle

The 2006–2008 election cycle represented the peak of organized labour's political success, as unions played an important role in shaping the liberal agenda, and then in helping Democrats to gain large majorities in Congress and elect Barack Obama president. The Service Employees International Union (SEIU) exerted especially strong influence in the political realm with its 1.8 million members and a highly effective member political mobilization program. The union also played a major role in shaping the Democrats' agenda between the 2006 and 2008 elections (Meyerson 1 February 2007). Perhaps most important, SEIU's demand for health care reform helped induce each of the three leading Democratic candidates to develop a national health care policy.

Spending by unions on the 2008 elections was estimated at $300 to $450 million, and the AFL-CIO claimed that more than 250,000 AFL-CIO volunteers participated in campaigns.[2] Unions put strong emphasis on reaching out to white working-class Americans, who have tended to vote Republican in recent elections. Canvassers stressed that Obama's economic policies would help ordinary working-class people, and sought to reassure voters about Obama's political beliefs and background, countering allegations that he was a socialist or a Moslem, or had ties to terrorists. The Steelworkers and other blue-collar worker unions concentrated their efforts on working-class voters in the populous swing states of Pennsylvania, Ohio, and Michigan (*Washington Post* 29 August 2008; *New York Times* 28 September 2008). These campaigns seemed to enjoy considerable success, as polls indicated that union household voters constituted 28 per cent and 27 per cent of the electorates in Ohio and Pennsylvania, respectively (Meyerson 10 November 2008). Further, exit polls indicated that 67 per cent of AFL-CIO union members voted for Obama, compared to 30 per cent for Republican presidential candidate John McCain.

2 See especially Meyerson (28 August 2008); *New York Times* (9 September 2008); and *Washington Post* (29 August 2008, 6 November 2008).

The Democratic Party, like the unions, utilized activists and activist strategies to strong effect. Veteran labour/political activist Marshal Ganz played a leading role in training over 3,000 organizers who in turn mobilized a claimed 1.5 million local volunteers. Ganz and other liberal activists later argued that Obama and his administration erred gravely by dismantling his campaign network after the 2008 election rather than using it to apply pressure in support of his policymaking agenda.[3] As we shall see, a very similar dynamic and dialog regarding grassroots activism has played out in Australia but with a proportionately larger union role.

California

Organized labour has contributed importantly to the Democratic Party's ability to maintain a strong grip on power in California. Besides mobilizing Latino workers to vote, it has also helped to groom Latino candidates and to forge political coalitions (Meyerson 30 September 2003, 17 May 2004). SEIU, UNITE-HERE, and the Los Angeles County Federation of Labor (LA Fed) have helped register and mobilize hundreds of thousands of new immigrant voters and turn out hundreds or even thousands of activists during elections to walk precincts and work phone banks in Los Angeles (*Los Angeles Times* 17 June 2007).

Much of labour's mobilizing ability derives from its successful Justice for Janitors campaigns, which have turned numerous Latino workers and their families into active union supporters. Also important was the revitalization of LA Fed. From the mid-1980s, LA Fed engaged several prominent former activists from the United Farm Workers, including Miguel Contreras, Elena Durazo and Marshall Ganz, who helped it develop a powerful political operation by the late 1990s (Frank and Wong 2004: 3–4; interview, LA Fed official, April 2009). To bolster the union movement's grassroots presence, LA Fed has established the Organization of Los Angeles Workers, which mobilizes union officials for election work and builds ties to minorities and local communities.

3 See Berman (2010), Dreier and Ganz (2009), and Ganz (2010).

Mutual benefit between organizing and political campaigns has been especially strong in the Los Angeles area, where unions and LA Fed have helped elect politicians, such as Antonio Villaraigosa, willing to support various labour initiatives. In 1999, as speaker of the California Assembly, Villaraigosa pushed the legislation necessary for one of SEIU's greatest triumphs, the organizing of 74,000 homecare workers in the late 1990s. As mayor of Los Angeles, Villaraigosa has supported UNITE-HERE's ongoing campaign to organize workers in airport hotels.

The Obama Administration

Leftist- and liberal-oriented opinion on the Obama administration has been mixed. Initially, many left-leaning observers made the case that the administration undertook an ambitious program with considerable success. The economic stimulus and health care policies were welcomed by the left, and the administration has pursued several union- or labour-friendly policies, including rescuing the auto industry, establishing a national health care system and establishing the Lilly Ledbetter Fair Pay Act to reduce sex discrimination. Efforts to revive manufacturing and enforce trade laws were also welcomed. Furthermore, Obama appointed a strongly pro-union politician, Hilda Solis, as secretary of labor.[4] However, labour activists were incensed that the administration never seriously attempted to reform immigration policy or to enact the Employee Free Choice Act (EFCA) to ease organizing woes. Many left-leaning commentators have lamented that Obama is weak at political strategizing and tends to allow Republicans the initiative in framing messages (though his more populist turn in early 2012 has revived expectations somewhat).

Whatever Obama's faults, it was the horrendous employment situation that became the main factor in the Democrats' 2010 electoral rout.

4 Fittingly, from the unions' perspective, Solis was originally elected largely because of the new activist union political agenda. Unions gave her crucial support in her first election against an incumbent Democrat judged insufficiently supportive of organized labour.

Employment anxieties aggravated the innate hostility of conservatives to the administration's policies, especially the economic stimulus and national health care. Anxiety also encouraged the rise of the Tea Party, groups of citizens angered by a belief that government was growing dangerously large. Tea Partiers helped crystallize a sense among conservatives that the administration was taking the country in a generally unconstitutional direction (Busch 2010). Even as the weak economy stoked anger and activism among conservatives, it discouraged many of the groups that supported the Democrats in 2008. Blacks, for example, continued to support Obama, but many reportedly lacked interest in the mid-term election (*Wall Street Journal* 11 October 2010). Similarly, the turnout of youth, who lean Democratic, fell considerably, while older voters, who lean Republican, had high voting rates.

In a year in which anti-government anger rendered incumbents especially vulnerable, outside money from corporations and rich conservatives appears to have played a decisive role in helping numerous Republican candidates defeat incumbent Democrats.[5] To be sure, rule changes on campaign financing enabled unions as well as corporations to spend more freely on political campaigns, and unions spent more than $200 million. Although union efforts probably helped the Democrats to save one or two Senate seats, they had little impact on House races.

Unions had greater difficulty in motivating members to participate or vote in 2010 than in 2006 or 2008, although the AFL-CIO claimed that its get-out-the-vote efforts resulted in union members backing union-endorsed candidates at a national rate of 64 per cent in the House and 62 per cent in the Senate (*Wall Street Journal* 4 November 2010). Not surprisingly, the one bright spot for Democrats and organized labour was California, thanks in large part to intensive union mobilization of Latinos (Meyerson 14 October 2010).

5 Center for Responsive Politics (4 November 2010). See also *New York Times* (3 November 2010) and *Los Angeles Times* (4 November 2010). Total spending on the 2010 election was estimated at around $4 billion, making it by far the most expensive mid-term contest in US history.

Australia

Until recently, Australian unions enjoyed a privileged position in political and economic decision making, in contrast to both America's excluded unions and Japan's 'included' (but not necessarily influential) mainstream unions. However, they saw their influence decline steadily from the 1980s when they agreed to the Accord, a policy program implemented under the Australian Labor Party (ALP) to bolster economic competitiveness. The left now regards the Accord as a misstep that led both the ALP and the union movement to drift toward neoliberalism and to slight the interests of working-class Australians. Like the AFL-CIO, the Australian Council of Trade Unions (ACTU) moved leftward in rhetoric and action in the 1990s as union activists became more concerned about the needs of women, minorities and vulnerable workers.

Much like their American counterparts, Australian unions came under strong political threat after conservatives won the 1996 election. Prime Minister John Howard's Coalition government (Howard's own Liberal Party and conservative partners) quickly revised labour laws to strengthen management control over workplaces. The threat deepened in 2004 when the Coalition gained control of the Senate, enabling it to pass the radical Work Choices Act, which swept away the existing employment structure and established in its place an individual- or market-based foundation for labour management (Ellem et al. 2005). Work Choices restricted union freedom of action, making it difficult to communicate with workers and conduct strikes, as well as giving employers strong rights to alter contracts.

Work Choices

However, Work Choices proved to be a disastrous error, as it led unionists to overcome their divisions and band together to wage an all-out struggle against Howard and the Coalition. Ironically, Work Choices was unnecessary to business because Howard's early revisions of labour law largely satisfied employer demands for stronger control of workplaces (Cooper and

Briggs 2009). But Howard was pushed by ideological conviction. He once stated, with possibly unintentional explicitness, 'We're not governing for the unions, we're governing for the employers' (cited in Barnes 2006: 369).

Although determined to defeat Howard, unionists were wary of Labor, which they saw as too distant from worker interests. Furthermore, the ALP, like Britain's Labour Party under Tony Blair, had taken pains to distance itself from unions. Consequently, Your Rights at Work (YR@W) was intended in part to assert a union political agenda independent of the ALP as well as achieve the immediate goal of winning the 2007 election and overthrowing Work Choices. Building (or rebuilding) ties to social movements and social activists was important to both goals.

Initially, union leaders lacked a clear strategy, since no ready model for mobilizing members for an all-out political campaign existed, but they had gained invaluable insights and experience from earlier struggles against the Coalition, including a healthy appreciation of the importance of public relations campaigns and well-organized social campaigns (Muir 2008). A clear strategy began to emerge as ACTU-commissioned research quickly determined that most people lacked awareness of the reforms but opposed them once they understood their content (Barnes 2007: 386). Union officials soon found that conversations and television commercials about employment concerns resonated with the public. In short, as occurred in the United States, perceptions of political threat led to much more strategic use of resources, including a stronger emphasis on direct contact with voters.

Author interviews with union officials in March and November 2008 indicated five especially critical points regarding YR@W. First, Your Rights at Work campaigns were run by unions, not the Labor Party. This reflected in part the belief of many unionists that the ALP's political operations, like its commitment to worker interests, were badly deficient. YR@W campaigns coordinated closely with ALP campaigns in some districts, but more often operated independently. Second, planners and organizers at all levels worked to develop focused campaign plans and practices to maximize voting impact, such as emphasizing face-to-face contact. Third, workplace campaigns to win worker support were important. Just as American unions made a strong effort to bring white working-class Americans back to the

Democratic fold, Australian unionists were concerned about large numbers of working-class voters who had backed Howard in 2004. Unions developed worker education campaign practices learned in part from the US's SEIU. Beginning in 2006, YR@W operatives contacted union members, often by phone, to engage them in conversations about the upcoming campaign. Fourth, grassroots activities and ties to social movements were emphasized, both to win the election and to create a durable movement for the future. Finally, unions were expected to make a strong commitment. Many reassigned numerous staff from new member organizing and member servicing to the political campaign, braving the risks of losing substantial income and disgruntling members.

Your Rights at Work initially targeted around 22 marginal (swing) seats important to deciding the coming election; as conditions evolved in the unions' favour, the number was increased somewhat. A major objective of YR@W organizers was to establish connections with social movements and community institutions. For example, YR@W organizer Linda Cargill started a 'Faith-based Campaign' in her electoral district, Deakin (eastern Melbourne suburbs). She and around ten other people active in local communities conducted discussion forums, contacted churches, and delivered presentations to social movement groups. They were accordingly able to establish ties to people concerned about non-labour issues, notably Howard's right-wing stances on environmental and immigration policies, and build a campaign apparatus from there.

Although Australian unionists studied American practices, they substantially adjusted any they borrowed to meet Australian conditions. American unions emphasize 'getting out the vote', encouraging groups such as low-income persons and members of union families to vote, confident that a majority will vote Democratic. But voting in Australia is mandatory, so YR@W instead emphasized raising awareness of the content of Work Choices, in effect encouraging voters to oppose the Coalition. Thus, in contrast to American union election campaigners, who generally directly support Democratic candidates, YR@W campaigners avoided urging voters to support Labor. The volunteers enabled the unions to campaign effectively with relatively little money. Hundreds of volunteers served as door-knockers, and organizers devoted considerable energy to ensuring that they were well prepared for their task.

Most of the districts where YR@W campaigns were waged saw large swings in voting from 2004 and victories for Labor Party candidates. While results are hard to verify quantitatively, YR@W clearly contributed strongly to the ALP victory, especially since Howard, unlike Bush, could boast a strong economic record.

The 2010 Election

As in the United States following the 2008 election, Australian unionists experienced considerable disappointment following the 2007 election, though for different reasons.[6] In contrast to the respect shown by Obama for unions and their agenda, Australian unionists were angered (though hardly surprised) by what they saw as dismissive treatment of unions and worker concerns by Prime Minister Kevin Rudd and other ALP leaders. Like the Democratic Party of Japan, as discussed below, the ALP is split between politicians preferring close ties to unions and those wanting greater distance. Nevertheless, unions did achieve their primary goal, the elimination of Work Choices, which was replaced by Fair Work Australia in 2009. From 2007 to 2009, union membership increased by 138,700, raising the organization rate by more than a point (to roughly 20 per cent), suggesting that government legislation indeed affects recruitment. However, construction-related unions such as the Electrical Trades Union (ETU) remain infuriated by the government's decision to maintain restrictive rules in their sectors.

In addition, the new government reportedly did poorly at 'selling' its policies. Union complaints notwithstanding, some observers believed that Rudd compiled a fairly good labour-related policymaking record, especially by raising the minimum wage and quickly overhauling employment legislation (of course, unions regarded that as minimum payback for their election contribution). Like Obama, however, Rudd reportedly

6 Information on the 2010 election draws heavily on 12 interviews conducted from 20–24 September with representatives of ACTU, CPSU, Australian Nursing Federation, NUW, and the Electrical Trades Union.

fared poorly at communicating his policy agenda to voters and in parrying conservative attacks. Consequently, ALP leaders precipitously replaced Rudd with Julia Gillard in May 2010 even though economic performance continued strong.

Most unions in 2010 never seriously considered not backing Labor[7] – the new Liberal leader Tony Abbott was as anti-union as Howard – but rank-and-file members were apathetic. Most union members contacted to work in the election declined or simply 'went through the motions', as one ACTU official acknowledged. There were exceptions, notably the Community and Public Sector Union (CPSU) and the Australia Nursing Federation. CPSU members remained motivated by memories of the Howard government's efforts to drive unions out of public sector workplaces. Strongly motivated by their desire to improve hospital conditions and secure better funding for aged care, the Nurses actively supported Labor's electoral campaign but also worked to put pressure on Labor ministers to support their policy agenda.

Despite those pockets of energy, unions lacked a compelling election message, and their campaigns were far less coordinated than in 2007. They compensated to considerable effect by charging that the Coalition intended to bring back Work Choices under some new guise. The ACTU's tagline became 'Work Choices: whatever the name, never again'. Thus YR@W had at least one very powerful and undeniable impact: three years on, the fear that employment rights could be lost still resonated strongly with many voters. Despite Abbott's well-known desire to shackle unions, he found himself compelled to disavow any intentions to revive Work Choices in order to limit its damage to Coalition electoral fortunes.

The 2010 election was widely labelled a 'near-death experience' for the government. Gillard adeptly overcame Labor's eventual one-seat disadvantage to the Coalition by recruiting independent members of Parliament to form a bare majority. The result was not necessarily displeasing to Australian unionists, who believe that ALP leaders would be forced to take union concerns more seriously.

7 An exception was ETU, which threw its support to the Greens.

Lasting Legacies of YR@W?

Much as Obama supporters hoped to turn his 2008 campaign into a permanent grassroots instrument for change, some ACTU strategists envisioned YR@W activists as a resource for waging continuous campaigns for progressive policies, and for countering big business influence. However, the ACTU decommissioned the YR@W organizers the day after the election. One union official lamented that 'we hadn't thought beyond that day'.

Despite the lack of direct follow-through, there are strong signs that YR@W continues to exert a political legacy on Australia. Officials in the National Union of Workers (NUW), for example, have built on the 2007 election activities by continuing to develop strategies for engaging voters. Like the US Democratic National Committee, it recently began programs to reach out to supporters in conservative-dominant areas to strengthen the sense of participation among all union or ALP supporters.

In addition, some unionists and activists credit YR@W with helping to inspire new campaign approaches. A community organizer for Liquor, Hospitality and Miscellaneous Union (LHMU), stated that YR@W exerted a 'powerful' effect on the union's highly regarded Clean Start campaign to organize cleaners, especially by providing inspiration to broaden the campaign by conducting community outreach programs (interview, September 2010). Another example is the experimental Sydney Alliance, which deploys local organizers to start up progressive grassroots campaigns. One intern noted that YR@W encouraged him to start working as an activist (interview, September 2010).

Japan

Patterns of political-electoral activism by Japanese unions contrast sharply to those of US and Australian unions. Whereas activism by American and Australia unions has intensified since the 1990s, social activism by Japan's mainstream unions has been declining since the 1950s in tandem with the decline of left-wing unionism. Today, labour-related grassroots activism results primarily from the efforts of activists outside of the major unions (as detailed by Endo, Takasu, and Suzuki in this volume) while major unions tend to emphasize the concerns of core workers in large enterprises. The lack of grassroots involvement notwithstanding, Japan's unions have been enthusiastic political participants since the 1940s, though their impact was greatly diluted because of ideological divisions among the unions, and because both labour-tied parties, the left-wing Socialist Party and the pro-business Democratic Socialist Party, were perpetually in opposition. Furthermore, Japan's private sector enterprise unions have usually supported politicians promoting the interests of their industries rather than those of workers per se.

In the 1970s, most cooperative unions strengthened their commitment to their firms. In keeping with their proclaimed core mission of protecting jobs within enterprises, they opted to moderate wage demands to protect competitiveness and to improve living standards primarily by participating in government policymaking. In comparative terms, the strategy was counter-intuitive, since meaningful union policymaking participation in European countries is predicated on the existence of strong social democratic-type parties and effective industrial unions. Nevertheless, the strategy became more strongly institutionalized in 1989 with the establishment of the national federation Rengo (presently representing about 6.8 million workers, roughly 16 per cent of the work force). Rengo was formed mainly by a merger of the left-wing national federation Sohyo with its conservative counterpart Domei. The new federation committed itself to labour-management cooperation (making Domei the winner of the sometimes bitter rivalry).

Rengo's primary function is, in principle, to lead the union movement's policymaking activities, while leaving collective bargaining to the industrial unions. Two main criticisms have ensued. The sympathetic criticism is that Rengo scores significant policymaking accomplishments, but fails to gain credit for them since the technocratic policymaking process draws little media or public attention. The harsh critique is that policymaking participation is a chimera because mainstream unions defer to managers, and because Rengo's policymaking agenda is overly broad and distant from real labour concerns (Igarashi 1994).

Not only does Rengo lack a practical political agenda (apart from promoting economic competitiveness), but it is bothered by continuing inter-union antagonisms. Many private sector unions, for example, have tacitly supported privatization and other neoliberal-tinged policies designed in part to weaken public sector unionism. These policies have reduced costs, but also eliminated jobs and worsened the decline in union membership, in turn weakening the union movement's political and policymaking influence (Nakakita 2008).

Internal frictions notwithstanding, Rengo stands as the major organizational supporter of the Democratic Party of Japan (DPJ) (Nakakita 2009; *Asahi* 3 March 2010). Rengo unions, especially Toyota Union and various regional public sector unions, have enabled the DPJ to establish crucial strongholds in Aichi Prefecture and Hokkaido, respectively (*Asahi* 30 June 2010). Also important in a country where political parties (save the long-dominant Liberal Democratic Party, LDP) have great difficulty developing grassroots organizations, Rengo unions provide local organizations and candidates for office in some 30 of the country's 47 *todofuken* (roughly equivalent to the US states). After winning a landslide electoral victory in August 2009, the DPJ held 308 of 480 seats in the Lower House, and 106 of 242 seats in the Upper House of Parliament. There were around 30 members of Parliament in the 'former Socialist Party' group and around 40 in the 'former Democratic Socialist Party' group (mostly union-origin candidates from former Sohyo and Domei unions); these included 57 officially connected to Rengo.[8] Although government subsidies now account for most funding for political parties, the Toyota and Panasonic unions are important funders for the DPJ (*Asahi* 1 October 2009), and unions provide a great amount of stealth funding to individual union-origin candidates.

8 One limit on union influence is that union-origin candidates tend to be elected to the less important Upper House.

The Rengo-DPJ alliance

Rengo began its existence with the objective of helping to bring about a government not headed by the Liberal Democratic Party, which has (along with its predecessors) dominated post-World War II Japanese politics. Rengo quickly accomplished its objective by playing a key role in brokering the formation of Hosokawa Morihiro's coalition government, which excluded the LDP, in 1993. That success proved short-lived, however, as the coalition collapsed within a year. In 1998, several opposition parties established the Democratic Party of Japan (DPJ), which succeeded the steadily collapsing Socialist Party (renamed the Social Democratic Party) as Japan's major opposition party. Rengo quickly threw its support to the DPJ, which has included most union-origin politicians.

The DPJ, created largely through mergers of small parties and defectors from the LDP and Socialist Party, is far from ideologically coherent. Despite the party's reliance on Rengo, many of its politicians are hostile to unions. During a brief turn as party president (2005–2006), neoliberal-leaning Maehara Seiji distanced the DPJ from organized labour. Ozawa Ichiro reversed course after succeeding Maehara as party president, in April 2006, by strengthening party-union ties. Ozawa was a shrewder political strategist than Maehara, but changing social conditions also favoured the shift. Rengo's (official) anti-neoliberal stance was not a political asset during the early 2000s when cost-cutting 'reform' was a popular issue, but growing unease about poverty and working conditions from mid-decade made unions more attractive political partners.

Ozawa formed close ties to Upper House Councillor Koshiishi Azuma of the teachers' union, Nikkyoso. Even after being forced to resign the presidency over a scandal, Ozawa's relationship with Koshiishi helped ensure the selection of his ally Hatoyama Yukio as party president in May 2009, and in turn ensured a strong Rengo voice inside the DPJ. Following the DPJ's election victory the following August, union-origin and union-affiliated politicians served in seven of the cabinet's sixteen posts. Most prominently, Naoshima Masayuki (Toyota Union) headed the Ministry of Economy, Trade and Industry (METI) and Hirano Hirofumi (Panasonic Union) served as chief cabinet secretary. In addition, Sengoku Yoshito, a lawyer with close ties to Jichiro, the 900,000-strong civil servants union, has been a major force in DPJ governments.

Hatoyama took office in September 2009 enjoying sky-high popularity ratings and relatively favourable economic conditions. The nation's powerful manufacturing industries were driving growth once again, providing the government important breathing space despite deteriorating conditions for low-wage workers. The DPJ's tagline 'from concrete to people' expressed its much welcomed intent of shifting spending from public works toward the social safety net. However, some proposals were neoliberal-tinged or simply contradictory. A scheme to stimulate the economy by eliminating auto tolls, for example, contradicted pledges to strengthen environmental policy and rectify the alarming budget deficit, and spread job fears in public transport sectors (*Hiroba Yunion* May 2010: 28–9).

In addition to policymaking muddles, the DPJ policy agenda was undermined by an intractable budget deficit – half of central government spending is borrowed, and nearly all regional governments are in severe financial straits as well. Moreover, much as Obama's Democrats were burdened with a recalcitrant Senate, the DPJ, despite holding nearly two-thirds of the Lower House seats, was forced to form an awkward coalition with the small Social Democratic Party and even smaller People's New Party to prevent its policies from being vetoed in the otherwise unimportant Upper House.

Pressure to adopt a more neoliberal stance grew stronger as conservative politicians, like their American counterparts, began to play effectively on voter frustrations. Consequently, a 'reduction' competition ensued during the 2010 election as most parties announced plans to slash government spending. Still, the conservative opposition remained generally unpopular, and during 2010 the DPJ was less bothered by the economy or the competition than by scandals, foreign policy and a steadily worsening image of incompetence.

Labour-related Policies

Despite a decade of clearly deteriorating labour market conditions, the DPJ lacked a clear employment strategy when it took office. The party has responded to the employment crisis by drawing up plans, still sketchy, to create millions of jobs in the environmental, health care, and tourism-leisure sectors. Rengo has naturally pushed for job creation, including demanding an employment-oriented fiscal policy (*Asahi* 21 April 2010). However, Rengo's own actions hardly accord with such demands. Most major Rengo unions remain reluctant to demand significant wage increases despite concern that years of weak consumption – partly a result of wage moderation aimed at maintaining manufacturing sector competitiveness – have undermined economic growth and job creation.

Nor has Rengo's strong presence in the government led the DPJ to adopt policies that consistently benefit workers (or even major unions). The most prominent pro-labour initiatives have been pushing up Japan's minimum wage and increasing social outlays, although socioeconomic pressures had helped begin to push these trends before the 2009 election. The minimum wage rose by 10 yen or more for four consecutive years from 2007 through 2010 as concern about rising poverty overrode strong objections by the business community. In addition, the government has increased coverage for measures such as social insurance, unemployment benefits and job training, though the minimum wage and most social outlays still remain very low compared to European countries. On the other hand, some unions felt undercut by specific policies. Unions in the hard-pressed railway sector were angered by the highway toll reduction policy, and auto unions felt that METI chief Naoshima failed to support their industry despite his ties to the auto industry.

A point important to this analysis is that the DPJ's pro-labour policies largely reflect the efforts of activists outside of mainstream labour. The DPJ made revision of the Temporary Worker Law one of its signature policy proposals, but this resulted from the success of individually-affiliated unions, anti-poverty NPO activists and enterprising journalists in exposing abuses and turning public opinion against temporary agency (*haken*) labour during the late 2000s. As other chapters note (Suzuki in this volume), these efforts culminated in early 2009 with the public relations triumph of *Hakenmura*, where Kan Naoto and other DPJ leaders made prominent appearances. In reality, however, both the DPJ and Rengo are internally divided about temporary workers. Some manufacturing sector unions, notably the Electronics Workers Federation (Denki Rengo), regard their employment as necessary to reduce costs to maintain competitiveness against firms in low-wage countries. The DPJ and the public lost interest in the measure as other problems mounted, and the final revision (approved in March 2012) was a loophole-ridden compromise that infuriated activists and will probably bring little change.

Similarly, the demand of tiny coalition partner People's New Party to modify the privatization of Japan Post (the post office) will have only a minor effect. Privatized and forced to execute severe labour cost-cutting policies around 2005, Japan Post now employs 210,000 non-regular workers, more than any other Japanese company. After People's New Party demanded that 100,000 non-regular workers be converted to *seishain* status, a de facto compromise emerged in which conversion would be limited to persons passing promotion tests (*Asahi* 2 July 2010: 7; 11 November 2010: 6). Ultimately, only a few thousand workers are likely to benefit. Similarly, Joho Roren, which represents employees in the NTT Group (telephone and telecommunication services), has opposed further restructuring that would cost jobs. Nevertheless, the Ministry of Internal Affairs and Communications has continued to press for restructuring even though one of Joho Roren's former officials was elected to the Upper House and named vice-minister in the same ministry (*Asahi* 10 July 2010).

Probably the DPJ's most dubious policy is mandating a 20 per cent reduction in national civil service personnel costs. Contrary to popular impressions, Japan's civil service is understaffed, and the steady pruning of numbers has entailed the hiring of ever larger numbers of non-regular workers (or increased contracting-out) to plug gaps. In addition, the International Labour Organization (ILO) has long complained about Japan's continual denial of strike and collective bargaining rights to public sector employees (*Asahi* 21 August 2010). Public sector unions were naturally angered, but DPJ and Rengo leaders defused the issue in part by tying it to restoration of union rights (essentially forcing civil servants to concede massive personnel and wage reductions to regain their basic labour rights). Public sector activists have resisted cost-cutting policies for years, but, like community union activists, they remain marginalized in the broader labour movement (interviews with public sector union representatives; Kansei Waakingu Pua Kenkyukai 2010).

The 2010 Election

As in the United States and Australia, unions in Japan saw their party follow up a great victory with a severe electoral setback in 2010.[9] Kan Naoto succeeded Hatoyama as prime minister in May 2010 and, with the Upper House election looming, promptly committed a major blunder by calling for a raise in the unpopular consumption tax. The DPJ lost its majority in the Upper House, winning only 44 seats to the LDP's 51, even though it easily outpolled the LDP, 41.2 million votes to 33.6 million. Lacking a majority in the Upper House, the DPJ was forced to attempt to cut deals to pass legislation even as its diminished standing made such manoeuvres excruciatingly difficult. Following the March 2011 Tohoku earthquake, political parties were unable even to cooperate on policies for disaster relief.[10]

Rengo's 2010 election performance indicated that its political influence continues a slow decline. The federation fielded 11 union candidates in proportional representation seats, of whom ten won, while five out of nine won in single-member districts. But the combined votes of Rengo union candidates in proportional districts fell from 1.82 million in 2007

9 See Taniguchi et al. (2010) on the 2010 election. The weakening of union motivation was a factor in defeat, as in the United States and Australia, though a much less important one.

10 Ironically, in view of the disaster, one of Kan's most important advisors was the recently deceased Sasamori Kiyoshi, a former Rengo president originally from the Tokyo Electric Power Company Workers Union. The union has funded Rengo, and the electric power companies the LDP, with both aiming to encourage development of nuclear power (*Japan Times* 1 August 2011).

to 1.59 million, even though more candidates ran.[11] Rengo officials are debating measures to restore worker support. For example, after learning that Toyota Union's Naoshima received fewer votes than expected in 2010, union officials began planning measures to verify whether members of the Auto Workers Union have voted in elections (*Asahi* 10 July 2010).

However, failure to try to develop a better political strategy is undoubtedly the more fundamental problem. The author was surprised to learn in one interview (in December 2010) that officials at a major Rengo regional branch have never thought about using election campaigns to mobilize workers. Union political action typically consists of union officials ordering members to distribute flyers and make phone calls, rather than seeking to motivate members to participate voluntarily or emphasizing face-to-face communication, the approaches now prioritized by American and Australian unionists.

In addition, the Rengo-DPJ partnership is troubled by perennial Japanese political problems, such as party instability and corruption. Ozawa is dogged by suspicions of shady financial dealings, which have in turn worsened the steady deterioration of the DPJ's public standing. Still, Ozawa is largely responsible for turning the DPJ into a potential ruling party, and dozens of DPJ legislators owe their political careers to him. Similarly, Rengo is indebted to him for providing the opportunity to strengthen its political voice. Accordingly, union-origin politicians, like the rest of the DPJ, have been deeply divided over how to deal with him (*Asahi* 4 September 2010; *Nikkei* 1 September 2010 evening edition).

11 See the JILPT website, http://www.jil.go.jp/kokunai/mm/roushi/20100820a.htm.

Conclusion

The 2007–2009 period marked the high tide of union political activism in the United States, Australia and Japan as electoral political action helped bring about major triumphs for political allies. In the United States and Australia, electoral success probably contributed to modest increases in membership. In both countries, success resulted in part from applying social movement tactics to political campaigning. These patterns differ somewhat from claims by Upchurch, Taylor and Mathers (2009) that unions are distancing themselves from political parties. Rather, lacking realistic alternatives, some unions have in certain respects drawn closer to political parties. They have become more effective partners, but also more demanding ones. In addition to using sophisticated mobilization techniques, they have increasingly acted as representatives of disadvantaged workers by campaigning for policies such as increases in minimum wages or improved health care policies, and they have adopted more aggressive means of pressuring politicians to support their agendas.

Nonetheless, 2010 saw union movements and their allies in all three case countries suffer severe election losses. To be sure, this largely reflected economic anxieties that exacted an unusually heavy toll on incumbents throughout the advanced economic democracies. Still, the setbacks indicated the limits of even sound strategies and effective mobilization.

The situation in Japan differed greatly from those in the United States and Australia. Union success in 2009 represented a payoff from years of steady insider political manoeuvring, but the lack of grassroots mobilization has been reflected in a policy agenda only partly responsive to union demands, and arguably detrimental overall to the interests of many workers. A comparison with Australian unions indicates other fundamental differences. Following the (alleged) failure of the Accord in the 1980s and 1990s, Australian unions became wary of economic policies that risked distancing them from worker concerns. However, Japanese unions remain fundamentally attached to cooperation with business, despite a lack of demonstrable results. At the same time, they have not developed strategies to politically mobilize workers despite steady long-term decline in basic economic policymaking influence and worrying increases in the low-wage work force. In short, the policy rationale for continued close support for the Democratic Party is unclear, but Japan's major unions, still enjoying embedded insider status, remain inclined to pursue their interests as technocratic rather than progressive social actors.

References

Baccaro, L., Hamman, K., Turner, L. (2003). 'The Politics of Labour Movement Revitalization: The Need for a Revitalized Perspective', *European Journal of Industrial Relations*, 9 (1), 119–33.

Barnes, A. (2006). 'Trade Unionism in 2005', *Journal of Industrial Relations*, 48 (3), 369–83.

Berman, A. (2010). *Herding Donkeys: The Fight to Rebuild the Democratic Party and Reshape American Politics.* New York: Farrar, Straus and Giroux.

Busch, A.E. (2010). 'The 2010 Midterm Elections: An Overview', *The Forum*, 8 (4). Available at: http://www.bepress.com/forum/vol8/iss4/art2.

Center for Responsive Politics. Various, Available at the OpenSecrets.org website. Available at: http://www.opensecrets.org/.

Cooper, R., Boggs, C. (2009). '"Trojan Horse" or "Vehicle for Organizing"? Non-Union Collective Agreement Making and Trade Unions in Australia', *Economic and Industrial Democracy*, 30 (1), 93–119.

Dreier, P., Ganz, M. (2009). 'We Have the Hope. Now Where's the Audacity?', *Washington Post*, August 30.

Ellem, B., Baird, M., Cooper, R., Lansbury, R. (2005). '*WorkChoices*: Myth-making at Work', *Journal of Australian Political Economy*, 56, 13–31.

Francia, P.L. (2006). *The Future of Organized Labor in American Politics*. New York: Columbia University Press.

Frank, L., Wong, K. (2004). 'Dynamic Political Mobilization: The Los Angeles County Federation of Labor', *WorkingUSA*, 8 (2), 155–81.

Ganz, M. (2010). 'How Obama Lost His Voice, and How He Can Get It Back', *Los Angeles Times*, November 3.

Glyn, A. (ed.) (2001). *Social Democracy in Neoliberal Times: The Left and Economic Policy since 1980*. Oxford: Oxford University Press.

Igarashi, J. (1994). 'Rengo no Seisaku Seido Sanka' (Rengo's Policy and Institutional Participation), *Kikan Rodo Ho* (Autumn), 6–24.

Kansei Waakingu Pua Kenkyukai. (ed.). (2010). *Nakuso! Kansei Waakingu Pua* (End It! Government-made Working Poor). Tokyo: Nihon Hyoronsha.

Meyerson, H. Various, *The American Prospect*. Available at http://www.prospect.org/cs/author?id=89.

Miura, M. (2008). 'Labor Politics During "the Lost Fifteen Years": From the Politics of Productivity to the Politics of Consumption', *Labor History*, 49 (2), 161–76.

Muir, K. (2008). *Worth Fighting For: Inside the Your Rights at Work Campaign*. Sydney: University of New South Wales Press.

Nakakita, K. (2009). 'Nihon no Rodo Seiji: Minshu-Shugi Taisei no Henyo to Rengo' (Japan's Labour Politics: Rengo and Changes in Democratic Structure). In T. Shinkawa, T. Shinoda (eds), *Rodo to Fukushi Kokka no Kanousei: Rodo Undo Saisei no Kokusai Hikaku*. Kyoto: Minerva Shobo.

Nakakita, K. (2008) 'Rengo to Seiji' (Rengo and Politics), *Seikatsu Keizai Seisaku*, No. 137 (June), 19–27.

Panitch, L., Leys, C. (2001). *The End of Parliamentary Socialism: From New Left to New Labour*. 2nd edition. London: Verso.

Savage, L. (2010). 'Contemporary Party-Union Relations in Canada', *Labor Studies Journal*, 36 (1) (March), 8–26.

Taniguchi, M., Sakaiya, S., Okawa, C., Uenohara, H. (2010). '2010-nen Sangiin Senkyo: Minshu Seiken ni Fuku Shufu?' (The 2010 Upper-House Election, Autumn Wind Blowing Against the DPJ), *Sekai*, No. 809 (October), 58–67.

Turner, L., Hurd, R.W. (2001). 'Building Social Movement Unionism'. In L. Turner, H. Katz, R. Hurd (eds) *Rekindling the Movement: Labor's Quest for Relevancy in the 21st Century*. Ithaca, NY: ILR Press.

Upchurch, M., Taylor, G., Mathers, A. (2009). 'The Crisis of "Social Democratic" Unionism: The "Opening Up" of Civil Society and the Prospects for Union Renewal in the United Kingdom, France, and Germany', *Labor Studies Journal*, 34 (4), 519–42.

KOSHI ENDO

9 Women's Labour NPOs and Women's Trade Unions in Japan

Introduction

Women's labour NPOs (non-profit organizations aimed at addressing women's labour issues) and women's trade unions (unions most of whose members are women) have been in the vanguard of protecting and expanding the employment rights of female wage earners in Japan over the last three decades, although the organizations are few and their membership is small. Why do these organizations exist? To put it differently, what relationship do these organizations have to the majority of trade unions in Japan, that is, to the in-house unions organized at individual companies? What are the characteristics of these organizations? How are they related to trade union revitalization in Japan?

Activists in women's labour NPOs have documented aspects of their organizations in Japanese, but there is little research on the organizations in Japanese or English (*cf.* Weathers 2005). This chapter uses Working Women's Network (WWN) as a case study of a women's labour NPO because it is one of the most famous women's labour NPOs in Japan, and in the history of its creation, it displays the essential features of women's labour NPOs in Japan. Furthermore, this author is one of WWN's few male members.

Women's trade unions have been specifically discussed in Japanese research papers, and Broadbent (2007) addresses the topic in English. Since women's trade unions are a type of individual affiliate union (IAU) and research on other types of IAUs has been presented in English (Urano & Stewart 2007, 2009; Suzuki 2008), this chapter addresses women's trade unions only briefly.

Why Does Japan Have Women's Labour NPOs and Women's Trade Unions?

Women's labour NPOs and women's trade unions exist because in-house unions are not sufficiently ready to protect and expand employment rights for female wage earners. Bound by their constitutions, as well as labour practices, in-house unions protect employment rights of only a limited scope of workers but do not extend their protection to other workers. Workers whose rights are not protected by in-house unions have formed independent organizations, such as women's labour NPOs and women's trade unions, to defend their own employment rights.

Workers whose rights are not protected by in-house unions

Workers not protected by in-house unions are roughly categorized into: (a) employees of small and medium-sized enterprises (SMEs); (b) non-regular or part-time employees and dispatched agency workers; and (c) female wage earners. Let me briefly outline each category.[1]

(a) In-house unions organize employees of large corporations but do not organize those of SMEs. The estimated rate of in-house union density is 46.2 per cent among private corporations with a 1,000 or more employees, while it is only 14.2 per cent among private corporations with 100–999 employees and 1.1 per cent among those with fewer than 100 employees (Basic Survey on Labour Unions 2009).

(b) Regular and full-time employees, as members, are protected by in-house unions, while these unions exclude non-regular or part-time employees and dispatched agency workers from their membership and protection. Those categorized as non-regular/ part-time employees or

1 The existence of workers not protected by in-house unions is deeply connected to the structure of the internal labour market in Japan (Benson et al. 2007; Keizer 2008).

dispatched agency workers account for 35.6 per cent of total wage earners and 55.3 per cent of female wage earners (Employment Status Survey 2007).

(c) In-house unions share with management a strong adherence to gender role norms, i.e., men are the breadwinners and women are the housewives, and believe that female workers should withdraw from the labour force while young. With this point of view, in-house unions do not protect female union members who continue to work for longer periods.[2]

It is not rare for women after graduating from high school or college to find jobs in large corporations, work as regular and full-time employees and become in-house union members. Actually, a small number of such women continue to work for a long period, but they are often differentiated from men and subject to discriminatory treatment in terms of promotions and pay increases. The major reasons for discrimination against women are that: (1) those women workers who remain on the job are regarded as exceptions because they do not fulfil the role of housewife; and (2) there is a strong adherence to gendered workplace norms that assigned female workers to be assistants to male workers. Male workers who are members of in-house unions share the same consciousness as management and acquiesce to management discrimination against long-term female workers.

The majority of female workers leave work in their twenties to thirties to marry or have and raise children and cease to be wage earners. It is often the case that when they come back to work and become wage earners again, they return as non-regular or part-time employees or employees of SMEs, and, in most cases, they are not union members.

There are two approaches available to workers not protected by in-house unions to protect their employment rights. One is to bring an action in court. Organizations supporting workers who stand as plaintiffs in labour cases have been created and developed separately from in-house unions. The other is to form trade unions separate from in-house unions. I will call this type of trade union an individual affiliate union (IAU).

2 Gerteis (2010) argues that leftist trade unions in Japan in the 1950s made use of female members for their political struggles but ignored their interests as wage earners (Endo 2010a).

At present, among the aforementioned three categories, namely, (a) SME employees, (b) non-regular/part-time employees and dispatched agency workers, and (c) female wage earners who in-house unions fail to protect, litigation is strongest in category (c). IAUs have sprung up among each of the three categories, with a noticeable increase from the late 1990s in IAU members who are non-regular/part-time/dispatched workers and female wage earners.

Labour Litigation and Plaintiff Support

Present day women wage earners frequently protect their rights through litigation. To understand this phenomenon, we need to take a look back at the history, since the end of the Second World War, of litigation and organizations that have supported plaintiffs in labour cases.

One of the first organizations to support litigants formed in 1950, during Japan's Red Purge. Directed by US Occupation forces, Japanese management fired Communist Party members and other leftist workers solely on the grounds of their affiliation with the Communist Party, despite provisions in the Constitution of Japan guaranteeing freedom of thought. Various organizations formed to support workers who sued their companies over wrongful termination. Yet, among the many cases, hardly any in-house unions supported terminated workers, even when they were union members. Litigation directly related to the Red Purge ended in the 1960s, but a new series of cases made their way to the courts.

During the 1960s, individual leftist workers or small groups of such workers, who were members of in-house unions at large corporations, filed lawsuits claiming that management discriminated against them for their leftist ideology.[3] These workers were members of groups within the in-house unions that opposed their unions' cooperative labour-management policies,

3 Endo (1997) gives a quantitative analysis of the reality of pay discrimination in one of these lawsuits, as well as the reality of pay discrimination against female workers. None of this evidence was disputed in the lawsuit.

or they were members of small in-house unions in conflict with the larger, in-house, management-cooperative unions.[4] Various organizations also formed to support these workers. While many cases against discrimination in wages and promotion were filed, mainstream in-house unions never supported the members who belonged to the anti-mainstream groups. Such cases started to decrease in the latter half of the 1980s.

From the latter half of the 1980s to the present, two new types of labour cases have been on the rise. One is the case in which the family members of workers who succumbed to *karoshi*, death from overwork (Kanai 2009), sue the state and firm management seeking a declaration that the worker's death was due to illness or injury that occurred in the course of work. Litigants claim compensation for damages arising from the employer's breach of its duty to provide security to its workers. The in-house union of which the deceased worker was a member has rarely supported the worker's surviving family. Various organizations have formed to support families involved in such labour cases.

A second type of case involves female workers who sue management, alleging gender discrimination in employment. Although the Act on Securing, Etc. of Equal Opportunity and Treatment between Men and Women in Employment (Equal Employment Opportunity Act, EEOA) enacted in 1985 is imperfect legislation, its passage made female workers more conscious of their rights and encouraged some to bring action in court. Some of these female workers were members of small leftist in-house unions, while others belonged to more management-cooperative in-house unions that failed to support their members' litigation. Various organizations formed to support those female workers.

Litigation was a natural approach to take for female workers who felt strongly that they were suffering gender discrimination, and it was

4 Even after the Red Purge, many in-house unions adopted policies on leftist movements. During the period from the latter half of the 1950s to the 1960s, members who supported the labour-management cooperation policy left these leftist in-house unions, and formed new in-house unions. The newly-formed in-house unions gradually increased members and became the majority, while the original leftist in-house unions lost members and became the minority.

also natural for their supporters to form organizations that supported the plaintiffs. This movement was based on the lessons that these women and their supporters learned from the experience of workers after the Second World War who lacked in-house union protection. The Working Women's Network (WWN) is one such labour NPO.

Individual Affiliate Unions (IAUs)

There is no particular qualification needed for a person to be a member of an individual affiliate union (IAU). In-house unions, in contrast, require their members to be workers employed by their particular company. IAU members consciously choose to join the unions, and IAUs organize workers across different companies.[5] In other words, IAUs can be formed by any type of worker, that is, they organize (a) employees of SMEs; (b) non-regular or part-time employees and dispatched agency workers; and (c) female wage earners.

IAUs provide labour issue counselling and try to persuade aggrieved workers to join the union. They explain that under Japanese labour law, IAUs can negotiate with employers on members' behalf. Another advantage of IAUs is their small size enables them to form networks easily with other IAUs as well as NPOs and experts (see Suzuki Chapter 3 in this volume).

According to my estimate, at present, there are about 300 IAUs in Japan with 30–50,000 members. Among them, 10–20,000 members are non-regular workers. The 300 IAUs can be divided into three types: Type 1 unions account for more than 200 IAUs, with Type 2 and Type 3 unions comprising the rest of IAUs (Endo 2011).

5 In Japan, there are a few trade unions which are neither in-house unions nor IAUs, such as the All Japan Seamen's Union, which is an industrial union, and the Japan Professional Baseball Players Association.

UNIONS SET UP BY REGIONAL TRADE UNION ORGANIZATIONS: TYPE 1

Sohyo (the General Council of Trade Unions of Japan), which was a central organization of trade unions, organized *chikuro*, local councils of in-house unions affiliated with Sohyo in each locality, until it was dissolved in 1989. In 1984, the *chikuro* of Edogawa Ward, Tokyo took a growing interest in the increase in part-time employees and set up the Edogawa Union, which admitted part-time employees in Edogawa Ward, irrespective of the companies where they work. The name of this union incorporates the English word *union*, which is written and pronounced as 'yunion' according to the Japanese (*katakana*) syllabary. This was the first trade union to use the Japanese-written form of the term *union* in its name. Its nomenclature emphasized that Edogawa Union was an individual affiliate union in which part-time employees could join based on their own decision.

As the Edogawa Union began to attract attention, similar 'yunions' were set up nationwide. 1988 saw the publication of *Komyuniti Yunion Sengen* [Community Union Manifesto], a book describing the activities of these unions and recommending the formation of this type of union. In 1989, the First National Meeting of Community Unions was held, and the Community Union National Network (CUNN) was established a year later. The CUNN was born, following the dissolution of Sohyo in 1989 and the inauguration of Rengo (Japanese Trade Union Confederation), and is still in existence today. Many unions which were set up under similar circumstances are referred to as *community unions*, which has become a common noun in Japanese (see Takasu in this volume).[6]

6 Organizations defined as IAUs in this chapter are referred to as *community unions* by some observers. I distinguish these two in this chapter for the following reasons. (1) Type 3 unions, including women's trade unions, do not fall within the category of community unions. (2) Some Type 1 unions use the term *chiki* [district] *union* or *local union* instead of the term *community union* in their names. *Chiki unions* and *local unions* refer to IAUs established by local chapters of Rengo and Zenroren (National Confederation of Trade Unions), respectively.

THE TRANSFORMATION OF IPPAN-KUMIAI: TYPE 2

In the 1960s, a new type of trade union, different from in-house unions, called *godoroso* [joint or amalgamated trade unions] was created. A significant feature of amalgamated trade unions is that their constitutions provide that workers join the organization based on their own volition. Theoretically, the constitution enables an amalgamated trade union to organize employees who belonged to different companies, in other words, to take non-regular or part-time employees, as well as employees of SMEs into its membership. This point distinguishes amalgamated trade unions from in-house unions because in-house union constitutions limit the people who qualify for membership to incumbent employees at the company. Many amalgamated trade unions use the term *ippan-kumiai* [general union] as part of their names. These amalgamated unions were in reality federations of small in-house unions of SMEs. They had few or no members who had joined them independently (see Takasu in this volume).

As time went by, some metropolitan area amalgamated unions gained new members who joined them independently, which is what they had originally intended to do, and among these new members, the number of non-regular employees rose. On the other hand, the percentage of members who belonged to in-house unions fell, a transformation that became obvious in the 1990s. Against this backdrop, some amalgamated unions which emphasized organizing individually affiliated members added the Japanese-written form *yunion* in their official or popular names.

UNIONS WHOSE MEMBERS ARE AMONG SPECIFIC CATEGORIES OF WORKERS: TYPE 3

In December 1993, the Tokyo Managers' Union was established, mainly targeting workers in managerial posts who would independently join. This may be the first union in Japan aimed at organizing a specific category of workers across company boundaries. Encouraged by the creation of this union, the Women's Union Tokyo was established in March 1995, followed by the Metropolitan Youth Union in December 2000. This movement further encouraged specific categories of workers, such as managers, female workers, and young workers, to form IAUs nationwide, with names that represent their attributes.

The Women's Union Tokyo and similar women's unions across Japan are categorized as women's trade unions for the purposes of this paper.

Women's trade unions

To the author's knowledge, as of 2010, there are nine women's trade unions in Japan. Among them, eight unions are regionally based (in Sapporo, Niigata, Tokyo, Kunitachi, Kanagawa, Nagoya, Osaka and Okayama), and women working at trading companies formed the other. It seems a few other women's trade unions once existed but have vanished. In general, these women's trade unions have a small membership, which fluctuates, and their organizational bases are unstable.

Women's Union Tokyo appears to have the most stable organizational base. Since its formation in 1995, it has always had at least one full-time officer, and its website has been updated periodically. With the collapse of Lehman Brothers, however, it experienced a significant decrease in members, down to about 150 in 2010, and fell into a financial crisis. It urgently solicited donations and currently manages to survive with such aid.

As a matter of course, women are the primary users of the women's trade union labour counselling services. Women's trade unions act through formal or informal collaboration with women's labour NPOs. Especially in Tokyo and Kanagawa, the women's trade unions have close relationships with the NPOs that manage shelters for battered women.

Working Women's Network (WWN)

Labour NPOs as non-profit organizations engage in counselling and supporting the jobless, foreign workers, women workers, agency workers, and so on.[7] To put it plainly, the role of labour NPOs in Japan is to protect

7 Although there are many such NPOs nationwide, few studies have discussed them (*cf.* Koseki 2011).

workers who are not protected by in-house unions. When female regular workers suffer discriminatory treatment but their in-house unions do not rectify the problem, they have no choice but to go to court. Therefore, there is a type of women's labour NPO that aims to support female workers who have brought actions before the court.

Working Women's Network (WWN) is one of the best-known women's labour NPOs in Japan. According to the information available on its website, the major objectives of WWN's current activities are to (a) eliminate 'indirect discrimination' and (b) rectify pay disparities between men and women and between regular and non-regular employees under the principle of equal pay for work of equal value. As its policy, WWN emphasizes lobbying activities targeting international organizations such as the United Nations and the International Labour Organization (ILO) to pressure the Japanese government to integrate the two objectives into national policy. WWN also carries out various other activities, such as supporting plaintiffs in legal actions brought to eliminate gender discrimination and providing seminars and other educational programs. Anyone who approves of WWN's objectives and activities can become a member by paying membership dues (http://wwn-net.org; as of 13 August 2010).

WWN was formed in Osaka in 1995. The immediate purpose of its formation was to support nine female workers who filed actions in 1995 against their companies for discriminating against women. They sued three major companies in the Sumitomo Group: Sumitomo Electric Industries, Ltd., Sumitomo Chemicals Co., Ltd., and Sumitomo Metal Industries, Ltd., all of which are based in Osaka. Although the nine plaintiffs were members of in-house unions at these Sumitomo companies, the unions refused to support the plaintiffs in their litigation. In supporting the nine plaintiffs when their in-house unions would not, it can be said that WWN has been a typical women's labour NPO from its birth.

To gain a deeper understanding of the features of WWN and the features of women's labour NPOs in Japan, we need to go back in history to the 1970s, to a time before WWN.

International Women's Year, 1975

An historical event, before the formation of WWN, was the formation of the Kokusai Fujin Nen Kita-ku no Kai [Group of Kita Ward for the International Women's Year, hereafter the Kita-ku no Kai] in Osaka, in 1975. This group, led by Reiko Shoji, started as a study group consisting mainly of women working in or around Osaka's Kita Ward.

The Kita-ku no Kai had the following three features (Hiromori 2004, 2005). (1) From the beginning, studying equal treatment in the workplace between men and women was a priority issue. (2) Although it was presumed that many of its members were officers of trade unions or engaged in social movements, the group provided all members with the opportunity to interact and study with one another beyond the boundaries of the organizations to which they belonged. These two features were important because while female union members at the time mainly appealed for maternity protection, the group functioned as a forum, separate from trade unions, where female workers were able to study and exchange opinions with one another regarding another issue, gender equality in employment. There were few groups at that time which had both of these important features. (3) Female lawyers participated in the group, because both law courts and a number of law firms were located in Kita Ward. Their participation influenced its subsequent development.

Until the first half of the 1970s, female union members, given the seniority system and gender role expectations, had demanded a *maternity protection system* which would enable them to continue working for a long period of time without suspending their careers, if they decided to get married or have and raise children. In other words, gender equality in employment was not an important demand (Watanabe 1976). The 1975 International Women's Year was regarded as an important turning point when the priority demand of leading female union members shifted from maternity protection to gender equality in employment. Kita-ku no Kai served as a driving force in this direction.[8]

8 Groups of working women similar to the Kita-ku no Kai formed in 1975, not only within Osaka City but nationwide. They were some of the original women's labour

Also in Osaka in 1975, female members of trading company unions formed Shosha Fujinmondai Kenkyukai [the Society for the Study of Working Women in Trading Companies].[9] Some of the members of this group also belonged to the Kita-ku no Kai. The members of the Society for the Study of Working Women in Trading Companies also shifted their efforts from a movement focusing on maternity protection to a movement aiming to rectify pay disparities between men and women.

In 1981, Danjo Chingin Sabetsu o Nakusu Osaka Renraku Kai [the Osaka Network for Elimination of Gender Pay Discrimination] was formed. It was led by Reiko Shoji and other women workers of the Kita-ku no Kai and female lawyers. The Society for the Study of Working Women in Trading Companies joined the network and formed the Trading Companies' Group and intensified its activities. In 1984, the Trading Companies' Group published a leaflet that presented an analysis of the actual conditions of pay discrimination against female workers at ten trading companies, and renamed itself Shosha ni Hataraku Josei no Kai [the Association of Women Working for Trading Companies] (Moriya 2000: 136–50; Moriya 2005: 143–60). The leader of this new group was Shizuko Koedo.

In 1985, the members of the Kita-ku no Kai for the International Women's Year, including Shoji and Koedo, participated in the Third World Conference on Women in Nairobi, and arranged a workshop. This was the first step in their international activities.

NPOs. The relationship of the national women's labour movement to the 1975 International Women's Year has not yet been sufficiently studied.

9 This group was formed by female union members who opposed the increasing tendency of in-house unions in the trading companies toward cooperating with the management. It acted as a forum for exchanging information on different trading companies.

Equal Employment Opportunity Act (EEOA) of 1985 – Despair led them to go to court –

Equal Employment Opportunity Act of 1985 was the most important legislation enacted as part of Japan's ratification of the 1979 Convention on the Elimination of All Forms of Discrimination against Women (CEDAW Convention). Despite the great expectation of women labour activists' for this legislation, what was actually enacted was a disappointing, lukewarm law.

In 1987, the Association of Women Working for Trading Companies published its second leaflet, *A Letter to CEDAW*, which claimed that the EEOA contravened the Convention. CEDAW (Committee on the Elimination of Discrimination against Women), a United Nations committee, promoted the effective enforcement of the CEDAW Convention in the States Parties. *A Letter to CEDAW* was given wide coverage by the media, and the Association of Women Working for Trading Companies translated the letter into English, and in 1991, its members visited the CEDAW office and submitted it to the Committee (Koedo 1998).

The Society for the Study of Working Women, a research and study organization of women workers and researchers, held a symposium to discuss equality in employment in Tokyo in 1992. Horne Kawashima Yoko, a researcher at Stanford University, was invited to speak on the principle developed in the United States of equal pay for work of equal value. It was the first introduction of this principle to female labour activists in Japan as an approach to rectify women's lower pay (Society for the Study of Working Women 1992).

The Association of Women Working for Trading Companies participated in this symposium and was deeply affected by this new principle. Labour activists of the traditional left, however, launched a campaign against the principle, as they were opposed to job analysis and job evaluation and were in favour of a seniority-based pay system. To confirm whether or not the traditional left's criticism was valid, a team, composed mainly of the members of the Association of Women Working for Trading Companies, went on a survey tour to the United States and Canada in August 1994, and published a report of their survey (Japan Pay Equity Society 1996).

After the tour, the principle of equal pay for work of equal value became the favored pay equity policy of female labour activists.[10]

With momentum from the passage of the EEOA, the number of legal actions filed by female workers demanding the elimination of gender discrimination in employment started to increase in the second half of the 1980s. For the primary purpose of learning from the experience gained in these actions, the Practical Network Seminar on the Equal Employment Opportunity Act, a series of study meetings, convened in Osaka on 19 occasions from 1990 to 1994. These study meetings provided female union members and workers with no union affiliation with the opportunity to interact and study with one another. One of the major organizers of the meeting was Lawyer Mitsuko Miyachi, who was also a member of the Kita-ku no Kai and the Osaka Network for Elimination of Gender Pay Discrimination.

On the occasion of one of the study meetings, a married woman working for a bank talked about her experience of having successfully received a promotion after charging the bank with discrimination against married female workers. Encouraged by this successful precedent, married women working for Sumitomo Life Insurance Company demanded, in 1992, promotions and pay increases, alleging discriminatory treatment of married female workers. They subsequently applied to a government agency for conciliation, a new type of dispute resolution proceedings under the EEOA.

10 To date, in two legal cases in which female workers alleged pay discrimination, a total of three written opinions have been submitted to the courts, analysing the state of discrimination through the lens of the principle of equal pay for work of equal value, and these opinions seem to have contributed to the rendering of judgments and terms of settlement in favour of the plaintiffs. There are various difficulties to overcome before putting the principle of equal pay for work of equal value into practice in employment conditions in Japan, where the practice of seniority-based pay is adopted at the majority of workplaces. Pilot studies have been conducted from the workers' viewpoints to find out how to overcome these difficulties. The first study targeted clerical work at trading companies. The second study focused on in-store work in supermarkets and in care-giving professions (e.g. caregivers and nurses). The third study is currently ongoing, addressing the work of municipal civil servants. Endo participated in the second study team, and is leading the third study team.

This case further encouraged women working for Sumitomo Electric, Sumitomo Chemicals, and Sumitomo Metal to organize, in 1993, to demand promotions and pay increases from their companies, claiming that the companies discriminated against female workers. In January 1994, these women flew to New York and observed the CEDAW session, where they were convinced that their claim was justified. On the occasion, they submitted a counter-report to CEDAW, *A Letter from Japan*, drafted by 13 lawyers and translated into English by Kita-ku no Kai. In 1994, they applied to the government agency for conciliation with claims against the three Sumitomo companies.

The case against Sumitomo Life Insurance and the other cases against the three Sumitomo companies all ended in vain, however, with the applications for conciliation dismissed without prejudice or offers of irrelevant conciliation. These efforts revealed that the conciliation proceedings under the EEOA were not at all effective. At this stage, with no option for the women workers of the three Sumitomo companies but to resort to the courts, they decided to file litigation on 8 August 1995.[11]

On 10 August, Working Women's Network (WWN) was formed to support the nine women who were standing as plaintiffs in the Sumitomo cases. The new organization was born from the predecessor organizations, namely, the Kita-ku no Kai, the Osaka Network for Elimination of Gender Pay Discrimination, the Association of Women Working for Trading Companies, and the Practical Network Seminar on the Equal Employment Opportunity Act (Miyachi 2005; Shoji and Koedo 2005). Since the unions to which these women belonged were in-house unions and wedded to labour-management cooperation, they expected no support. WWN took the place of their unions.

11 In addition to the lawsuits against the three Sumitomo companies, 12 women working for Sumitomo Life Insurance filed a lawsuit against the company on 11 December 1995. The judgment in the first instance was rendered for the plaintiffs in 2001, and the High Court issued a recommendation for settlement in favour of the plaintiffs in 2002. In the Sumitomo Life Insurance Case, Endo prepared a written opinion as requested by the plaintiffs and submitted it to the court of first instance.

WWN's Supporting Activities

The judgment in the first instance for the Sumitomo Electric Case was rendered in 2000, and that of the Sumitomo Chemicals Case, in 2001. Both judgments were against the plaintiffs and both plaintiffs appealed to the High Court. In the Sumitomo Electric Case, however, the High Court issued a recommendation in December 2003 for settlement in favour of the plaintiffs.

The successful settlement in the Sumitomo Electric Case was significant and, in a sense, determined the direction of the other two Sumitomo cases. In the Sumitomo Chemicals Case, the High Court issued a recommendation for settlement in favour of the plaintiffs in 2004, and in the Sumitomo Metal Case, the judgment in the first instance was rendered for the plaintiffs in 2005, and the High Court issued a recommendation for settlement in favour of the plaintiffs in 2006 (http://wwn-net.org; as of 13 August 2010).

In the course of litigation, WWN supported the plaintiffs in diverse ways. Among its supporting activities, the most characteristic and the most conducive to the successful settlement in the Sumitomo Electric Case was its lobbying of CEDAW in 2003.

WWN attended the CEDAW Working Group pre-session held in New York in February 2003, and expressed the following views on the situation in Japan: (1) the employment management categories and the track-based personnel management system constitute 'indirect discrimination'; (2) the government's guidelines under the EEOA are inappropriate because they provide that discrimination is determined by comparison only within the same employment management category, whereas discrimination should be determined across different categories; (3) discrimination should be eliminated without delay. These views were a clear rebuttal to the reasons given by the court that rendered the judgment against the plaintiffs in the Sumitomo Electric Case. WWN also attended the CEDAW session held in New York in July and reiterated its views while lobbying CEDAW members. These efforts came to fruition, and CEDAW's final comments to the Japanese government in August included many of WWN's views.

In response to the presiding judge's offer to commence settlement proceedings, the plaintiffs submitted a settlement proposal to the court in September. The proposal demanded that the Japanese government put into practice the measures mentioned in CEDAW's final comments. In December 2003, the presiding judge proposed the terms of settlement, which, unprecedentedly, contained a preamble that reflected the plaintiffs' settlement proposal. The plaintiffs' promotions were mentioned in the main body of the terms, despite that the plaintiffs had failed to demand it in court because they lacked relevant personnel material. The plaintiffs accepted the settlement proposal, and the cases were successfully settled. Upon reaching settlement with the plaintiffs, Sumitomo Electric also promoted female co-workers who were not party to the suit (Miyachi 2005).

The plaintiffs had no access to relevant personnel materials because the Sumitomo companies refused to provide the material. Further, the in-house unions refused to hand over personnel material in their possession, despite the recommendation of the Japan Federation of Bar Associations (JFBA) that the unions provide the personnel materials to the plaintiffs (Miyachi 1998).

Comment should be made here on the three points of WWN's activities in 2003. The first point is that, despite the long-held assumption that employees gain most when their unions work with management through collective bargaining and negotiations, such a path turned out to be completely ineffective in improving the working conditions for the plaintiffs. On the contrary, the plaintiffs' in-house unions were obstacles that led the plaintiffs to litigation. Supported by international lobbying carried out by WWN, the plaintiffs fashioned their lawsuits to reflect the outcome of the lobbying and finally succeeded in improving their working conditions. What the legal cases above suggest is that, in the process of eliminating discrimination against female workers, in-house unions may be not merely useless, but obstructive, whereas women's labour NPOs have proven to be far more helpful.

Second, the approach of improving women's working conditions through litigation, WWN's international lobbying and the introduction of CEDAW's recommendations, for which WWN had lobbied, could not have been attained without the experience, accumulated since the 1970s, of women's labour NPOs. Furthermore, the experience, accumulated since the 1970s, of women's labour NPOs was completely independent from in-house unions. Despite their independence from in-house unions, or rather, thanks to their independence from in-house unions, women's labor NPOs have successfully accumulated experience from their own activities over a long period of time, and have gained from this approach.

Third, the link between WWN's international lobbying and improving women's working conditions was, in fact, not extraordinary in two respects but was ground-breaking in another. First, WWN's successful intervention at CEDAW can be regarded as a typical example of an NPO or NGO in a country lobbying the United Nations or the ILO and submitting a counter-report. It is not unusual for the United Nations or the ILO to place as much or more importance on the counter-report of an NPO or NGO than on the official report of the country's government. Considering that national governments tend to be male-dominated, it is understandable for the United Nations or the ILO to turn to an organization mainly composed of women to acquire information that concerns women. This is in a sense a product of the gender perspective of these international organizations.

Second, it has happened more than once in the modern history of Japan that labour reforms have made progress due to the external pressure exerted by international labour standards. Historians of Japanese labour often point out that the Japanese government's shift in labour policy toward a tolerant stance on trade unions in the 1920s came after becoming a member of the ILO, and labour reforms carried out during the occupation period immediately after the end of the Second World War were promoted by external pressure. The 1985 passage of the EEOA is another example. There was previously no precedent, however, for a Japanese labour NPO or NGO to apply such pressure. In this respect, WWN introduced a new epoch of external pressure in Japan's labour history.

Contemporary calls for legislative measures

Now that the lawsuits against the three Sumitomo companies have been concluded, WWN's activities emphasize demands for legislative measures.

First of all, WWN requests complete enforcement of the ban on 'indirect discrimination,' a ban that has been enshrined in revisions to the EEOA in 2007, as well as the introduction of the ban on discrimination under employment management categories and the track-based personnel management system. The second demand is the establishment in law of the principle of equal pay for work of equal value. The approach to be taken will be similar to the precedent of the WWN campaign, that is, to create external pressure toward ensuring the complete enforcement in Japan of the UN Convention on the Elimination of All Forms of Discrimination against Women, as well as the ILO Convention concerning Equal Remuneration for Men and Women Workers for Work of Equal Value (Equal Remuneration Convention 1951).

Some successful results have already been made thus far: the EEOA was revised in 2007 to prohibit 'indirect discrimination', and the Diet passed an additional resolution to review the 2007 revision to the EEOA five years later. Also, in the spring of 2010, the Ministry of Health, Labour and Welfare prepared and published a manual that recommends the introduction of job analysis and job evaluation for the purpose of improving the treatment of part-time employees. Job analysis and job evaluation are the prerequisites for the enforcement of the principle of equal pay for work of equal value.[12]

Conclusion: What is *trade union revitalization*?

When viewed from the vantage point of women's labour NPOs and women's trade unions, what does trade union revitalization in Japanese society mean? To put it simply, it means that existing trade unions, most of which are in-house unions, should break away from the conventional

12 The approach to job analysis and job evaluation recommended by the Ministry's manual is defective from the workers' viewpoint. However, the manual can be appreciated as groundbreaking because in Japan, job analysis and job evaluation are currently not accepted by many employers and in-house unions (Endo 2010b).

labour movement and its policies that are based on the concept of 'male breadwinner family'. Because in-house unions have pursued such concepts of family in their movements and policies, women's labour NPOs and women's trade unions have been formed and have developed as movements aimed at improving working conditions for female wage earners, a goal which cannot be attained by in-house unions. In other words, what women's labour NPOs and women's trade unions advocate is that there can be no trade union revitalization that is not sensitive to gender issues.

Shuto (2009) investigated the degree Rengo and its affiliate trade unions have broken away from the conventional concept of 'male breadwinner family', and judged that there has been little progress. Unfortunately, this is a valid judgment. In this situation, further development of women's labour NPOs and women's trade unions is required to force Rengo and its affiliate trade unions to break away from their concept of family and to make efforts toward trade union revitalization.

References

Benson, J. et al. (2007). 'The Prospect for Gender Diversity in Japanese Employment', *International Journal of Human Resource Management*, 18 (5), 890–907.

Broadbent, K. (2007). 'Sisters Organising in Japan and Korea: the Development of Women-only Unions', *Industrial Relations Journal*, 38 (3), 229–51.

Endo, K. (2011). 'Hiseiki Rodosha no Soshiki-ka – Kigyōnai Kumiai to Kojin Kamei Yunion' (Organizing of Non-regular workers – In-house Unions and Individual Affiliate Unions (IAUs)), *Keieironshū* (Meiji Business Review), 58 (3), 1–16.

Endo, K. (2010a). 'Book Review: C. Gerteis *Gender Struggles: Wage-Earning Women and Male-Dominated Unions in Postwar Japan*', *Social Science Japan Journal*, 13 (2), 284–86.

Endo, K. (2010b). 'Seiki to Hiseiki no Chingin Kakusa – Shokumu Bunseki, Shokumu Hyōka kara Kangaeru' (Pay Disparities Between Regular and Non-Regular Workers – From the Perspective of Job Analysis and Job Evaluation), *Gekkan Jichiken* (August), 63–9.

Endo, K. (1997). 'Sex and Union Member Discrimination under the *Satei* System in the Japanese Firm', *Review of Radical Political Economics*, 29 (2), 26–44.

Gerteis, C. (2010). *Gender Struggles: Wage-Earning Women and Male-Dominated Unions in Postwar Japan*. Cambridge, Mass: Harvard University Press.

Hiromori, N. (2005). 'Josei no Rodoken ni tsuite no Manabi – Hataraku Josei no Gakushu Katsudo no Jirei kara' (Study on Women's Right to Work – Examples of Learning Activities of Working Women). In M. Takahashi, T. Makiishi (eds), *Jendā to Seijin Kyoiku*. Tokyo: Sofusha.

Hiromori, N. (2004). 'Josei no Rodoken ni kakawaru Gakushu Katsudo no Tenkaito Hataraku Josei no Enpawāmento – *Kokusai Fujin-nen Kita-ku no Kai* wo Jirei to shite' (Advancement of Learning Activities on Women's Right to Work and the Empowerment of Women – Taking the *Kita-ku no Kai for the International Women's Year* as an Example), *Tohoku Daigaku Daigakuin Kyoiku Kenkyuka Kenkyu Nenpo* (Annual Study Report of Study of Tohoku University, Graduate School of Education), No. 52, 135–61.

Japan Pay Equity Society. (1996). *Byodo heno Charenji* (Challenge to Equity). Osaka: Japan Pay Equity Society.

Kanai, A. (2009). '"Karoshi" (Work to Death) in Japan', *Journal of Business Ethics*, 84, 209–16.

Keizer, A.B. (2008). 'Non-regular Employment in Japan: Continued and Renewed Dualities', *Work, Employment and Society*, 22 (1), 407–25.

Koedo, S. (1998). 'Sogoshosha no Hataraku Josei' (Women Working at General Trading Companies). In H. Fujii, T. Watanabe (ed.), *Nihon Kigyō no Hataraku Josei Tachi*. Kyoto: Minerva Shobo.

Koseki, T. (2011). 'Rodo NPO no Tokushitsu – Kojin Kamei Yunion tono Taihi, Kanren ni oite' (Characteristics of Labour UNPs, as Compared with and in Relation to Individual Affiliate Unions). Unpublished manuscript.

Miyachi, M. (2005). 'Teiso Zenshi' (History Before Litigation). In WWN (Working Women's Network) (ed.), *Danjo Chingin Sabetsu Saiban: Kojo Ryozoku ni Makenakatta Onnatachi*. Tokyo: Akashi Shoten.

Miyachi, M. (1998). 'Rodo Kumiai to Joho Kaiji – Sumitomo Sankigyo Rodo Kumiai he no Nichibenren Kankoku wo megutte' (Labour Unions and Information Disclosure – Recommendation by the Japan Federation of Bar Associations to the Labour Unions of the Three Sumitomo Companies), *Rodo Horitsu Junpo*, No. 1432 (May 25), pp. 6–21.

Moriya, T. (2005). *Nihon Kigyo he no Seikashugi Donyu* (Introduction of the Performance-based Pay System into Japanese Companies). Tokyo: Moriyama Shoten.

Moriya, T. (2000). *Gekido no Sogoshosha*. Tokyo: Moriyama Shoten.

Shoji, R., Koedo, S. (2005). 'WWN to tomoni' (Acting together with WWN). In WWN (ed.), *Danjo Chingin Sabetsu Saiban: Kojo Ryozoku ni Makenakatta Onnatachi*. Tokyo, Akashi Shoten.

Shuto, W. (2009). 'Josei to rōdō kumiai – Dansei kaseginushi moderu no shikaku kara' (Women and Trade Unions – From the Perspective of the Male Breadwinner model). In N. Hisamoto (ed.), *Rōshi Komyunikēshon* (Labour-management Communication). Kyoto: Minerva Shobo.

Society for the Study of Working Women. (1992). *Koyo Byodo no Saizensen* (Frontline of the Movement Toward Equality in Employment). Tokyo: Iwanami Shoten.

Suzuki, A. (2008). 'Community Unions in Japan: Similarities and Differences of Region-based Labour Movements between Japan and Other Industrialized Countries', *Economic and Industrial Democracy*, 29 (4), 492–520.

Urano, E.I., Stewart, P. (2009). 'Beyond Organized Labor in Japan – The Case of the Japanese Community Union Federation'. In J. McBride, I. Greenwood (eds), *Community Unionism: A Comparative Analysis of Concepts and Contexts*. New York: Palgrave Macmillan.

Urano, E.I., Stewart, P. (2007). 'Including the Excluded Workers?: The Challenges of Japan's Kanagawa City Union', *WorkingUSA*, 10 (1), 103–23.

Watanabe, M. (1976). 'Fujin to Rodo Undo' (Women and Labour Movements). In *Jurist, Sogo Tokushu: Gendai no josei*. Tokyo: Yuhikaku.

Weathers, C. (2005). 'In Search of Strategic Partners: Japan's Campaign for Equal Opportunity', *Social Science Japan Journal*, 8 (1), 69–89.

HEIWON KWON

10 Success While Others Fail: Union Strategy against Railway Restructuring in South Korea[1]

Introduction

In the last few decades, globalization has led to the weakening of organized labour and a sense of crisis in much the same way as it has affected other sectors of the world economy. Labour restructuring and layoffs have become widespread, creating massive job losses and reducing union bargaining leverage. The public sector is no exception. In fact, the hitherto protected public sector is considered a hindrance to competitiveness and has become a major target of market reform. In this context, public sector unions have had a difficult time retaining their bargaining power.

Yet, although public sector restructuring has swept almost every nation and led to the privatization of many industries, unions have influenced restructuring processes differently. In some cases, unions have subordinated themselves to the unilateral process of restructuring, while in others they have fought hard but unsuccessfully to protect labour interests. In other cases, unions have been more effective in opposing unilateral restructuring.

This chapter focuses on identifying factors that explain variations in the strategic effectiveness of trade unions. It presents a framework that pays attention to both changes in political opportunities and union strategic

1 This chapter is a slightly modified version of 'A Union Campaign Against Railway Industry Privatization in South Korea: What Explains Its Relative Success?', published in *the Korean Journal of Industrial Relations* (Vol. 21, No. 4, 2011). The editorial board of the journal kindly granted permission for its publication as a chapter in this volume.

capabilities. In particular, it suggests that a union's ability to develop and mobilize power resources is central to explaining differences in the outcomes of restructuring.

Drawing upon this framework, I conduct a case analysis of the Korean Railway Workers' Union (KRWU or Railway Workers) to investigate the union's strategic response to railway restructuring in South Korea. The Korean Railway Workers' Union strongly opposed government plans to privatize the railway industry, and, ultimately, the government officially withdrew the railway privatization policy and decided to maintain public operation of the railway system. Moreover, the union obtained considerable concessions in 2003 from the government by negotiating the April 20th union-government agreement, which incorporated almost all the Railway Workers' major demands. The union's interests were reflected in the final railway restructuring legislation.

Yet the relative success of the KRWU is not generalizable to other unions in Korea. On the contrary, there exists wide, within-country variation in the strategic effectiveness of trade unions. What conditions explain the relative success of the KRWU? Why did the government grant the Railway Workers considerable concessions? This chapter focuses its analysis on changes in political conditions and the KRWU's strategic choices. Using the KRWU's opposition to railway privatization as a case study, I argue that the extent of political opportunities provided by changing political contingencies shapes the strategic context for unions. If political opportunities increase, unions encounter more favourable conditions. Yet the increase in political opportunities neither automatically raises the power resources of unions nor directly determines the outcome of restructuring. In fact, it is the variation in the strategic ability of unions that determines the variety of outcomes. In this respect, this chapter underscores that the KRWU's strategic abilities ensured that its interests would be reflected in the final design of the railway restructuring.

I begin this chapter by presenting an analytical framework that emphasizes the central place of strategic capability in explaining the varied restructuring outcomes. I then briefly review the railway restructuring process in Korea. The following section focuses on how changes in political contingency explain the specific strategic context in which the Railway Workers operate. That section is followed by an analysis of union strategy. I argue that although political resources provided by changes in political contingency increase opportunities for unions, successful union gains do not result unless unions develop strategic abilities to exploit favourable conditions. Hence, I highlight the strategic capabilities of the KRWU to explain its relative success. A final section summarizes the findings of the study and considers practical implications for union strategies.

Sources of Variation: Strategic Capabilities of Trade Unions

Studies in the past have sought to understand the diversity of restructuring outcomes by relying on an institutionalist framework. For example, institutionalist accounts of industrial relations have often pointed to distinct national institutions that explain cross-national differences in union abilities to influence restructuring decisions. Unions in coordinated or corporatist countries have retained their influence thanks to the institutional arrangements that accommodate a high level of labour involvement in decision-making. By contrast, unions in more liberal or market-based countries lack institutional resources to curb management discretion and thus have become increasingly ineffectual (Turner 1991; Ferner 1994; Thelen 2001). From this perspective, variation in union influence is due to institutionally embedded forms of union power: in coordinated countries, organized labour is integrated into corporatist bargaining systems whereby they have extensive participatory rights. In contrast, in countries where organized labour lacks institutional access to the polity, management is more likely to gain unilateral authority over weak unions.

Yet, national institutional variables cannot fully account for differences in strategic effectiveness among unions in the same country. In this respect, it is noteworthy that a number of studies have raised questions about the stability of national institutions and have emphasized the fragmentation and weakening of industrial relations institutions. Instead they draw attention to growing differences in practices across firms and workplaces within countries (Locke 1992; Katz and Darbishire 2000; Frost 2000; Doellgast 2006). For them, subnational variation derives from the different strategic choices of managers and unions. In line with these studies, this chapter draws upon a strategic choice framework to explain subnational variation in restructuring outcomes. This approach is useful in explaining varied union effects in non-coordinated countries. Here we are faced with the question of why some unions are more influential than others despite an absence of a stable institutional structure for labour incorporation. In fact, Korean unions were all constrained by a lack of institutional resources. Still some unions had considerable policy influence over restructuring designs while many others remained far less influential. In this respect, it is noteworthy that 'in light of weak institutional structures for stakeholder participation, the strategic choices of the companies and unions have played a far stronger role in determining the variation of outcomes' (Turner 1991, cited in Batt and Darbishire 1997: 68). In coordinated countries, the presence of corporatist regulation reduces within-country variation by narrowing employer discretion. Such is not the case of more liberal, market-based countries where lack of labour integrative institutions produces wider variation. Hence, the strategic capabilities of trade unions become all the more important in countries with weak corporatist traditions.

Changes in political contingencies also condition trade union choices. If those changes increase political opportunities for unions, they are in a more advantageous position to leverage the bargaining process. Yet, an increase in political opportunities does not necessarily lead to successful union gains unless unions can exploit favourable situations. To ensure that the restructuring outcomes incorporate some benefits and protections for labour, trade unions should develop strategies to counteract employer or government initiatives. Thus, the dimension of union strategic ability becomes the key variable in explaining differences in the degree of union success. Specifically, unions should be able to mobilize both their internal constituencies and external support. Internal solidarity and membership involvement are essential for leveraging the bargaining process, and mobilizing political and social support provides power resources that complement institutionally weak, labour positions. Drawing upon these arguments, this chapter highlights three union capabilities central to understanding differences in the strategic effectiveness of unions: the ability to educate and mobilize members; the ability to create and multiply political channels; and the ability to build broad, social coalitions and appeal to public interests.

The Launch of Railway Privatization and Restructuring in South Korea

The railway privatization plan was decided at a cabinet meeting of the Kim Dae Jung government in March 1999 (Commission for Railway Restructuring 2001: 1). The government considered privatization the most effective means to raise efficiency in railway transport and argued that the Korean National Railroad (KNR)[2] could never eliminate chronic deficits unless it underwent a fundamental restructuring and established an autonomous, management system through privatization (MOCT and KNR 2000; KNR 2000b; MOCT 2001a). Such an initiative was part of a broader public sector restructuring program pushed by the government. When Kim Dae Jung took office in February 1998 amid a severe economic crisis and IMF bailout of the South Korean economy, his administration immediately launched a radical public sector restructuring program within the framework of IMF, structural reform guidelines. For this, the government established the Planning and Budget Committee (PBC),[3]

2 The Korean National Railroad had been a state-run authority until January 2005 when KNR was split into the Korea Railroad Corporation (KORAIL), the public corporation for railway transportation services and the Korea Rail Network Authority (KRNA), the public authority in charge of railroad construction.

3 The Planning and Budget Committee was under direct presidential control based on Article 19 of the National Government Organization Act, and the president of the Committee was appointed by President Kim Dae Jung. The committee, going beyond the boundary of individual ministries and covering the whole of the public sector, took charge of the privatization of a wide range of public industries. The Committee merged with the National Budget Administration to become the Ministry of Planning and Budget in May 1999.

which not only took charge of state budget planning but also had the task of leading the process of public sector reform. The initiative was far more comprehensive in its scope than previous government efforts. It aimed at privatizing 19 corporations[4] and their 55 subsidiaries, and it also imposed detailed restructuring guidelines including workforce reduction and corporate restructuring on the targeted companies (PBC 1998). KNR was not included in the targeted public companies for privatization at the time, but ultimately the Kim Dae Jung government concluded that railway privatization was the best means to raise railway competitiveness and began to push a tight and speedy privatization program. According to the initial government plan of 1999, privatization would be achieved by January 2002, within just a year and a half of announcing the railway privatization plan (MOCT 2000). This plan was modified after a fine-tuning process among the Ministry of Planning and Budget (MPB), the Ministry of Construction and Transport (MOCT) and KNR. In supporting the original government plan, the MPB endorsed the most radical form of privatization. It also argued for the divided ownership of passenger operations, freight operations and vehicle maintenance (the horizontal separation) along with the vertical separation of service operations and infrastructure. By contrast, KNR supported an integrated privatization plan by opposing the horizontal split of the railway operation company, and it sought a delay in the final privatization until 2004 as it expected to spend at least two years and seven months transferring ownership. The MOCT sided with KNR on the time schedule (MOCT 2000). The finalized government plan proposed

4 According to the second privatization plan of the Kim Dae Jung government, which was announced on 4 August 1998 (only one month after the announcement of the first plan), the targeted public corporations for privatization are: Korea Telecom, Korea Tobacco and Ginseng Corp., Daehan Oil Pipeline Corp., Korea Minting and Security Printing Corp., Korea Agro-fisheries Trade Corp., Korea Resources Corp., Korea Trade Investment Promotion Agency, Korea National Housing Corp., Korea Expressway Corp., Korea Appraisal Board, Korea Electric Power Corp., Korea Gas Corp., Korea District Heating Corp., Korea Tourism Organization, Korea Rural Corp., Korea Coal Corp., Korea National Oil Corp., Korea Land Corp. and Korea Water Resources Corp.

a gradual privatization process of: 1) the vertical separation of railway operations and infrastructure (to be achieved by 2002); 2) the transformation of KNR from a government organization to a public corporation (to be achieved during 2003–2004); and 3) the ownership transfer of the railway operations corporation to private companies and the creation of a competitive market by selling government shares and giving private service providers free access to railways (to be achieved during 2005–2010) (MOCT 2001a). Based on this scheme, the government introduced two bills in the National Assembly in December 2001: the Basic Law on the Development and Restructuring of the Railway Industry and the Railroad Corporation Act. The bills statutorily defined the method of restructuring based on a split between railway infrastructure and operations. While the newly established Railroad Construction Authority would remain a government authority taking responsibility for railroad construction as well as its maintenance and repair, the Korean Railroad Operations Corp. would be set up to manage operation services, which would be gradually privatized. In short, the law envisioned completely handing the railway operation company over to private companies. According to Article 18 of the Law, 'the state will sell government shares of the Korean Railroad Operations Corp. to private parties in consideration of business conditions of the latter' (MOCT 2001a: 10).

Deliberation of the bills, however, was delayed in the Assembly, and consequently, the bills were not passed until Kim Dae Jung's term ended in February 2003. The change in the leadership of the Railway Workers in May 2001 and the mounting opposition of the union to the passage of the railway reform bills played a central role in postponing the legislation. Hence, the task of railway restructuring and related legislation fell to the government of Roh Moo Hyun who took office on 25 February 2003. Railway restructuring took a new turn when Roh's presidential transition committee reviewed the railway restructuring policy. Roh had promised to withdraw the privatization plan during his electoral campaign. Such political change made it possible for the KRWU to escalate pressure on the new government.

In the end, the Basic Law on the Development of the Railway Industry and the Railroad Infrastructure Authority Act were enacted after the passage of the bills in the National Assembly on 30 June 2003. The legislation split KNR into KORAIL, the service operations company, and the Korea Rail Network Authority (KRNA), the railroad construction authority. The contents of the final legislation shared the same framework of a vertical split between operations and infrastructure as the Kim Dae Jung government's proposed law. The new bill deleted the privatization clause, though. Corporatization (the change of organizational structure of the KNR from a government authority to a corporation) was a substitute for privatization, not a preliminary step to ownership transfer. As a result, KORAIL has continued to be a public corporation with 100 per cent government ownership. In addition, the government conceded on other restructuring issues. Above all, the law also included clauses that guaranteed employment security and safeguard measures against the deterioration of working conditions (MOCT 2003). Thus, the KRWU not only prevented the passage of the privatization bills but also gained major concessions from the government and KNR on the terms and conditions of employment.

The following sections explain how the KRWU succeeded in derailing the government restructuring plan and negotiating a labour-protecting agreement. They shed light on both changes in political contingency and the development of strategic union capabilities.

Changes in Political Contingency

For public sector unions, because they operate through the political process, political resources are more important than market power for gaining leverage in the bargaining process. The centrality of political resources makes it important to consider the changing characteristics of political contingency. By political contingency I mean the forces that act on public enterprises: 'formal rules and targets, ministerial intervention, the policies of political parties, public opinion, the demands and investigations of a variety of other state bodies, including parliamentary select committees or state committees of enquiry, and the pressure and claims of public user bodies and private sector interest groups' (Ferner 1988: 10). Changing political contingency can provide or constrain trade union opportunities. If the range of political resources widens through changes in the political environment, unions can increase points of engagement and gain allies who could help them pressure their counterparts. If, on the contrary, the range of political resources narrows, unions are less likely to oppose the other bargaining parties as limited resources constrain unions to act defensively.

In this respect and at the time of the Korean Railway restructuring, changes in political contingencies increased political opportunities for the KRWU. First, although the privatization of KNR was decided in March 1999, it was only a year later that the Kim Dae Jung government announced the final railway privatization plan. In the meantime, the political contingency changed as the economic discipline brought about by the Korean financial crisis came to be loosened.[5] During the crisis period, the government had an uncompromising attitude that advocated for a fast-paced push for public sector restructuring. This made it difficult for trade unions and political dissidents to raise objections to the government drive. But when the government finalized the railway restructuring plan, the immediate need for crisis management fell less heavily on the government. This easing in the political climate opened space for labour-sided policy contenders to voice their opposition to the PBC-led process of unilateral restructuring. Despite the government's continued avoidance of labour integration at peak-level negotiations, political opportunities increased for the KRWU.

Second, the tension between the MPB (the resultant merger between the PBC and the National Budget Administration), the MOCT and KNR also contributed to an increase in opportunities for the Railway Workers. Unlike the earlier privatization push, which was overwhelmingly dominated by the PBC's guidelines, this new attempt at railway restructuring constituted a more contested political sphere, which put a brake on the

5 After two years of crisis, Kim Dae Jung declared that the economy had recovered from its economic crisis on the grounds that macroeconomic data proved that Korea's economic growth in 1999 ranked highest among the 29 members of OECD. See 'Retrospect on Korean Economy: The Restoration of Korean Economy', *Yeohap News*, 11 December 1999.

PBC's unilateral leadership. There were conflicting views among political authorities on the timing and method of restructuring that required many rounds of negotiations before its finalization. As seen in the previous section, KNR objected to the MPB's heedless drive towards railway privatization and proposed to delay the process (KNR 2000a; MOCT 2000). Hence, the coherence of the political control of the PBC (later the MPB) weakened during the plan's adjustment period.

The 2002 presidential election brought about yet another distinctive change in the political environment. First, the electoral campaign widened the political space in which the KRWU could publicize its claims and obtain broad support from various political constituencies. In the electoral context, political parties and their candidates become more responsive to the demands of various social groups (including trade unions) as competing candidates strive to win elections by expanding their electoral base. The KRWU sent the presidential candidates a questionnaire to which not only the sympathetic Korean Democratic Labour Party candidate but also those of the other major parties responded. For example, Democratic Party candidate Roh Moo Hyun, who later was elected president, promised to revise the privatization policy for network utilities including the railway. Even the candidate of the right-wing Grand National Party stated that the party opposed privatization of KNR and promised to pursue railway restructuring in a cautious way. Regarding other restructuring issues, the candidates of the Democratic Party and the Grand National Party avoided directly responding to union demands. Nonetheless, the presidential election made it possible for the Railway Workers to increase political pressure on the parties. Moreover, the candidates acknowledged a need to engage in good faith negotiations, ensuring the union greater participation in restructuring decisions. Such a process helped delay the implementation of the railway privatization plan as well as block the passage of the related privatization bills in the National Assembly.

Political opportunities continued to expand after Roh Moo Hyun's election in December 2002. As he promised to hold back on steps towards privatizing network utilities, the KRWU was in an advantageous position to pressure the new government to keep its public pledge. In fact, the new president officially announced that he would revise the privatization plan for the railway and gas industries.[6] There was no doubt that such a policy switch threw more weight behind the KRWU's campaign to halt the hasty move towards railway privatization. In line with this switch, the presidential transition committee also announced that the new Administration would discard the previous government's railway privatization plan and that it would take into account the opinions of not only the related ministries but also industrial experts and civic groups in drawing up a relevant restructuring plan. Together, these processes of political negotiation created an environment whereby the Railway Workers found greater opportunities to push its demands more aggressively.

In sum, the increase in political opportunities provided a favourable strategic condition for the KRWU. Yet increases in the political opportunities do not necessarily improve outcomes. Indeed, if the KRWU had failed to develop effective strategic capabilities, it would not have been successful in negotiating labour-protective agreements with the government. For this reason, the next section will highlight the KRWU's strategic capabilities in influencing the process and outcomes of railway restructuring. But before analysing the strategic abilities of the union, I first examine changes in the micro-politics of KRWU and their implications for union strategies.

The Changes in the Internal Political Dynamics of the KRWU

When the Kim Dae Jung government decided to privatize the railway industry in 1999, the KRWU set up the 'Emergency Committee to Challenge Privatization' to carry on a campaign against privatization and began organizing a series of mass protests. The union leadership's call for collective

6 Roh Moo Hyun declared in a speech to foreign businessmen that he would modify the privatization plan for network utilities. And in several occasions later on, he recapitulated his intention to postpone the railway privatization and revise the plan on the basis of social agreement (See *The Korea Economic Daily*, 12 January 2006).

action was unprecedented. The Railway Workers had had a long history of labour peace under conservative leadership and a reputation for being 'very docile and pro-government' (Kang 2002: 174). In fact, despite a union democratization movement that burgeoned after a first-ever, wild-cat strike led by locomotive drivers in July 1988, the leadership faced no significant challenge until the mid-1990s (KRWU 1997). The union's conservatism gave way in the late 1990s with the government's push for railway restructuring. While union members felt a heightened concern for job security, they were frustrated by their passive leadership, whose quiescence prodded rank-and-file support for a movement for union democratization. Faced with both increasing membership discontent and the threat of leadership replacement, union leaders felt obliged to adopt confrontational tactics and declared a joint strike in November 2000 with the Korea National Electricity Workers Union (KNEWU) against public sector restructuring. Union member support for the strike turned out to be 81 per cent in the union ballot with a 94 per cent voter turnout (Kang 2002: 245), evidence of member determination to take collective action and an expectation for strong measures from their leaders. Still, the union leadership called off their first-ever planned strike after an agreement on railway restructuring was made at the Tripartite Commission on 10 December 2000.

Although the agreement stated the need for a postponement of the original railway privatization plan, it fell far short of expectations. Members were frustrated by union leaders' consent to the targeted employment cuts and considered cancellation of the strike unjustifiable. Such defiance was confirmed when a union democratization movement group, the Korean Democracy Railroad Labour (KDRL) group harshly criticized the leadership and organized an independent ballot on the agreement in which 9,036 members participated, 85 per cent of whom opposed the agreement (Kang 2002: 246). Eventually, the opposition defeated the old leadership in the May 2001 election. The leadership change fundamentally altered labour relations at KNR as it brought an end to decades of labour quiescence. Above all, the timing of the leadership replacement coincided with the escalating discontent of union members with government policy. In response to this discontent, the new leadership broke radically from the union's cooperative past and built on militant tactics to confront the government-led railway privatization and restructuring.

Leadership change occurred in May 2001 at the time when the Kim Dae Jung government pushed the railway restructuring plan forward. In a sense, the changes in the internal politics of the union, fuelled by a fear of deteriorating employment conditions, augmented membership resources for the KRWU as union members responded increasingly favourably to the new leadership. As a result, the new leadership's appeal to strike against the privatization bills garnered a 72.23 per cent approval in a vote that turned out 92.06 per cent of the membership (KRWU 2002).

Despite a high level of leadership support, the internal organization of the union was fragile and susceptible to government backlash. It lacked embedded institutional structures to hold and develop a cohesive countervailing power, and since it was the dissident group's first experience with leadership, the leadership was constrained by the lack of a stable bargaining relationship with management. Similarly, it lacked well-organized communication networks within the union that could link union leaders with the rank-and-file members. In addition, the tension among different factions of union activists threatened internal solidarity and undermined leadership authority. Indeed, when the new leadership reached an agreement regarding the February 25th strike with KNR on 27 February 2002, leftist activists criticized the leadership for accepting the agreement without ensuring the complete withdrawal of the government plan.[7] The government and KNR also hit the union with a mass disciplinary action in the aftermath of the strike, despite a union security clause in the February 27th Agreement. The disciplinary action resulted in the imprisonment of eight union officers, including the president of the KRWU, 57 lawsuits, the dismissal of 24 union members and a 1.6 billion won claim for losses and damages from the strike (KRWU, 2002: 533).

In sum, the internal political condition of the Railway Workers provided as many opportunities as constraints for the union. The potential for membership mobilization capacity was at its highest with the leadership

7 Related to the privatization issue, the February 27th Agreement stated that 'both union and management will make efforts for public development of the railway' without official withdrawal of the previous privatization plan. It contained other clauses such as gradual workforce supplementation, reduction of working hours, an increase in fringe benefits and union security.

change. Yet, the institutional basis of the union was too weak for the new leadership to address the challenges from both leftist unionists and the employer violation of the union-management agreement. Hence, membership mobilization capacity could not be sustained unless the new leadership developed strategies to engage members in union activism and mobilize a variety of power resources.

Strategies of the KRWU

With weak institutional and organizational bases, the new leadership of the KRWU had the task of increasing membership participation and power resources, but the strategic capability that played a key role in achieving positive bargaining outcomes was not predetermined. In fact, three resources of power were necessary for the union to leverage bargaining power: membership resources, political resources and broad-based social resources. The Railway Workers were relatively successful in mobilizing these resources thanks to effective strategies in developing and renewing these three levers of union power. If we consider that membership resources refer to collective cohesion among union members, it is necessary that unions strengthen internal solidarity by being able to educate and mobilize their members. Similarly, political resources increase when unions create political channels to voice opinions and pressure the government. Lastly, the range of social resources depends on mobilizing broad, social support by building alliances with other unions and other social constituencies. This section examines the KRWU strategies by focusing on these three dimensions.

The ability to educate and mobilize members

When the new leadership took power for the first time after a decade-long union democratization movement in May 2001, the internal organization of the Railway Workers was not well-established and had weak institutional legacies. Union leaders focused on establishing communication channels between union executives, stewards and lay members and increased efforts to fortify the regional and local bases of the union. This led to a series of thorough membership education sessions held at regional offices and a variety of activities such as a performance tour held at major railway stations. During July, August and September 2001, the Kim Jae Kil leadership organized forty educational sessions in five regional divisions (KRWU 2002: 115). It also held twenty-three performances of a propaganda play, *Journey on Railway Tracks* [*Cheoloyeokjung*] in the winter of 2001–2002, aimed at informing union members and the general public of the negative aspects of the railway privatization policy. By organizing the performances, the KRWU also sought to build coalitions with local civil society organizations and strengthen the organizational basis of its regional divisions (KRWU 2002). The leadership then launched a series of 29 educational meetings in five regional divisions to inform members about union demands for 2002's special collective bargaining. For sure, tackling privatization and other restructuring issues often required instant membership mobilization that hindered the establishment of day-to-day organizational activities on a more long-term basis. Despite these limits, the KRWU demonstrated a relatively strong mobilization capacity. In the first place, the escalation of the union democratization movement gave momentum for membership mobilization. Leadership efforts for intense membership education further sustained the high mobilization capacity.

Although internal tension among different factions within the union democratization movement existed, they did not undermine union cohesion. When criticism arose within activist groups towards the union-management agreement of February 2002, the KRWU's leadership asserted its authority by organizing ratification votes from 11–13 March in which a majority of members voted (70.3 per cent) (KRWU 2002: 533). The union also organized a by-election when the strategic capacity of leadership was undermined by the previously-noted, KNR-initiated disciplinary action against the strikers. This union-organized by-election paved the way for a new democratic leadership (with Chun Hwan-Kyu elected president). This sustained membership commitment rebuilt the Railway Workers internal organization.

Membership mobilization efforts continued under the new Chun Hwan-Kyu leadership. Upon taking office on 8 August 2002, the new leadership concentrated all its resources on the contract struggle and held membership rallies at its regional divisions. It also organized nationwide, mass demonstrations both independently and in conjunction with the National Joint Committee for Opposing Privatization to exert pressures on KNR. Its goal was to turn the half-success of the February 25th strike into a complete success by forcing management to adhere to the February 27th Agreement (KRWU 2003). In response to the KNR and the government's provocative disciplinary action and violation of the Agreement, the new leadership resorted primarily to confrontational tactics to force the employer into good faith negotiations. Yet membership education lagged in comparison to the previous leadership's efforts because of a tight contract bargaining schedule. The new leadership had to move quickly on to the contract struggle as soon as it took office and had little time to organize intensive membership education. Still, it sought to increase membership participation by other means. First, it encouraged members to attend union meetings and organized two ballots, one on November 4th for changing the national umbrella organization and the other one on February 17th to 19th for strike action.[8] It also set up an 'unfair labour practice report centre' and urged members to file grievances against management attacks on union activities. Lastly, it mobilized mass rallies and a week-long campaign of 'work to rule' from April 11th to 18th to draw public attention to safety issues and gain public support for the strike (KRWU 2003). These activities contributed to the maintenance of the political vitality of the union, without which union mobilization capacity could not be sustained. In sum, the KRWU leadership demonstrated a relatively high capacity to educate

8 The vote for changing the KRWU's national confederation affiliation from the Federation of Korean Trade Unions (FKTU) to the more militant Korean Confederation of Trade Unions (KCTU) had a high rate of membership participation with a 94.08 per cent voter turnout. As a result of this vote (with 54.02 per cent in support of the change), KRWU left the FKTU to affiliate with the KCTU (KRWU, 2003: 393). With a turnout of 89.9 per cent, 51.62 per cent of members voted in favour of strike action (KRWU, ibid: 106).

and mobilize union members. This resulted in an increase in membership resources that enhanced the collective cohesion of the union and helped overcome its weak institutional and organizational basis.

The ability to exert political pressure through multiple channels

Besides membership resources, public sector unions need to mobilize political resources to increase their bargaining power. In fact, as public enterprises are politically regulated and their labour relations are highly political, public sector unions' strength rests chiefly on political resources that help them exert pressure on government. For the same reason, political contingencies that augment or reduce political resources have a significant impact on union strategies. As I have already discussed, political changes favourably conditioned the strategic formulation of the KRWU by providing greater opportunities for more leverage in political bargaining with the government.

Yet, the Railway Workers could only be strategically effective by taking advantage of political opportunities and mobilizing political resources. If they failed to develop strategic, political capabilities, increased opportunities would have meant nothing to the union. In this respect, they relied on a dual strategy combining negotiations and confrontation. While they tried to utilize various confrontational tactics to increase pressure on the government, they also made efforts to persuade the government to bargain directly with the union. For this, the union multiplied its political channels to the political parties, government officers and politicians and used them to support union claims. Increasing its allies within the polity gave the KRWU points of pressure on the government when Roh Moo Hyun, the candidate of the Democratic Party, was elected. Thus, the union demanded the new government keep its election pledges, conveyed a written opinion on railway restructuring to the presidential transition committee and held a discussion meeting with the committee on 22 January 2003 (KRWU 2003). Besides these official contacts, the union leadership also increased informal contacts with committee members and government officials to convince them to incorporate union demands into the final design of railway restructuring.

Among the committee members, there were those whose labour movement backgrounds increased communicative channels for the union. The KRWU leadership took advantage of these contacts to influence policy-making (personal interview). The Railway Workers also contacted members of the Construction and Transportation Committee of the National Assembly to secure their endorsements of the union proposals (KRWU 2003).

In sum, the Railway Workers made persistent efforts to extend political channels and use them to increase their bargaining leverage and succeeded in persuading the government to negotiate directly with the union. It is also noteworthy that the ability to negotiate a union-government agreement was actually backed up by a mobilization of mass opposition, which put effective pressures on the government. According to the KRWU leadership, bargaining with the government could not go beyond ritualized formal talks unless backed up by the mobilizing power of the union (KRWU 2003: 139). Similarly, the union also had to build external solidarity links through horizontal coordination among unions and other social groups to retain its influence over restructuring decisions. This leads us to emphasize the importance of the third strategic ability of KRWU: the ability to mobilize public support through building social coalitions.

The ability to mobilize social support through coalition-building

The Railway Workers viewed social coalition-building as an important source of bargaining power and constantly tried to build broad alliances with external groups. They pursued these efforts in three areas. First, the union sought to carry out joint research with progressive academia and labour policy practitioners to frame its campaign in a more effective way and develop alternatives to the railway privatization policy. This outreach, in turn, contributed to finding labour allies among government officials, members of political parties and broader constituents of civil society, and the research findings provided the KRWU with a firmer rationale for union claims that it could build upon to mobilize support. It also helped dissipate negative public images of the union as a narrow interest group that fought solely for its own sake.

Second, it actively sought to forge inter-union alliances with other public sector unions. 'The most remarkable efforts were seen in the launch of the "Joint Alliance of Public Sector Unions for Blocking Privatization of National Key Industries" at the end of October 2001' (Kang 2002: 249). Those efforts brought together the KRWU and the Korean Gas Corporation Union, the Power Plant Industry Union, the Korea Electric Technology Union, the High Speed Rail Union and the District Heating Corporation Union. Indeed, the joint strike with the allied unions increased the bargaining power of the KRWU as the coordinated strike overcame individual union weaknesses and expanded their collective power resources. The Railway Workers continued to consolidate the strategic alliance with other public sector unions under the Chun Hwan Kyu leadership, notably with the Power Plant Industry Union.

Lastly, the KRWU also began to connect itself to broader social movement and civil society organizations. The union tried to organize joint actions with the National Joint Committee for Opposing Privatization and Overseas Sales of Public Industries, a coalition of forty-two organizations that included the two national labour confederations (FKTU and KCTU), the Korean Democratic Labour Party, various labour movement organizations, religious organizations, civil society movement organizations and student movement organizations. The union allied itself with these diverse social groups and mobilized public support by organizing and participating in the coordinated campaign. For this, the KRWU framed the campaign as a defence of public needs. It argued that railway privatization would sacrifice public interests for profitability and that the right to universal services for the socially-disadvantaged would be undermined by a profit-centred railway operation, which would eliminate unprofitable railway lines to the detriment of public needs. It also called public attention to safety issues as private ownership could reduce investment in railway facilities and create a risk of fatal accidents. As an alternative, it advocated a public railway model that would increase government investment to develop further railway infrastructure and improve public services. Based on this, the union assembled a social coalition in defence of public interests against service cutbacks. Hence, the Chun Hwan Kyu leadership continued to participate in activities of and support the National Joint Committee. As the social coalition broadened the range of power resources for the union, the Railway Workers continued exerting pressure while bargaining with the government. The coalition also helped the union draw attention to its campaign and gain broader public support. Indeed, social coalition-building was indispensable to maintaining momentum for the union's campaign and retain union influence over the restructuring process.

During the second round of the campaign, membership support was on the decline, although membership participation remained high with 89.9 per cent of voter turnout. In fact, support for strike action reached 72.23 per cent during the earlier Kim Jae Kil leadership but decreased to 57.42 per cent under Chun Hwan Kyu's leadership. It was vital to retain and renew the mobilizing power of the union. Social coalition-building contributed to enhancing union mobilization capacities without which the KRWU may have been unable to force the government to negotiate.

Assessing the Strategic Effectiveness of the KRWU

As we saw in the previous section, the KRWU developed and enhanced its strategic capabilities over the course of restructuring, which allowed the union to obtain considerable concessions from government. Substantial union gains are evidenced by both the union-government agreement of 20 April 2003 and the final contents of the Basic Law on the Development of Railway Industry.

To start with, the initial union demands and the final negotiated agreement of 20 April illustrate that the KRWU succeeded in ensuring its interests (see Table 10.1). First, it forced the government to abandon the railway privatization policy. Although the Roh Moo Hyun administration had publicly announced that it would revise the privatization policy, it never officially called it off, but in the end, the government complied with union demands and stipulated the withdrawal of railway privatization in the agreement. The Railway Workers also secured remarkable gains in other areas. The agreement clearly stated that 'for safe train operation, the single-driver system will not be adopted and that it will hire additional workers because of the shortage caused by such action'. The April 20th Agreement achieved long-time union objectives when it secured a management agreement for 'the reinstatement of laid off workers' and for 'the cancellation of lawsuits against the union'. The KRWU had during the campaign against privatization called for the recruitment of new workers to supplement workforce shortages and the reinstatement of dismissed workers (KRWU 2003: 194, 195).

Table 10.1 Comparison of Union Demands and Contents of the April 20th Agreement

Issues	Union Demands	April 20th Agreement
Privatization	Withdrawal of the pending National Assembly railway privatization bill	Withdrawal of the previous privatization plan and search for alternatives considering the public nature of the railway industry
Railway Restructuring	Cancellation of the railway restructuring model based on the separation of infrastructure and operation; social consensus building for developing a public model of railway restructuring	Search for alternatives such as integrating maintenance into railway operations; pursuit of railway reform through consultation and consensus-building among interested parties.
Workforce Increase	Withdrawal of proposed single-driver system; supplementing workforce shortages by recruiting new staff	Withdrawal of single-driver system; supplementing workforce shortages by assuring 1,500 new staff by late-June; gradual recruitment of 1,358 employees by late-December for personnel required by new businesses.
Reinstatement of laid-off workers	Reinstatement of laid-off workers	New hires of 45 laid-off workers by late July.
Lawsuit	Withdrawal of lawsuits against union members	The annulment of provisional seizure of union assets/ individual salaries; annulment of damage suits

Source: KRWU (2003)

Public post-mortems of the agreement confirmed the KRWU's groundbreaking achievements. First, the union itself considered the agreement as 'the victory of railway workers'. Furthermore, the strong dissatisfaction of the conservative media with the bargaining results evidenced union success. Here are excerpts from newspaper editorials:

- 'The principle of dialogue and compromise that the government advocated degenerated into asymmetric concessions by management...The government ignored the principle and unilaterally empowered the union'. (*Chosun Ilbo*, 22 April 2003)
- 'The government set a bad precedent by subordinating itself to union pressures and by proving that the government could be pushed down by force'. (*JoongAng Ilbo* Editorial, 22 April 2003)
- 'The government had announced that it would take a firm stand against excessive union demands. But the result was the accommodation of almost all union demands'. (*Segye Ilbo* Editorial, 22 April 2003)

In short, conservative forces expressed their deep frustration with the bargaining results. Yet, the written agreement itself did not guarantee union success as employers could breach the agreement and implement decisions unilaterally. In fact, the union had entered into a strained relationship with the government after the April 20th Agreement and went on strike just two months after the agreement had been signed. Mobilization for a strike against passage of railway restructuring bills on 28 June 2003 took place immediately after Assembly member Lee Ho-Ung introduced them in the Assembly on June 9th. The KRWU considered this a violation of the agreement that promised to undertake railway reform through social consensus. It demanded postponing legislation until September on the grounds that it needed to go through an internal fine-tuning process to come up with a reasonable restructuring plan based on membership consensus. The government, however, ignored its demand and took steps to pass the legislation. The June 28th strike opposed the move, but it failed in preventing the Assembly from passing the bills. The Basic Law on the Development of the Railway Industry and the Railroad Infrastructure Act passed the Assembly's plenary session on 30 June 2003.

Nonetheless, the final contents of the bills contained major concessions from the government. They reflected union interests in many respects, evidenced by a comparison of the Ministry of Construction and Transport's proposed 2001 railway privatization bill and the final legislation of 2003. As shown in Table 10.2, with regards to railway privatization, the previous bills contained articles laying out the groundwork for gradual privatization, such as 'gradual sales of government shares to private investors' (Article 18) and 'contracting out some lines to private operators' (Article 24). The Basic Law, as enacted, deleted all these articles and eliminated the legal basis for gradual privatization. In addition, the Basic Law clarified a guarantee of employment security by stipulating 'comprehensive employment transfer' (Article 25) and 'protection of transferred workers from a deterioration in working conditions and severance pay' (Article 25).

The changes from (A) to (B) as indicated in Table 10.2 meant more than a mere modification of legal provisions. There was a fundamental difference between the two. While the proposed bill (A) was drafted to lay the foundation for the privatization of railway operations, the enacted bill (B) eliminated that very groundwork and reflected the incorporation of union interests related to employment security and working conditions, which were also beneficial to labour.

In short, the transition from (A) to (B) indicates the labour-mediated character of railway restructuring. Consequently, the KRWU utterly derailed the privatization plan and contributed to changing the shape of railway restructuring. Moreover, it also succeeded in negotiating agreements on employment security and labour-protective measures that had not been incorporated in the previous restructuring plan. The Railway Workers also prevented compulsory employment reduction. As we have seen, they called for management to abandon the single-driver system and hire new employees to make up for workforce shortages. In this process, the KRWU convincingly argued safety depended on sufficient staff levels for the safety of train operations. It also succeeded in reinstating laid-off workers. Hence, although the Ministry of Planning and Budget intended to carry out employment cuts at KNR from 1999, this process was held back by union efforts to reverse workforce shortages and prevent compulsory reductions. The result was a very modest reduction from 1999 to 2001 of 487 jobs which was accomplished through natural attrition.

These job losses were far below the targeted number of reductions set by KNR in 1999, losses of 1,506 jobs for 1999, 2,346 in 2000, and 341 in 2001 (Kang 2002).[9] These numbers contrast with other public sector restructuring cases where management implemented massive employment reductions without being significantly challenged by union.

Table 10.2 Comparison of 2001 and 2003 Railway Restructuring

	2001 Bills (A)	Finalized 2003 Bills (B)
General Direction	Establishment of an efficient private sector for railway operations based on a market economy	Pursuit of efficiency and public interests
Form of Corporation	Korean Railway Corporation. A stock company with 100% government shares that will be regulated by the Act for Structural Reform and Privatization of Public Enterprises	Public Corporation. A non-stock government-investment company regulated by Government Invested Enterprise Regulation Act
Privatization	'Gradual sales to private investors' (Article 18)	Elimination of Article 18
Contracting Out to Private Sector	Contracting out of operation and management of railway lines to private investors (Article 24)	Elimination of Article 24
Employment Protection	Not specified	– Comprehensive employment transfer (Article 25). – Protective measures against the deterioration in working conditions and severance pay (Article 25).

Source: MOCT (2001b, 2003)

9 In the mid-1990s, KNR implemented its employment reduction plan through a massive compulsory retirement of senior workers. More than 2,500 compulsory redundancies occurred in 1998 when KNR lowered the retirement age of manual workers by one year. Yet from 1999 onward KNR failed to meet its targeted reductions. The main reason for this failure was effective union opposition to the proposed employment cuts (Kang 2002: 207).

Concluding Remarks

This chapter has examined the labour-mediated process of railway restructuring in South Korea. Contrary to the expectation that countries with weak labour-integrative institutions will undergo employer-led, market-driven unilateral restructuring, the case of the KRWU shows that a union's strategic ability can make a difference in the process and outcomes of public sector restructuring. Where unions are able to mobilize countervailing power, they succeed in negotiating labour-protective agreements. Where unions lack such strategic abilities, restructuring is led by unilateral managerial decisions that erode union influence. In the latter cases, restructuring outcomes are often detrimental to labour, with deterioration in terms and conditions of employment. In short, the findings of this study assert the explanatory power of unions' strategic choice in explaining divergent outcomes. In fact, it is unlikely that restructuring outcomes will converge within the same national units because different strategic choices create substantial subnational variations. In this respect, it is noteworthy that the strategies of the KRWU contributed to its relative success even within a non-participatory institutional arrangement.

Among the findings, the strategic importance of coalition-building provides a particularly useful reference for union practice in neoliberal countries. Indeed, trade unions that have restricted participatory rights are less likely to succeed when they rely solely on traditional bargaining tactics and minimize efforts to reach out to broad social constituencies. The mobilization of society-wide support provides trade unions with power resources that complement weak bargaining power. Indeed, a number of labour researchers have connected the strategic innovations of unions to social mobilization. For them, coalition building is an effective way of expanding available resources to break through existing constraints, and trade unions are more able to revitalize themselves when they adopt social mobilization approaches (Johnston 2001; Hurd et al. 2003; Frege and Kelly 2004; Turner and Cornfield 2007). More recently, Gentile and Tarrow have argued that union success is associated with the use of a 'citizenship rights protest repertoire' in countries where labour's political and institutional categorization is weak (Gentile and Tarrow 2009). The findings of this study also support the arguments of this previous research. Indeed, the successful union campaign by the KRWU drew not only upon its political-organizational resources but also upon its ability to frame its campaign as a defence of citizenship rights to meet public needs. The union avoided being identified as pursuing narrow, economic interests and strove to encompass broad, social concerns to recruit public opinion. Coalition-building was central in mobilizing social support, which eventually contributed to an increase in bargaining power.

Yet, social coalition-building cannot be the sole component of successful union strategies. In fact, this analysis of the Railway Workers highlights three union strategic abilities: the ability to sustain high level of union vitality by educating and mobilizing members; the ability to create and multiply political channels; and the ability to build broad, social coalitions. The union developed and enhanced these three strategic capabilities despite institutional constraints. Taking advantage of its strategic capabilities, it increased and mobilized union power resources. If this case analysis provides a snapshot of social movement unionism, it does so by pointing to the importance of both internal and external solidarity. Rank-and-file mobilization is central to renewing and sustaining the vitality of trade unions. It is the fundamental basis of union cohesion. At the same time, trade unions need to transcend their narrow, sectional interests and build broad, social alliances for the defence of citizenship rights as well as public goods.

References

Batt, R., Darbishire, O. (1997). 'Institutional Determinants of Deregulation and Restructuring in Telecommunications: Britain, Germany and the United States Compared', *International Contributions to Labour Studies*, Vol. 7, 59–79.

Commission for Railway Restructuring. (2001). *The Status of Railway Restructuring (Privatization)*. July 2001 (in Korean).

Doellgast, V. (2006). 'Negotiating Flexibility: the Politics of Call Center Restructuring in the US and Germany'. Unpublished Dissertation. Cornell University, Ithaca. NY.

Ferner, A. (1988). *Governments, Managers and Industrial Relations: Public Enterprises and their Political Environment*. Oxford: Blackwell Publishers.
Ferner, A. (1994). 'The State as Employer'. In R. Hyman, A. Ferner (eds), *New Frontiers in European Industrial Relations*. Oxford: Blackwell Publishers.
Frege, C., Kelly, J. (eds) (2004). *Varieties of Unionism: Strategies for Union Revitalization in a Globalizing Economy*. Oxford: Oxford University Press.
Frost, A.C. (2000). 'Explaining Variation in Workplace Restructuring: the Role of Local Union Capabilities', *Industrial and Labor Relations Review*, 53 (4), 559–78.
Gentile, A., Tarrow, S. (2009). 'Charles Tilly, Globalization, and Labor's Citizen Rights', *European Political Science Review*, 1 (3), 1–29.
Hurd, R., Milkman, R., Turner, L. (2003). 'Reviving the American Labour Movement: Institutions and Mobilization', *European Journal of Industrial Relations*, 9 (1), 99–117.
Johnston, P. (1994). *Success While Others Fail: Social Movement Unionism and the Public Workplace*. Ithaca, NY: ILR Press.
Kang, C-H. (2002). 'The Process of Privatization in the Korean National Railroad and Its Implication for Employment Relations and Union Strategy'. Unpublished Dissertation, University of Leeds, Leeds University Business School.
Katz, H.C., Darbishire, O. (2000). *Converging Divergences: Worldwide Changes in Employment Systems*. Ithaca, NY: Cornell University Press.
Korean National Railroad (KNR). (2000a). 'The Method for Railway Restructuring and Timeline' (in Korean).
KNR. (2000b). 'Understanding the Railway Privatization' (in Korean).
Korean Railway Workers Union (KRWU). (1997). *50 Years of History of Korean Railway* (in Korean).
KRWU. (2002). 'Report on 2001 Union Activities' (in Korean).
KRWU. (2003). 'Report on 2002 Union Activities' (in Korean).
Locke, R. (1992). 'The Decline of the National Union in Italy: Lessons for Comparative Industrial Relations Theory', *Industrial and Labor Relations Review*, 45 (2), 229–49.
Ministry of Construction and Transport (MOCT). (2000). 'The Status of Railway Restructuring' (in Korean).
MOCT. (2001a). 'The Basic Scheme of Railway Restructuring' (in Korean).
MOCT. (2001b). 'The Basic Law on the Development and Restructuring of Railway Industry' (in Korean).
MOCT. (2003). 'The Basic Law on the Development of Railway Industry' (in Korean).
Planning and Budget Committee (PBC). (1998). 'The Second Plan for Privatization and Management Reform of Public Enterprises', 4 August 1998 (in Korean).

Thelen, K. (2001). 'Varieties of Labor Politics in the Developed Democracies'. In P. Hall, D. Soskice (eds), *Varieties of Capitalism*. New York: Cambridge University Press.
Turner, L. (1991). *Democracy at Work: Changing World Markets and the Future of Labor Unions*. Ithaca, NY: Cornell University Press.
Turner, L., Cornfield, D. (eds) (2007). *Labor in the New Urban Battlegrounds: Local Solidarity in a Global Economy*. Ithaca, NY: Cornell University Press.

HIROHIKO TAKASU

11 The Formation of a Region-based Amalgamated Union Movement and Its Possibilities[1]

Introduction

The aim of this chapter is to describe the history of the region-based amalgamated union [*Chiiki Godoroso*] movement in the post-World War II era in Japan and to consider its possibilities and limitations and the clues it holds for the revitalization of the Japanese labour movement. Before explaining what region-based amalgamated unions are, I will review the better-known enterprise-based unions, which have had a leading role in the Japanese labour movement throughout the post-World War II era. The vast majority of trade unions in post-war Japan have been enterprise-based unions that organize workers by individual enterprises or workplaces (Shirai 1986: 98; Shirai 1979). Industrial unions or industrial labour organizations are federations of these enterprise-based unions in each industry. The federations come together to form national confederations such as Rengo (Japanese Trade Union Confederation) and Zenroren (National Confederation of Trade Unions). Generally, it is the enterprise-based unions rather than industrial federations that have the right to bargain collectively, give strike orders and reach agreements with the employer. Thus, one of the characteristics of Japanese trade unions is that industrial federations seldom negotiate directly with the employers on labour issues. The main function of industrial federations and national confederations has been to coordinate strategies, e.g., for the Annual Spring Labour Offensive [*Shunto*], to provide information to

1 This chapter, originally written in Japanese, was translated by Seiichi Yamasaki.

enterprise-based unions and to formulate political demands for industrial, social and labour policy and to work to realize those demands.

Enterprise-based unions are compatible with the employment practices known as Japanese-style management, an internal labour market based on long-term employment and a seniority-based wage system for regular employees (Shirai 1986: 101–2; 1979: 34–41). Therefore, most members of enterprise-based unions are regular workers and, until recently, these unions were inactive in organizing irregular workers, such as temporary, contract, part-time and dispatched workers. Nor did they organize workers in subsidiary or subcontracting companies. Consequently, organizing irregular workers and workers in the small- and medium-sized enterprises (hereafter SME) has lagged behind.

Alongside the enterprise unions, there have always been region-based amalgamated unions, even though their names and organizing targets have changed over the years. Region-based amalgamated unions organize individual workers in different enterprises in a certain area, but they also allow affiliation of enterprise-based unions. Half a century ago, labour law scholar Inejiro Numata defined a region-based amalgamated union as 'a cross-enterprise regional organization of SME workers, aiming to be an entity union with an individual affiliation basis'. 'But' he observed, 'the realities are diverse' (Numata 1963: 3).

Workers in SMEs and irregular workers such as temporary, part-time, fixed-term contract and dispatched workers are outside the internal labour market of a typical large company with its long-term employment and seniority-based wage. Instead they must find work in a local external labour market characterized by low wages and unstable working conditions. Region-based amalgamated unions, which organize individual workers from different enterprises in a given region, have offered an effective means to organize these workers.

From an international comparison perspective, these region-based amalgamated unions and especially the 'community union' variant (more on this below) are quite similar to worker centres in the United States. The only difference is that region-based amalgamated unions have the right to conduct collective bargaining. According to Japan's Trade Union Law, even if a union organizes only one worker in an enterprise, the employer has to bargain with the union. Thus, Japan's region-based amalgamated unions can function as minority unions. These unions have welcomed individual members and non-majority groups of workers because the unions seek to improve the working conditions in the enterprise and organize the majority of workers there. Similarly, these unions have negotiated on behalf of the workers who join the union after being dismissed. If they manage to reverse the dismissal and win reinstatement, they have created an opportunity to organize other workers in the workplace.

Thus, region-based amalgamated unions have been an efficient tool for organizing workers in SMEs, and irregular workers generally. Looking back at the history of the Japanese labour movement, various types of region-based amalgamated unions have emerged and declined, according to circumstances.

Roughly speaking, we can say there are two types of region-based amalgamated unions. One is the type created as a policy of the national confederations. The earliest case is in the 1950s. Sohyo (General Council of Trade Unions of Japan), the leftist national confederation, collected donations from its members to hire over 300 organizers who were assigned to local organizations where they devoted themselves to organizing workers in the SME sector. Region-based amalgamated unions of this type sprang up in various areas culminating in the formation of Sohyo's National Union of General Workers (NUGW, Sohyo Zenkoku Ippan Rodokumiai), which grew to over 130,000 members in the 1970s. In the 1980s, though, while the movement to unify national confederations gained power under the influence of the large enterprise unions, the NUGW lost momentum. After the formation of Rengo in 1989, the NUGW split into three streams (see below).

The second type of region-based amalgamated unions is the community union that emerged in mid-1980s, 30 years after the formation of the NUGW. From the late 1980s to early 1990s, region-based amalgamated unions sprang up nationwide, naming themselves 'Tokyo Yunion' or 'Fukuoka Yunion', after the region in which they were located, instead of 'Rodo Kumiai', the standard Japanese term for a trade union. The new name 'Yunion' sounded fresh and approachable to unorganized workers. These unions prioritized labour counselling for unorganized workers and organizing irregular workers. Since Sohyo's local organizations were dissolved after the formation of Rengo in 1989, community unions have become the focal point of efforts to build region-based labour movements.

The national confederations started to pay attention to the second type of region-based amalgamated union, the community union, as a means to organize the unorganized. In 1996, the main national confederation, Rengo, adopted a policy of forming regional unions [*Chiiki Yunion*] in each prefecture, and in 2002, Zenroren, the national confederation friendly with the Japanese Communist Party also adopted a policy of forming local unions [*Rokaru Yunion*]. Although the region-based amalgamated unions were not part of the main stream of the Japanese labour movement, they acted as intermediaries between unorganized workers and the labour movement and created diverse movements.

This chapter describes the formation process and characteristics of the NUGW, the community unions, and the region-based amalgamated unions established by the existing national confederations (Rengo and Zenroren). Finally, the chapter will briefly examine the challenges and possibilities for region-based amalgamated unions. This chapter includes materials from participatory observation from 1990 to 2003 when I was an organizer and later general secretary of NUGW Tokyo South. I also draw on interviews with various informants and previous studies and other information.

Formation and Decline of the NUGW

'Chutai' Organizer

The post-war upsurge in the Japanese labour movement reached its peak in 1949 when union density was estimated at 55.8 per cent. The combination of the Red Purge and austerity measures under the Dodge Line[2] led to a rapid decline in union density to 38.2 per cent in 1953. Mass dismiss-

2 Joseph Dodge was a chairman of the Bank of Detroit and served as an economic advisor to the post-war Japanese Government. He drafted a financial and monetary

als were rampant in the public sector and large enterprises, where union density was high. Unions in these sectors fought back but were defeated or suffered severe setbacks (Hyodo 2006: 8–9). Through the post-war economic recovery process, the 'dual structure' of the contemporary economy was established; the wage disparity between the large enterprises and the unorganized SMEs widened and sweatshop conditions and the violation of workers' human rights in the latter lingered. In 1954, however, an outburst of 'human rights disputes' in the Omi Silk Mill (Omi Kenshi), stock exchanges, local banks and other SMEs brought public attention to the conditions of SME workers, who had been left behind in the 10 year post-war recovery.

The left-wing national confederation, Sohyo,[3] the largest labour confederation at the time, adopted 'Measures for the SMEs and an Action Program for Workers' Struggle' at its 5th Annual General Meeting held in 1954, and at its 6th Annual General Meeting the following year, outlined a policy for organizing SME workers. The main contents of the policy were: '(1) to address the unorganized workers in SMEs, amalgamated unions will be set up in regions and districts, (2) region-based amalgamated unions will form a district committee at the level of Sohyo's district (prefecture-level) labour councils, and district committees will try to form a national committee in turn, and (3) when there is a need to reorganize region-based amalgamated unions, they will be reorganized along industrial lines' (Sohyo 1986: 294).

---

contraction policy called the 'Dodge Line', which succeeded in controlling inflation. But it led to bankruptcies and mass dismissals, due to the ensuing deflation.

3 In the late-1940s after the World War, the JCP affiliated 'Sanbetsu Kaigi' (Congress of Industrial Unions of Japan) was the main national confederation but was nearly annihilated by the Red Purge and mass dismissals of 1949 and 1950. Unions critical of JCP domination formed Sohyo in 1950 with aid from the US occupation. The leadership of Sohyo was in the hands of the non-JCP left (the leftwing of the JSP) and it became the mainstream of the Japanese labour movement. After the 1960s, large enterprise-based unions adopted a labour-management cooperative line and opted to switch their affiliation from Sohyo to the rightwing confederation Domei (Japanese Confederation of Labour). Thereafter, Sohyo remained as a national confederation centred in the public sector. The unification of labour by large enterprise-based unions brought about the dissolution of Sohyo in 1989.

In 1956, Sohyo started to levy a compulsory donation of ¥3 for every member to hire 90 SME organizers (*Chutai* [literally 'in charge of SMEs'] organizer) and to dispatch them to its district and region organizations all over the country. In 1959, it approved a donation of ¥50 per member, and the number of regional organizers and national organizers in Sohyo was increased to 263. These organizers, mostly in their twenties and thirties, were dispatched to district labour councils [*Chi-Kenpyo*] or to regional labour councils [*Chikuro*])[4] where they organized the unorganized into region-based amalgamated unions. Thus, with unions in the public sector and big enterprise unions providing money and human resources, a full-scale effort to organize SME workers at the local level started (Numata 1963: 1–12; Hamamura 2003: 20–1; Hyodo 2006: 17–19; Okamura 1976: 216–27; Matsui 2010: 14–18, 23–40; Watanabe 2003, 171–2; Iwai 1960: 15–21; Takeyama 1981: 174–209).

Formation and Development of the NUGW – A Unified Union Movement

In 1955, under the direction of Sohyo, region-based amalgamated unions across the nation gathered to form a 'National Liaison Committee of General Amalgamated Unions' (NUGW). At that time, Sohyo was trying

4 *Chi-Kenpyo* is an abbreviated name for district labour councils at the prefectural level and *Chikuro* for regional labour councils at the city and county level. These organizations included not only Sohyo affiliates but also enterprise-based unions and regional organizations of industrial federations affiliated to Churitsuroren, a third national confederation, and independent enterprise-based unions not affiliated to any federation or confederation. These district and regional organizations had no institutional relations with Sohyo, but they played the role of district and regional organizations of Sohyo in actual practice. Most of the *Chi-Kenpyo* and *Chikuro* were dissolved after the formation of Rengo, but some changed names such as Peace Centre or Regional Labour Council Centre to carry on the issues not taken up by Rengo. A small number of these district/regional organizations have continued to exist as regional organizations of Zenroren or independent organizations not affiliated to Rengo. *Chi-Kenpyo* is equivalent to an AFL-CIO state federation in the United States and *Chikuro* is equivalent to a Central Labour Council.

to strengthen its regional representation structures by setting up 1,000 regional labour councils, which were to help *chutai* organizers organize the unorganized and support the regional structure of the NUGW (Matsui 2010: 31–8).

In 1960, the 6th Annual General Meeting of the NUGW resolved to 'change its name to Sohyo NUGW' and set a goal of 'making the union a general amalgamated union to which individual workers can affiliate, with its structure consisting of unified regional organizations' (Numata 1963: 2). By centralizing collective bargaining, strike orders, the ability to finalize agreements and authority over dues collection, strike and mutual aid funds at the district (prefectural level) headquarters, Sohyo NUGW aimed to break away from '*Chusho-Roren*' type structures, i.e., the federation of enterprise-based union locals in SMEs. In this way, the NUGW set up a policy to restructure itself into a 'unified union' [*toitsu roso*] in which members were affiliated directly and not through enterprise-based unions.

The organizers of the NUGW were young activists in their twenties and thirties and were used to learning from each other across the political barriers that existed between the Japan Communist Party (JCP) and the Japan Socialist Party (JSP). In December 1960, learning from the experiences of unified unions, such as the Hiroshima General Workers' Union and the Kochi General Workers' Union (both affiliated with the JCP), activists in Tokyo set up a JSP-affiliated Eastern General Unified Union. Similar unified unions were formed in and around Tokyo. But the mainstream of the NUGW unions remained a mixture of federations of enterprise-based locals and individually-affiliated members. It was difficult for region-based amalgamated unions, many of which had started as federations of enterprise-based locals, to overcome the resistance from enterprise-based locals and to transform themselves into unified unions.

On 8 April 1964, on the eve of a strike planned by the Federation of Public Corporation and Government Employees Unions, the JCP issued a statement appealing to the union to cancel the strike. The antagonism between the JSP-affiliated mainstream of Sohyo and the JCP-affiliated opposition became decisive. The NUGW bore the brunt of the crisis as internal conflict between JCP-affiliated members and JSP-affiliated members became irreparable. In Tokyo, two regional organizations came into being when the Eastern General Unified Workers' Union withdrew from the Tokyo District Headquarters, which was dominated by the JCP, and affiliated directly with the NUGW national headquarters. Similar splits followed in other districts. In this way, the unified union movement stopped its practice of learning and working across the political divides, and the NUGW national headquarters ceased to function effectively (Matsui 2010: 41–109; Watanabe 2003: 170–82; NUGW Thirtieth Anniversary Committee 1985: 139–54).

Nevertheless, the NUGW continued its effort to organize the unorganized with the support of district and regional labour councils and through the activities of *chutai* organizers. Its membership grew throughout the 1960s and the first half of the 1970s. Former student activists also joined the movement to organize the unorganized. The NUGW was involved in an increasing number of labour disputes in SMEs and scored many organizing victories in this sector, bringing the movement and organization to its height. Union membership grew from 65,000 in 1960 to over 100,000 in 1964 and 139,000 in 1975 (Takasu 1995; NUGW Thirtieth Anniversary Committee 1985: 85; interviews with Keiichi Tajima, 9 December 2009, 21 January 2010; interview with Ichiro Endo, 21 January 2010).

Formation of Rengo – Split and Downfall of the NUGW

From the 1960s to the 1970s, the leadership of the large enterprise union movement gradually fell into the hands of the Japan Council of Metal Workers' Unions (IMF-JC) and the Japanese Confederation of Labour (Domei), both of which tended towards labour-management cooperation. Sohyo, whose main members were public sector unions, gradually lost power. The regional organizer system became a burden to Sohyo, so the number of organizers fell off in the 1970s from its peak of 338 in 1967. Also, there were many cases where organizers became bogged down in the every-day business of district and regional labour councils rather than focused on new organizing (Okamura 1976: 237–40; Hamamura 2003: 25; Hyodo 2006: 20–1).

When the large enterprise unions led the unification of the national confederations to form Rengo in 1989, the NUGW's regional organizations chose sides and split three ways: the Rengo-affiliated NUGW, Zenroren NUGW, and the Zenrokyo-affiliated National Council of NUGW.[5] Some regional organizations remained neutral (interview with Keiichi Tajima, 9 December 2009). Due to the process of restructuring of regional organizations that followed the formation of Rengo, most district and regional labour councils that supported the NUGW either dissolved or lost influence, and the power of the NUGW movement dissipated. The Rengo-affiliated NUGW in particular suffered a drastic decline in membership. The union merged with the All Japan Prefectural and Municipal Workers Union (Jichiro) in 2006 and reorganized as the NUGW Council of Jichiro. The present membership of the Council is approximately 30,000 (interviews with Keiichi Tajima, 9 December 2009, 21 January 2010). Zenroren NUGW has a membership of 27,000 (2009 Labour Union Basic Survey) and the Zenrokyo-affiliated National Council of NUGW has 10,000 members (interview with Ichiro Endo, 21 January 2010). The estimated membership of regional organizations that withdrew from the NUGW and joined the Community Union National Network (the CUNN, see below) is 4,500.

The NUGW movement declined for the following reasons: (1) Sohyo and the regional and district labour councils that had supported the NUGW movement declined; (2) antagonisms between political tendencies in the NUGW, especially between the JCP and the JSP, weakened the NUGW headquarters and led to the post-Rengo three-way split; (3) activities of the NUGW depended on the initiative of a limited number of experienced organizers, which made a generational change among organizers difficult; (4) the 'principle of industrial reorganization' forced affiliate unions to withdraw from the NUGW and move to other industrial unions and pressured enterprise-based locals to leave the NUGW to join federations

5 Zenrokyo was formed in 1989 as a 'joint struggle organization' of mainly non-JCP left unions (leftwing JSP-affiliated and independent unions) opposed to the formation of Rengo.

of company unions (interview with Keiichi Tajima, 9 December 2009); (5) SME unions proved difficult to maintain due to vulnerability of the businesses, high turnover of workers, and anti-union tendencies of management, all of which resulted in frequent labour disputes and an inability to establish stable labour-management relations (interview with Keiichi Tajima, 9 December 2009); and (6) a failure to cope effectively with the changing industrial structures after the 1973 oil crisis (especially the decline of small- and medium-sized manufacturing industry and the expansion of tertiary industry) and changes in the labour market (e.g., the increase of irregular workers, especially women part-time workers).

Though the NUGW declined, regional labour councils across the nation started labour counselling activity in the 1980s, and a new type of region-based amalgamated union, 'Yunion', was formed as a bargaining agent for unorganized workers who came for labour counselling. These are the 'community unions' which are addressed in the next section. Community unions can be said to be a response by the region-based labour movement to the causes that triggered the downfall of the NUGW movement. Besides labour counselling, regional organizations of the NUGW started to organize irregular workers and workers in the tertiary industry. These organizations changed their style of activity and transformed themselves into community unions. The following section will deal with the community union movement together with the subsequent developments of the NUGW movement.

Community Unions – a New Type of Region-based Amalgamated Unions[6]

The Emergence and Development of Community Unions

In the wake of the oil crisis in 1973, manufacturing streamlined its workforce and the weight of the tertiary service industry began to rise. Enterprises actively took advantage of women part-time workers as a low-wage and easily dispensable workforce. The proportion of short-hour (below 35 hours per week) women workers in non-agriculture and non-forestry industries increased from 12.2 per cent in 1970 to 19.3 per cent in 1980 and rose to 27.9 per cent in 1990 (Labour Force Survey). In the meantime, union density, which had been steady at around 35 per cent from the mid-1950s, began its decline in 1975, dropping to 31.1 per cent in 1980 and to 25.4 per cent in 1990 (see Table A.4 in the Appendix). During the 1980s' national confederation unification movement, organizers and activists in the district and regional labour councils expressed profound anxiety about the future of the region-based labour movement. They feared that the new national confederation might not carry on the region-based labour movement and its institutions; organizers tried to revitalize the labour movement at the local community level.

In 1981, the Katsushika-ward Labour Union Council and the Nankatsu NUGW in Eastern Tokyo began a hotline for part-time workers called 'Part 110',[7] which triggered a nationwide expansion of labour counselling activity. Not only part-time workers, but other workers came to consult, and the number of consultations rose. Many of the problems were not resolved on the phone. Issues related to contingent workers, such as part-time and contracted-out workers, were not being addressed by the existing enterprise-based unions. Collective bargaining rights were effectively

6 See Takasu 2010b for details on the formation and development of community unions.

7 'Part 110' means an emergency call service for part-time workers. '110' is an emergency phone number, equivalent to 911 in the United States.

employed in tackling these issues without relying on existing unions, and small unions were set up to facilitate collective bargaining. Regional labour councils began forming new region-based amalgamated unions. In 1983 Union Higoro and the Ishikawa Workers' Union were formed, followed by the Edogawa Union in 1984. This was the birth of a new region-based amalgamated union movement, which Ikuro Takagi, a prominent labour economist, later named 'community unions'. Amidst the dissolution and decline of district and regional labour councils that accompanied the formation of Rengo, community unions were set up across the nation as a new institution for the region-based labour movement. In 1989, activists from the community unions gathered to hold the first Community Union National Exchange Meeting and the Community Union National Network (the CUNN) was formed in 1990 (Obata 1993; Obata 2003a, 2003b; Mizutani 2003; Nagamine 2003; Takagi 2000; Community Union Study Group 1988).

The number of unions affiliated with the CUNN was 31 in December 1987, 64 in August 1993 and currently is 72 in 30 prefectures with a total membership of approximately 15,000 (as of November 2010) (Community Union Study Group 1988: 236; CUNN 1993: 246–7; interview with Tetsufumi Okamoto, 21 January 2010).

Characteristics of Community Unions

Community unions came from three main sources (Takagi 2000: 55; Obata 2003ab). Some were formed on the basis of regional labour councils (e.g. the Edogawa Union, the Kobe Workers' Union, the Mukogawa Union, Union Fukuoka [currently Rengo Fukuoka Union]). These community unions had to seek a new basis after the dissolution and decline of the regional labour councils. Others were formed as a result of the secession of regional organizations from the NUGW (e.g., the Sapporo General Union [Sapporo Chiiki Roso], the Tokyo Union, Union Mie). These unions have enterprise-based locals in addition to individually-affiliated members and are larger in size than other community unions. Finally, community unions have also arisen from the citizens' movement and the women's movement. (e.g., Hokusetsu Community Union, Women's Union Kanagawa).

These community unions have different organizational characteristics and activities, due to their different origins. The CUNN conducted a survey of 44 community unions in 26 prefectures in 2006 and published the findings in its newsletter under the title 'This is the typical image of a union in 2006' (CUNN 2006: 14):

> The union was established in 1992 and currently has 208 members, of whom 60 per cent are male and 40 per cent female. The membership has increased since last year. There are 8 locals, and 35 per cent of the members belong to locals. Thirty-five per cent of the members are irregular workers, of which 10 per cent are part-timers, and 10 per cent are dispatched workers. The union has 15 migrant worker members. The initiation fee is ¥3,019, union dues are ¥1,128 per month, and mutual aid fund fees are ¥569 per month. The annual budget is ¥6.82 million with one paid staff member. The union does not have an independent office, but shares an office. There are 13 executive committee members, who meet once a month. A newsletter to connect the union and members is published monthly. The union has a website and is planning to have a mailing list on the internet.

In summary, a typical community union has a membership of several dozen to several hundred, one paid full-time staff member and union dues of ¥1,000 per month per member. It is quite vulnerable, its continued existence depending on the passion and devotion of its staff and volunteers. Therefore, community unions try to form networks in the community so that they can receive the support and cooperation of other unions and citizens' movements.

Organizing in New Fields

In the 1990s, with the burst of the bubble economy and the prolonged recession, organizing in new fields took place mainly through labour counselling. Since the late 1980s, the number of newcomer migrant workers had grown rapidly. NUGW Tokyo South started organizing language teachers with proper visas in the mid-1970s. In the early 1990s, Zentoitsu Union and the Kanagawa City Union embarked on organizing undocumented or overstaying migrant workers (from South Asia, Korea and Africa) in the hundreds. This was followed by organizing South American workers of Japanese descent (from Brazil and Peru, for example) and foreign trainees and technical interns. Efforts to organize migrant workers spread across the nation. The unions organizing migrant workers and support organizations joined together to establish the Solidarity Network with Migrants Japan (Ijuren) in 1997.

Women and managerial workers who had been the target of retrenchment were the second new field of organizing. In the mid-1990s, the Tokyo Managers' Union and the Women's Union Tokyo were set up in NUGW Tokyo and later became independent. The managers' unions and women's unions were also established in cities other than Tokyo (see Endo in this volume).

The third was the young workers movement. From the late 1990s to 2000s, jobs held by young workers became increasingly non-regular because companies refrained from hiring regular workers. As a reaction to this tendency, the General Union for Young Workers in Tokyo (Shutoken Seinen Yunion) was set up in 2000, followed by the Part-timer, Arbeiter, Freeter & Foreign Worker Union (Freeter Zenpan Roso) and the Dispatched Workers' Union (Haken Yunion). These unions are composed mainly of young workers and are very active to date.

The Formation of Networks, Leading to Hakenmura

The formation of the Community Union National Network (the CUNN) was the beginning of a network-type movement. Unlike conventional trade union organizations, its executive committee has no hierarchical power over its local organizations. Independent affiliate unions form a loose network and support and exchange experiences with each other through the CUNN's annual national exchange meeting and other activities.

During the 1990s, community unions and other region-based amalgamated unions set up many issue-oriented networks: the Temporary Agency Workers' Network, Part-timers' Study Group for Women's Working Life, Equal Opportunity Law Network and Fixed-term Contract Workers' Right Network, together with labour lawyers, labour researchers and labour-related NGOs. These four networks launched a National Campaign to Stop Revision of the Labour Standards Law, spearheaded by non-regular workers themselves in 1997 and 1998. The three national confederations, Rengo, Zenroren and Zenrokyo, sent representatives and solidarity messages to Campaign rallies and meetings: this was the first instance, after the formation of Rengo, of different political streams in the labour movement converging on a common space, and it served as a model for the network-type movements that followed (Takasu 2002; Takasu 1998).

In October 2007, the Anti-Poverty Network was established to 'link for a humane life'. Its constituents included dispatched and contract workers, freeters,[8] multiple debtors, single-mothers, domestic violence victims, disabled people and patients, homeless people, migrant workers, pensioners, recipients of welfare benefits and supporters of these people, such as lawyers, judicial scriveners (*shiho shoshi*) and trade unionists. Against the backdrop of spreading poverty and social disparity in the late 2000s, the Anti-Poverty Network served as a catalyst for the convergence of the region-based amalgamated union movement and the anti-poverty movement (Yuasa 2008; Yuasa 2009; Interview with Makoto Kawazoe, 9 March 2009; interview with Shigeru Ojima, 6 April 2009; interview with Keiichi Ito, 15 April 2009; interviews with Katsuyasu Iida, 17 February and 2 May 2009; interview with Ichiro Endo, 16 February 2009).

In autumn 2008, following the Lehman Shock, there was a burst of dispatched workers and non-regular workers in the export-dependent production industries, especially the auto industry, who lost their jobs. Region-based amalgamated unions and other unions involved in labour counselling started to realize that something quite different was going to happen towards the end of that year. In consultation with the Anti-Poverty Network, they decided to put up a year-end emergency camp for the unemployed [*Toshikoshi Hakenmura*] in Hibiya Park, right in front of the Ministry of Heath, Labour and Welfare building, from 31 December to 5 January, when government offices and employment security offices would be closed. (Utsunomiya 2009; Toshikoshi Hakenmura Jikkoiinkai 2009: 204).

8 Reiko Kosugi (2005: 6) defines freeters as 'youth who do not find employment as *sei-shain* (full-time tenured employees) and work in untenured short-term and/or part-time jobs after leaving school (either by graduation or by dropping out)'.

That more than 500 workers came to the camp seeking shelter, made visible how serious it was for the workers to lose both their jobs and their homes at once, and how weak the safety net was. Labour counselling up to that point had proven inadequate to cope with this grave situation. What the out-of-work needed in addition to labour consultation was livelihood counselling to address welfare benefits, multiple debt and housing problems. These needs led to the convergence of labour and social movements, especially the anti-poverty movement. An executive committee of anonymous members organized the camp; the committee's representative was Makoto Yuasa, the director of the Anti-Poverty Network and unaffiliated with any political stream in the labour movement. Consequently, Rengo, Zenroren and Zenrokyo could direct money and human resources to the effort, and grass-roots and social movement activists, ordinary workers, students and citizens could cooperate and volunteer to support the end-of-year/new year camp.

It was also significant that the various streams of the labour movement and other social movements were able to work together on a common project, everyone sharing tasks for which they were best suited. This was the first time since the formation of Rengo 20 years earlier that the labour movement cooperated on such a large scale with social movements.

In this way, the region-based amalgamated union movement with community unions at its centre converged with the social movements, particularly the anti-poverty movement, and, by involving national confederations, brought about the *Hakenmura* in the 2008 year-end. This was a huge breakthrough and an important turning point for the region-based amalgamated unions and the community union movement. The driving force for the breakthrough was labour counselling and the dire situation of the workers who lost their jobs and housing simultaneously and sought help at the camp.

The following figure (Figure 11.1) depicts the structure of the aforementioned movements. Rengo, Zenroren, Zenrokyo, community unions, region-based amalgamated unions, and various social movements are connected through the Anti-Poverty Network and *Hakenmura* (Takasu 2010a).

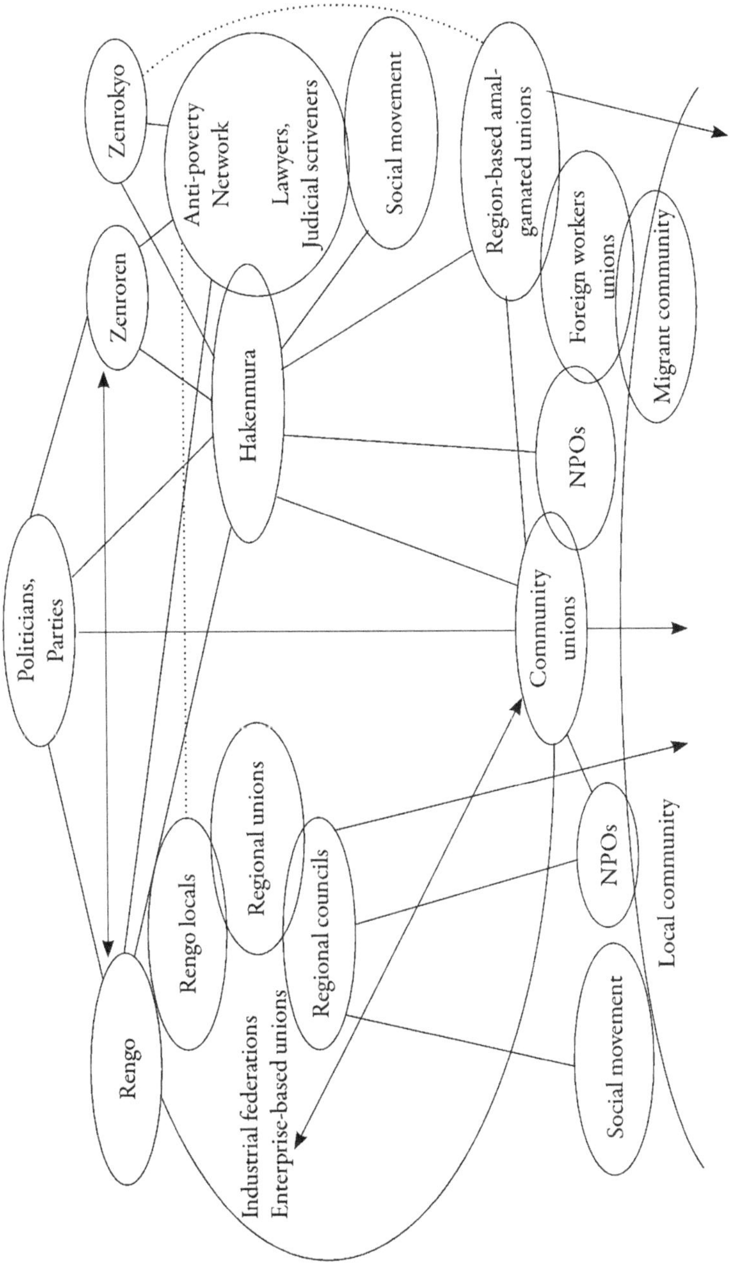

Figure 11.1 Rengo, Zenroren, Zenrokyo, community unions, region-based amalgamated unions, and various social movements were connected through Anti-poverty Network and Hakenmura in the 2008 year-end.

National Confederations and Regional (Local) Unions

In 1989, four confederations of labour merged to form Rengo. The merger was led by the large enterprise unions. But trade unions friendly with the JCP formed Zenroren, and leftwing JSP-affiliated unions and independent unions formed Zenrokyo, resulting in a new split of the labour front.[9]

In post-bubble mid-1990s, the depression deepened, forcing enterprises to retrench further, cutting the number of regular workers drastically and increasing the number of irregular workers. Neoliberal deregulation policies were pursued and labour laws were deregulated. The unemployment rate rose to 5 per cent in 2001. Union density continued to fall (from 26.1 per cent in 1989 to 24.0 per cent in 1995) and from 1995 the absolute number of union members began to fall (see Table A.3 and A.4 in the Appendix). The national confederations started new organizing drives to cope with these situations.

Rengo and its Regional Unions[10]

RENGO'S ORGANIZING DRIVE

Initially, Rengo intended to dissolve the regional labour councils and district labour councils that had formed the regional base of the Sohyo-led labour movement, and shift to an industry-oriented movement. Faced with decreasing membership, though, Rengo leadership considered creating some sort of institutions at the local level that could conduct organizing drives. Rengo's regional councils (local organizations at the city and district

9 The membership of Rengo in 1990 was 7,641,000 and Zenroren 835,000 (1,340,000 according to a survey of Zenroren Organizing Department) and Zenrokyo 290,000. The total number of union members was 12,264,000 at the time (Labor Union Basic Survey 1990).

10 See Takasu 2010b for details on Rengo organizing drives and its regional unions.

level, equivalent to Sohyo's erstwhile regional labour councils) were forbidden to collect their own dues and many of them had no independent office or full-time staff, making them unsuitable for conducting organizing drives. Instead, Rengo looked to the model of community unions.

In 1996, Rengo decided to set up regional unions at the level of its prefectural organizations (organizations equivalent to the district labour councils of the Sohyo era and to state federations in the United States). Rengo tried to persuade the leaders of industrial unions who opposed the move by saying, 'While holding to the industrial affiliation principle, Rengo has to have many windows on organizing. Regional unions are a temporary landing on the way to industrial affiliation' (interviews with Hitoshi Takahashi, 17 December 2008 and 21 April 2009). Rengo set a concrete organizing target for the industrial federations and prefectural Rengo organizations (1.1 million new members in three years) and tried to accomplish it by setting up an organizing drive subsidy and by clarifying the role and jurisdiction of each organization, signalling a change from the principle that organizing was the job of industrial federations: now Rengo headquarters and its prefectural organizations would be actively engaged in organizing.

But progress was slow, so Rengo inaugurated a free telephone service for labour counselling and union organizing and decided to create a 'staff advisor' position based on new funding measures in 1998. The term 'organizer' was avoided because it was reminiscent of the *chutai* organizers of Sohyo. These staff advisors were retirees in their 60s, since regular staff would be too costly. As of September 2009, two advisors were assigned to Rengo headquarters and 92 advisors to prefectural organizations, respectively. Thus, a system to organize the unorganized at the prefectural level was set up, enabling Rengo to advance from labour counselling to organizing (Hayakawa 2006: 73–83; interviews with Hitoshi Takahashi, 17 December 2008 and 21 April 2009).

In the late 1990s, Rengo sought to change its style of action from that based on the large-enterprise unions. In its 2001 Biannual General Meeting proceedings and a report titled '21st Century Vision: Rengo Movement Opening Up the 21st Century', Rengo acknowledged the crisis of the trade union movement and the limitations of enterprise-based unions. Rengo aimed at a 'welfare society based on labour' as an alternative to an enterprise-centred society and market ideology, and at building 'a social labour movement representing all the working people in an alliance with NPOs and civic groups'. Thus, at least on paper, a change of strategy took place.

In 2005, Rengo introduced a plan to set up '100 model regional councils' with the aim of achieving a 'Rengo movement based in the local community and close to the people' and allocated funds for the policy. Four hundred and eighty-one regional councils across the nation were reorganized and consolidated, and subsidies were given to 106 of them for the funding of an officer and a staff person to convert the regional councils into bases for labour-livelihood counselling and union organizing, in cooperation with local NPOs and social movement groups. In its 10th Biannual General Meeting, Rengo initiated a Centre for Non-Regular Employment (Hiseiki Rodo Senta) for 'the solidarity of all workers'. The Centre was an attempt by the confederation to carry out a kind of 'social movement unionism', based on the twin strategies of region-based labour movements and of solidarity campaigns of all workers, especially non-regular workers. In late 2008, Rengo joined the *Hakenmura* movement. In 2009, a decision was made to add 200 regional councils to the original 106 to serve as a base for local organizing. In addition, Rengo raised dues to support that effort, from the present ¥50 to ¥55 (per month per member) in January 2011 to ¥60 in January 2012 (Takahashi 2008; Tatsui 2008; interview with Yoji Tatsui, 9 December 2009; interviews with Toshio Ootsuka, 25 February and 30 March 2009; interviews with Hitoshi Takahashi, 17 December 2008 and 21 April 2009; interview with Takuya Seryu, 18 December 2008). As a result of these measures, union density stabilized and grew slightly (from 18.1 per cent in 2008 to 18.5 per cent in 2009).

OVERVIEW OF RENGO REGIONAL UNIONS

Rengo adopted a policy to set up regional unions in 1996 through its prefectural organizations. According to the 11th Rengo Regular General Meeting proceedings, as of September 2009 45 prefectural organizations had organized regional unions, representing 15,500 members. The typical membership of a regional union is 344, slightly larger than that of the community unions affiliated with the CUNN. Rengo Union Tokyo (with a membership of 4,220 from 90 enterprise-based unions [locals] and 110 individual affiliation members) and Rengo Hokkaido Regional Union (3,133 members) are by far the largest regional unions, constituting more than half of the total membership. They are followed by 6 unions with memberships between 500 and 1,000. The rest are far smaller: 17 unions with 100 to 300 members and 20 unions with fewer than 100 members.

Rengo used most of the regional unions for the purpose of collective bargaining on behalf of individual affiliated members and for facilitating affiliation of small-sized enterprise unions formed through labour counselling to Rengo's prefectural organizations. Not many regional unions are active in typical community union-type activities such as solidarity actions and exchange programs, with the exception of those unions in Sapporo, Fukuoka, Miyazaki and Kagoshima.

Zenroren and Its Local Unions[11]

ZENROREN AND ITS ORGANIZING DRIVE POLICY

Trade unions friendly with the JCP formed Zenroren in 1989 (1.34 million members according to a survey by the Zenroren Organizing Department) to oppose the dissolution of Sohyo and the formation of Rengo. Two thirds of Zenroren's affiliated unions represent state and local government employees and other public service sector workers in schools and hospitals, and the rest are industrial organizations representing workers in the SME sector.

The downsizing of regular public employees starting in the late 1990s led Zenroren's membership to fall rapidly from the peak it reached in 1998. Faced with this crisis, Zenroren formulated a new organizing drive policy in 2002. From July 2004 to July 2007, it drew on a three-year Organizing Drive Fund, posted 12 organizers to various regional blocs and formed local unions. Though these organizers were posted for only three years,

11 See Takasu 2010b for details on Zenroren organizing drives and its local unions.

they had positive effects on Zenroren. In 2008, the confederation allocated monies to an Organizing Drive Budget in place of the temporary Fund and set up a Contingent Workers' Action Centre (CWAC, Hiseiki Koyo Rodosha Zenkoku Senta). It was also decided that 'more than 20 per cent of (Zenroren's) budget should be allocated to organizing'. From the autumn of 2008, Zenroren's prefectural federations [*chiho soshiki*], its local unions, and the All Japan Metal and Information Machinery Workers' Union (JMIU, one of its affiliates) counselled dismissed dispatch and fixed-term workers. At year's end, in 2008, Zenroren actively supported the *Hakenmura*. This experience inspired the prefectural federations to engage in labour-and-livelihood counselling, resulting in rapid membership growth in the local unions.

Zenroren had 1.2 million members in 2009, slightly less than the previous year. The confederation has managed to stop the decline in membership by allocating funds for organizing and by strenuous organizing efforts, despite disadvantageous factors such as the reduction of regular public service workers and the mass retirement of baby-boom generation workers (Terama 2010a; Hayakawa 2006: 53–89; interview with Seiji Terama, 21 January 2010).

OVERVIEW OF LOCAL UNIONS

Zenroren defines its local unions as 'trade unions, which any worker can join as an individual, irrespective of industry or employment status; their aim is to meet the urgent needs of workers across the region' (Zenroren 2002: 4). They resemble the region-based amalgamated unions affiliated with other confederations. They affiliate directly to the prefectural or regional federations of Zenroren. As of July 2010, according to the 2010 Zenroren Biannual General Meeting proceedings, there were 152 such local unions with a membership of 11,338.

Zenroren local unions originated in proposals by the Democratic Youth League (a youth organization affiliated with the JCP) in the early 1980s (the same time as community unions were being organized). At the end of the 1980s, when confederation reorganization was taking place, the local unions gradually declined and nearly died out (Asami 2010: 176). As of 1989, there were only 39 Zenroren-affiliated local unions, with a membership of 1,008. Throughout the 1990s, membership stagnated.

Membership of local unions gradually increased in the 2000s, and in 2002 the number of local unions grew to 83, doubling over the previous decade; membership was at 3,020. The confederation decided at its 20th Biannual General Meeting in 2002 to 'strive to form local unions in every prefecture as tools to organize the unorganized across industries'. To facilitate the formation, it was decided that 'the local union exchange meetings will be held for the exchange of information and experiences and for learning from each other's activities'.

The membership of local unions grew steadily after 2004 when Zenroren adopted policies of setting up an organizing drive fund, posting Zenroren organizers to various prefectural federations, creating standing labour counselling centres, and establishing the system of regional mutual aid funds. From 2008 onwards, local unions actively organized dismissed irregular workers, and membership jumped by 4,390 in one year: a breakthrough for the local union movement.

A snapshot of a typical local union can be seen from the Zenroren document 'Organizational Realities of Zenroren Local Unions' (Zenroren 2009). Here is a summary. The average membership of the 135 local unions stood at 76.7. Membership ranged from single digits to over 400. There were 61 enterprise-level locals (*bunkai*) in 39 local unions. Average union dues were ¥843 per month: there was a wide range of dues rates, from just over ¥100 to over ¥2,000, ¥1,000 a more typical amount. One third of local unions had supporting or associate member systems. Associate members or supporting members accounted for 12.2 per cent of the membership and paid lower dues. The average annual budget of a local union was ¥960,000. 41.5 per cent of the unions had full-time staff and the average number of full-time staff was 1.56. Most staff members were retirees, pensioners, dismissed workers, or workers who had other full-time jobs at prefectural or regional federations of Zenroren or other organizations. Due to fiscal constraints, there were few full-time staff members working solely for local unions.

In summary, most local unions are individual-based organizations (there are relatively few enterprise-based locals), supported by full-time staff members from regional organizations of Zenroren and activists from regional organizations of Zenroren affiliate unions. These local unions have grown rapidly in these few years because they have the advantage of a nationwide network and can offer counselling in areas where Rengo is not present.

Zenrokyo and the Region-based Amalgamated Union Movement

Zenrokyo was formed in 1989 as a 'joint struggle organization' of mainly non-JCP left unions (leftwing JSP-affiliated and independent unions) opposed to the formation of Rengo. Its membership was 290,000 in 1989 and 140,000 in 2009, according to the Labor Union Basic Survey. Affiliates with a significant membership are the National Railway Workers' Union and the public employee unions in the Tokyo Metropolitan Government. Zenrokyo has a weak national office and no organizing functions.

One of the affiliates of Zenrokyo is the National Council of the NUGW. Regional organizations of the NUGW that broke away from the main body of the NUGW at the time of the formation of Rengo formed the National Council in 1991 with a membership of 10,000. Enterprise-based unions in SMEs and region-based amalgamated unions formed in the 1990s joined the National Council afterwards. These Zenrokyo-affiliated region-based amalgamated unions are quite independent and responsive to the changes in the labour market. They have created managers' and women's unions, played important roles in supporting and organizing foreign and migrant workers, engaged in new types of labour disputes through labour counselling and publicized them, provided a secretary for the Solidarity Network with Migrants Japan (Ijuren), and served as the secretariat for the National Campaign Against the Revision of the Labour Standards Law in 1997–1998. From my point of view as a participant observer, the Zenrokyo-affiliated region-based amalgamated unions have been mostly transformed into community unions.

Challenges and Possibilities of Region-based Amalgamated Unions

Thus far, this chapter has looked back on the history of region-based amalgamated unions in the post-war labour movement. We will now examine the challenges and possibilities of region-based amalgamated unions.

National Confederations and Region-based Amalgamated Unions

The Sohyo-affiliated NUGW, Rengo regional unions and Zenroren local unions were all region-based amalgamated unions created by the national confederations to organize the unorganized. The confederations funded them through donations and dues (by collecting special dues or by raising general dues) and staffed them with organizers or advisors from the confederations' regional organizations. Without resources from the confederations, it would have been hard for region-based amalgamated unions to develop.

Is it possible for region-based amalgamated unions established by national confederations to become self-reliant and active? In the case of the NUGW, Sohyo's district and regional labour councils already had independent budgets and were carrying out diverse campaigns. Moreover, the regional organizations of the NUGW launched various movements with their talented and politically-diverse, full-time staff and organizers. These regional organizations were connected loosely to each other, and were not under strong control from the national headquarters. These factors enabled the NUGW's regional organizations, in close association with Sohyo's regional labour councils, to build diverse movements. On the other hand, the national headquarters of the NUGW was weak and unable to direct a comprehensive movement for NUGW as a whole due to the antagonism between the JCP and the JSP.

What about Rengo's regional unions? Rengo started by negating the independent movement of district and regional labour councils, prohibiting its regional councils from collecting their own dues and running them, as a rule, by subsidies from Rengo headquarters and its prefectural organizations. Rengo has a centrally controlled organization, in which the autonomous activities of its regional councils are restricted. This creates an environment unfavourable for independent moves, although there are slight discrepancies or exceptions due to differences in constituent unions and in the personality of union officers and staff members. The same could be said of prefectural organizations of Rengo. Advisors assigned to them are running labour counselling and organizing drives but are not in a good position to organize a new movement. Consequently, many of Rengo's regional unions are just entities for collective bargaining for individual members who join the union through labour counselling, or pools for enterprise-based unions which have no industrial federation with which to affiliate. They lack solidarity and mutual aid activities in which members participate, although there are rare exceptions in a few regional unions (e.g., Kagoshima, Miyazaki, Fukuoka and Sapporo) (interview with Terumi Shimizu, 17 February 2010).

Rengo has resolved to raise dues to finance full-time officers or staff in its 300 regional councils within the next few years. The increase is only ¥10 per month for each member, but it is of great significance that Rengo, whose base is enterprise-based unions, has decided to support the region-based labour movement financially. If this is carried out, there is a possibility that the regional councils might become more active and link up with the regional unions to revive the region-based labour movement. The prospect is uncertain at the moment, though.

In the case of Zenroren's local unions, we can identify two types of unions: those unions whose main function is to provide collective bargaining assistance and those unions which promote solidarity and membership participation. At this point, it is not certain which type is going to be dominant among local unions. The confederation is holding a biannual national exchange meeting of local unions to exchange experiences and to activate the local union movement. The financial base of the local unions, however, is very weak with an average annual revenue of only ¥629,000 (Oh 2010: 50). They seem to survive only through the support of Zenroren's regional organizations.

Challenges for Self-reliant Region-based Amalgamated Unions

Community unions formed on the basis of regional labour councils had to become self-reliant after the formation of Rengo and the dissolution and diminishing of regional labour councils. They presently face the problem of securing a financial base for their continued existence and expansion. The same applies to regional organizations of the NUGW.

The average annual revenue of community unions is ¥6.82 million (CUNN 2006: 14). The average number of full-time staff is just one and the typical union is maintained by the long working hours of its staff. Community unions survive only because of the dedication and years-long experience of their full-time staff and the support they receive from many volunteers. It is difficult for unions in Japan to get funds from private funding agencies, so the only effective means to strengthen a union's financial base is to increase its membership. As for the membership, half of community unions are increasing their membership (Oh 2010: 53), whereas the remaining half are losing, so they are not increasing as a whole (interview with Tetsufumi Okamoto, 15 November 2010). The method of organizing is only through one-on-one labour counselling, making it difficult to organize on a large scale. Some unions have set up support groups for organizing or associate member systems and are collecting donations and dues from supporters to strengthen their financial base, but there is no apparent prospect of changing the situation in the short- or medium-term.

Generational Change of Organizers

Experienced organizers played important roles in the formation of the region-based amalgamated unions: the *chutai* organizers at the start of Sohyo's NUGW, the advisors and labour counsellors from Rengo's prefectural organizations and the full-time staff from Zenroren's prefectural and regional federations. Sohyo *chutai* organizers were young, in their twenties and thirties and had the energy to carry out labour disputes and create new areas of activity. By contrast, due to financial restraints, the staff in charge of organizing for Rengo and Zenroren are mostly retired activists in their

60s and lack the energy of youth, although they have years of experience in the labour movement. In the case of Rengo, most staff members are from enterprise-based unions in the public sector and big enterprises, without actual knowledge of the realities of contingent workers and SME workplaces, and they lack experience in organizing.

A quarter century has passed since the emergence of the community unions, and the first generation of activists is reaching retirement age. Especially important is the huge challenge posed by the retirement of the '68 generation, who experienced the student and social movements of that time and have led the labour movement to this point. How can they hand over the experience and know-how of this layer to the next generation? The know-how of labour counselling and organizing has to be learned through actual participation and experience. Activism must be deliberately and conscientiously handed-over to younger organizers, but, it is difficult for community unions to employ young organizers and educate them considering that most community unions have only one or two full-time staff members. The difficulty of generational change is aggravated by the difficulty of finding new jobs for middle-aged organizers. This situation is the same for regional organizations of the NUGW.

In general, region-based amalgamated unions are centred around their full-time organizers with day-to-day activity heavily dependent on organizers, on whom union members also rely. Consequently, unions tend to become service-model unions, and activism declines. The big challenge is how to change these unions into organizing-model unions with the lively participation of their members.

Models of Organization and Movement

Throughout the sixty-year history of the region-based amalgamated unions, there have been many attempts to find the appropriate model of organization and movement. It is important to learn from the historic experience and to look for a future model of organization and movement for regional amalgamated unions. As mentioned above, Sohyo NUGW attempted to overcome the limitations of enterprise-based unions (locals) by transforming itself from a federation of enterprise-based unions in the

SMEs to a unified union, based on individual affiliation, organizing across enterprises. A typical example of this union type has been Zentoitsu (All United Workers' Union), but it has had only moderate success, since the concentration of power and money at the top meant concentration of power in the hands of the full-time staff and conflict between them has lead to a split in the union (Matsui 2010). Many regional organizations of the NUGW, on the other hand, failed to transform themselves into united unions and are still operating as federations of enterprise-based unions in the SMEs. Although there was a period in the 1960s and 1970s when they were activated by political movements and labour dispute support activities, when the movement receded members returned to their workplaces and the union strengthened its standing as a federation of enterprise unions (Takasu 1995).

Community unions are smaller in size and have a high percentage of individual members, lacking the qualities of a federation of enterprise-based unions (locals), but when community unions expand and organize enterprise units, they naturally face the same challenges. The General Union for Young Workers of Tokyo (Shutoken Seinen Yunion) used to have enterprise-based locals, but was faced with barriers created by the enterprise-oriented consciousness of its members. The union now has converted to locals based on administrative districts and is organizing meetings of its members based on district-based locals (interview with Makoto Kawazoe, 9 March 2009).

It is still a great challenge for region-based amalgamated unions to overcome the limitations posed by enterprise-based locals and to promote the genuine region-based movement.

Labour Counselling and the Formation of a Network

Labour counselling for unorganized workers is the most important activity for region-based amalgamated unions and provides a kind of emergency support for unorganized workers in the region. It is also a means to identify the issues facing the workers. Unions handle from dozens to several hundred labour-and-livelihood counselling cases annually (OISR 2010: 9–13; Oh 2010: 53–6). Through counselling, the situation and issues of unorganized and contingent workers become apparent. This is not the case for enterprise-based unions and industrial federations mainly organizing regular workers. Whenever labour laws change, or personnel and labour management policies change, new issues come up in labour counselling. It becomes clear what demands should be made on the government and employers and what sort of organization and movement are needed to solve the issue.

Region-based amalgamated unions actively involved in labour counselling are organizing new categories of workers, bringing new issues into the labour movement and relaying messages to the labour movement and the public. In order to solve counselling cases and larger issues raised through counselling, they have a strong natural inclination to network by connecting with other unions, NPOs and social movement groups both in the region and nationwide. Successful examples were the National Campaign to Stop Revision of the Labour Standards Law (1997–1998) and the *Hakenmura* (from the year-end of 2008 to the beginning of 2009), in which the mass media reported on the efforts of the region-based amalgamated unions on the same footing as the efforts of Rengo: a stark contrast with the inward-focused enterprise-based unions and industrial federations that are self-contained in their enterprise or industry and have lost their social identity.

Conclusion

To summarize, the greatest challenge for all streams of region-based amalgamated unions is to secure their financial base. Rengo has succeeded in raising its dues to strengthen its regional councils, but other streams have not been able to increase their financial resources. Generational change and training young organizers are challenges common to all amalgamated unions. In the area of union models, the challenge is how to overcome the limitations of enterprise-based unions and create cross-enterprise solidarity and a participatory union movement that is less dependent on full-time organizers. The key issue here is the participation of young workers. The challenges are huge.

If region-based amalgamated unions can form a broad network with other social movements by calling attention to the issues raised in labour counselling, they might be able to move the government and the mainstream labour movement by gaining support from the public. The success of the *Hakenmura* shows that this is possible.

The membership of Sohyo NUGW was around 130,000 at its peak in the mid 1970s. The total number of members of the region-based amalgamated unions taken up in this chapter is 112,526, roughly the same as that of Sohyo NUGW. When the steep decline of the total union force in Japan is taken into consideration, region-based amalgamated unions are faring well.[12] Though they constitute only 1 per cent of the 10 million union members in Japan, if they are effective in publicly addressing the challenges of the day, region-based amalgamated unions can play a significant role in the labour movement and revitalize it by involving the mainstream unions in the most important struggles of the day.

References

Asami, K. (2010). 'Nihon no Rodo Kumiai: Kaikaku wo Meguru Ronten to Kadai' (Japanese Labour Movement: Issues and Challenges of its Reformation). In T. Kitagawa, K. Asami (eds), *21 Seiki eno Chousen 6: Shakai Undo: Soshiki, Shiso.* Tokyo: Nihon Keizai Hyoronsha.

Hamamura, A. (2003). 'Godoroso kara Komyuniti Yunion he' (From Amalgamated Unions to Community Unions). In A. Hamamura, T. Nagamine (eds), *Kumiai Kino no Tayosei to Kanosei.* Tokyo: Hosei Daigaku Shuppan Kyoku.

Hayakawa, S. (2006). 'Rengo to Zenroren no Soshiki Kakudai Senryaku' (Organizing Drives of Rengo and Zenroren). In A. Suzuki, S. Hayakawa (eds), *Rodo Kumiai no Soshiki Kakudai Senryaku.* Tokyo: Ochanomizu shobo.

12 The total union force in Japan was at its height in 1994 at 12,698,000 members (estimated union density 24.1 per cent), but has decreased to 10,054,000 (18.5 per cent) by 2010 (figures from Labour Force Survey which are slightly different from those in Table 3 and 4 in Appendix).

Hyodo, A. (2006). 'Nihon no Rodo Kumiai Undo ni Okeru Soshikika Katsudo no Shiteki Tenkai: Haisengo kara Kodo Seichoki madewo Chushin ni' (The Historical Development of Organizing Activities in the Japanese Trade Union Movement: Focusing the Period from the End of the World War to the Rapid Growth Period). In A. Suzuki, S. Hayakawa (eds), *Rodo Kumiai no Soshiki Kakudai Senryaku*. Tokyo: Ochanomizu shobo.

Iwai, A. (1960). 'Sohyo no Misoshiki Rodosha Soshikika Undo to Godo Rodo Kumiai' (Organizing Activities of Sohyo and Amalgamated Unions), *Nihon Rodo Kyokai Zassi*, Vol. 16, 15–21.

Komyuniti Yunion Zenkoku Nettowaku. (ed.) (2006). *CUNN*, No.24.

Komyuniti Yunion Zenkoku Nettowaku. (ed.) (1993). *Yunion, Ningen, Nettowaku: Komyuniti Yunion Sengen Part 2* (Union, People, Network: Community Union Manifesto Part 2). Tokyo: Daiichi Shorin.

Komyuniti Yunion Kenkyukai. (ed.) (1988). *Komyuniti Yunion Sengen* (Community Union Manifesto). Tokyo: Daiichi Shorin.

Koseirodo sho (Ministry of Health, Labour and Welfare). (various years) *Rodo Ryoku Chosa* (Labour Force Survey).

Koseirodo sho (Ministry of Health, Labour and Welfare). (various years) *Rodo Kumiai Kiso Chosa* (Labor Union Basic Survey).

Kosugi, R. (2005). 'Problems of *Freeters* and "NEETs" under the Recovering Economy', *Social Science Japan*, No.32, 6–7.

Matsui, Y. (2010). *Godoroso no Kensho: Sono Rekishi to Ronri* (Examination of Amalgamated Union: Its History and Logic). Tokyo: Fukuin.

Nagamine, T. (2003). 'Komyuniti Yunion Undo no 20 Nen' (20 Years of the Community Union Movement). In A. Hamamura, T. Nagamine (eds), *Kumiai Kino no Tayosei to Kanosei*. Tokyo: Hosei Daigaku Shuppan Kyoku.

Numata, I. (ed.) (1963). *Godoroso no Kenkyu* (The Study of Amalgamated Unions). Rodo Hogaku Kenkyujo.

Obata, Y. (1993). 'Komyuniti Yunion Undo no Totatsuten to Kadai' (The Achievements and Challenges of Community Unions). In Komyuniti Yunion Zenkoku Nettowaku (ed), *Yunion, Ningen, Nettowaku: Komyuniti Yunion Sengen Part 2*. Tokyo: Daiichi Shorin.

Obata, Y. (2003a). 'Komyuniti Yunion Undo no Totatsuten to Tenbo (jo)' (The Achievements and Prospects of Community Unions 1), *Rodo Horitsu Junpo*, No. 1560, 41–5.

Obata, Y. (2003b). 'Komyuniti Yunion Undo no Totatsuten to Tenbo (ge)' (The Achievements and Prospects of Community Unions 2), *Rodo Horitsu Junpo*, No. 1562, 79–85.

Oh, H. 2010. 'Godoroso no Genjo: Kobetsu Rodo Funso Kaiketsu ni Kanren shite' (Present Situation of Amalgamated Unions: Concerning Individual Labour Dispute Settlement), *Nihon Rodo Kenkyu Zasshi*, No. 604: 47–65.

OISR (the Ohara Institute for Social Research) (2010). 'Kojin Kamei Kumiai no Katsudo ni Kansuru Anketo Chosakekka Hokoku' (A Report on the Results of the Survey on Individually-Affiliated Unions' Activities), the Ohara Institute for Social Research Working Paper No.41.

Okamura, S. (1976). 'Orugu Seido no Rekishiteki Hensen' (Historical Transition of Organizer System). In Nihon Rodo Kumiai Sohyo Gikai (ed), *Orugu*. Tokyo: Rodokyoiku Senta.

Rengo. (2001). *21 Seiki wo Kirihiraku Rengo Undo: 21 Seiki Bijon* (Rengo Movement Opening Up the 21st Century: The 21st Century Vision). In Rengo Biannual General Meeting Papers.

Shirai, T. (1986). *Rodo Kumiai Dokuhon* (Trade Union Reader). Tokyo: Toyo Keizai Shinposha.

Shirai, T. (1979). *Kigyobestsu Rodo Kumiai* (Enterprise-based Unions) Revised Edition. Tokyo: Chuko Shinsho.

Sohyo. (ed.) (1986). *Sohyo 30 Nen Shiryoshu 1* (Sohyo 30 Years Data File 1). Tokyo: Rodokyoiku Senta.

Takagi, I. (2000). 'Komyuniti Union no Soshiki to Katsudo' (Organization and Activities of Community Union), *Shakai Seisaku Gakkaishi*, 3, 53–70.

Takahashi, H. (2008). 'Jidai no Tenkanten ni Tatte: Shakaiteki Rodo Undo to Chuo Rofukukyo no Kadai' (At the Turning Point of the Era: The Challenges of the Social Labour Movement and Chuo Rofukukyo), *Rodo Horitsu Junpo*, No. 1687/ 1688, 98–105.

Takasu, H. (2010a). 'Rodo Kumiai Undo no Shin Tenkai: Shakai Undo Yunionizumu no Kanosei: Nichibei wo Hikaku shite' (New Developments in the Trade Union Movement: The Possibilities of Social Movement Unionism, A Comparison between Japan and the US), *Shakai Seisaku*, 2 (1), 51–63.

Takasu, H. (2010b). 'Tokushu 1: Yunion Undo no Kesei to Genjo: Hosei Daigaku Ohara Shakai Mondai Kenkyujo' (The Formation and the Current State of the Community Union Movement), *Nihon Rodo Nenkan*, No.80, 40–68.

Takasu, H. (2003). 'Labor Dispute and Organizing among Foreign Workers in NUGW Tokyo South', *BULLETIN*: Center for Transnational Labor Studies, No. 8.

Takasu, H. (2002). 'New Developments in the Japanese Labor Movement Fighting Against Non-standardization of Employment by the Koizumi Government's Structural Reforms', *BULLETIN*: Center for Transnational Labor Studies, No. 7.

Takasu, H. (1998). 'Rodo Kijun Ho Kaiaku Soshi! Watashitachino Tatakai' (Stop the Revision of the Labour Reform Law! This is our Struggle), *Kikan Rodosha no Kenri*, Vol. 225, 24–8.

Takasu, H. (1995). 'Gendai Nihon no Chusho Kigyo ni okeru Rodo Undo: Taikoteki Rodo Undo no Totatsu Ten to Taian Senryaku Undo no Kanosei: Zenkoku Ippan Rodo Kumiai Tokyo Namubu Shibu. A Bunkai no Jirei Kenkyu' (Japanese Labour Movement in SMEs: The Achievements of the Oppositional Labour Movement and the Possibilities of Alternative Strategy Movement: A Case Study of a Local of NUGW Tokyo South), Master's thesis, Graduate School of Economic Science, Saitama University.

Takeyama, H. (1981). 'Sohyo no Chusho Kigyo Rodosha Taisaku, Zenkoku Ippan Rodo Kumiai no Kessei to Orugu Haichi' (Sohyo's Policy on SME Workers: The Formation of NUGW and the Placement of Organizers). In Y. Kuramochi, *Sengo Chusho Kigyo Sogishi*, Tokyo: Rodo Kyoiku Senta (in Japanese).

Tatsui, Y. (2008). 'Hiseiki Koyo ni Taisuru Rengo no Torikumi' (Rengo's Activities toward Contingent Employment), *Rodo Horitsu Junpo*, No. 1663/1664, 35–9.

Tejima, S. (1990). 'Chiiki wo Shokuba to suru Rodosha no tame no Soshikika no Keiken' (The Experience in Organizing Workers Whose Workplace Is in the Local Community). In Rodo Mondai Jissen Shirizu (ed.), *Rodo Kumiai wo Tsukuru*. Tokyo: Otsuki Shoten.

Terama, S. (2010). 'Hiseiki Rodosha no Soshikika to Rodo Kumiai Kaikaku no Hoko' (The Organizing of Contingent Workers and the Direction of Trade Union Reform), *Rodo Horitsu Junpo*, No. 1713, 25–35.

Toshikoshi Hakenmura Jikko Iinkai. (2009). *Hakenmura: Kuni o Ugokashita 6 Kakan* (*Hakenmura*: 6 Days that Shook the Nation). Tokyo: Mainichi Shinbunsha.

Utsunomiya, K., Yuasa, M. (eds) (2009). *Hakenmura: Nani ga Towarete Irunoka* (*Hakenmura*: What was the issue?). Tokyo: Iwanami Shoten.

Watanabe, T. (2003). *Koseki: Hokkaido Gyogyo Kosha no 28 Nen* (The Tracks: The 28 Years of Hokkaido Fishing Public Corporation Union). Tokyo: Dojidaisha.

Yuasa, M. (2009). 'Rodo Undo to Shakai Hosho Undo ga Futatabi Te wo Tsunagu Toki ga Yattekita: Hinkon no Genjo to Hanhinkon Undo' (The Time Has Come Again for the Labour Movement and the Social Security Movement to Join Hands: The current situation of Poverty and Anti-Poverty Movement), *Rodo Horitsu Junpo*, No.1696, 72–8.

Yuasa, M. (2008). *Hanhinkon: Suberidai Shakai karano Dasshutsu* (Anti-Poverty: Exit from the 'Slide' Society). Tokyo: Iwanami Shinsho.

Zenkoku Ippan 30 Shunnen Jikko Iinkai. (1985). *Sohyo Zenkoku Ippan 30 Nen Shiroshu* (Sohyo NUGW 30th Anniversary Data File).

Zenroren. (2009). *Zenroren Rokaru Yunion no Soshiki Jittai* (Organizational Realities of Zenroren Local Unions). In *Zenroren Biannual General Meeting Papers.*
Zenroren. (2002). *Rokaru Yunion Zenkoku Koryu Shukai Mondai Teiki (an)* (Local Union National Exchange Meeting Proposals).

Interviews: positions are at the time of the interview

Endo, Ichiro. Secretary General, National Council of NUGW; Steering Committee Member, Zenrokyo (16 February 2009, 21 January 2010 Telephone).
Iida, Katsuyasu. Secretary General, Tokyo Occupational Health and Safety Centre; Steering Committee Member, Shitamachi Union (17 February 2009, 2 May 2009 Telephone).
Ito, Keiichi. Zenroren Director of Research (15 April 2009).
Kawazoe, Makoto. Secretary General, General Union for Youth Workers of Tokyo (9 March 2009).
Ojima, Shigeru. Rengo Executive Director, Department of Economic and Social Policy (6 April 2009).
Okamoto, Tetsufumi. CUNN Director General (15 November 2010 Telephone).
Otsuka, Toshio. Rengo Executive Director of Department of Organizational Affairs (25 February 2009, 30 March 2009).
Seryu, Takuya. Ex-Rengo Officer (17 December 2008).
Shimizu, Terumi. Secretary General, Rengo Fukuoka Union (17 February 2010).
Tajima, Keiichi. Rengo Central Advisor, NUGW Ex-President (9 December 2009, 21 January 2010, Telephone).
Takahashi, Hitoshi. Former Rengo Assistant General Secretary; Director General Chuo Rofukukyo (17, December 2008, 21 April 2009).
Tatsui, Yoji. Rengo Executive Director, Centre for Non-Regular Employment (17 April 2009).
Terama, Seiji. Zenroren Director, Organizing Department (9 December 2009, 21 January 2010).

Appendix

Table A.1 Employment by Sector: Japan, Korea and the United States (unit: %)

Japan							
	1980	1985	1990	1995	2000	2005	2010
Industry (excluding Construction)	25	26	25	23	21	19	17
Construction	9	9	9	10	10	9	8
Service	54	56	59	61	64	68	71
Others	17	9	7	6	5	4	4

Korea			
	2000	2005	2010
Industry (excluding Construction)	21	18	17
Construction	7	8	7
Service	61	65	68
Others	11	9	8

United States							
	1980	1985	1990	1995	2000	2005	2010
Industry (excluding Construction)	23	19	17	16	15	12	11
Construction	6	7	7	6	7	8	7
Service	66	71	73	75	76	79	81
Others	5	3	3	3	2	1	1

Source: OECD StatExtract
(http://stats.oecd.org/Index.aspx?DataSetCode=UN_DEN). As of 21 December 2011.

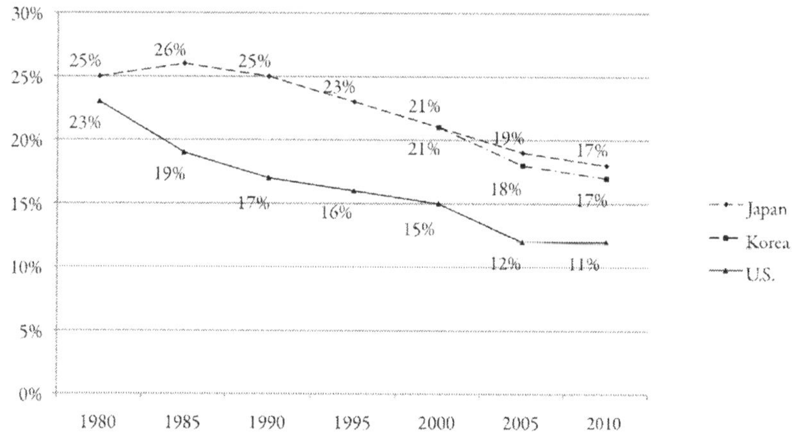

Figure A.1 Percentage of Industrial Employees (excluding Construction): Japan, Korea and the United States, 1980–2010

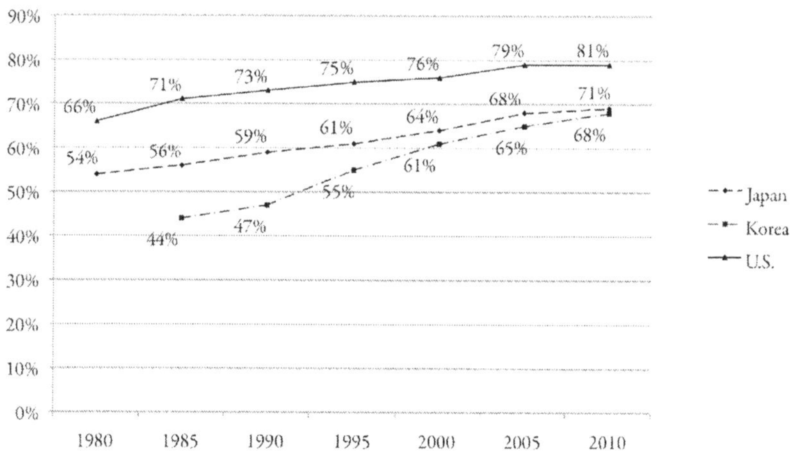

Figure A.2 Percentage of Service Sector Employees: Japan, Korea and the United States, 1980–2010

Source: OECD StatExtract (http://stats.oecd.org/Index.aspx?DataSetCode=UN_DEN). As of 20 December 2011.

Table A.2 Annual Growth in GDP: Japan, Korea and the United States, 1980–2010 (unit: %)

Year	Japan	Korea	U.S.
1980	2.8	-1.9	-0.3
1981	4.2	7.4	2.5
1982	3.4	8.3	-2.0
1983	3.1	12.2	4.5
1984	4.5	9.9	7.2
1985	6.3	7.5	4.1
1986	2.8	12.2	3.4
1987	4.1	12.3	3.2
1988	7.1	11.7	4.1
1989	5.4	6.8	3.6
1990	5.6	9.3	1.9
1991	3.3	9.7	-0.3
1992	0.8	5.8	3.4
1993	0.2	6.3	2.9
1994	0.9	8.8	4.1
1995	1.9	8.9	2.5
1996	2.6	7.2	3.8
1997	1.6	5.8	4.5
1998	-2.0	-5.7	4.4
1999	-0.1	10.7	4.9
2000	2.9	8.8	4.2
2001	0.2	4.0	1.1
2002	0.3	7.2	1.8
2003	1.4	2.8	2.6
2004	2.7	4.6	3.5
2005	1.9	4.0	3.1
2006	2.0	5.2	2.7

2007	2.4	5.1	1.9
2008	-1.2	2.3	-0.4
2009	-6.3	0.3	-3.5
2010	(E)4.0	6.2	3.0

(E) estimated value

Source: OECD StatExtract (http://stats.oecd.org/Index.aspx?DatasetCode=SNA_TABLE1). As of 21 December 2011.

Table A.3 Union Membership: Japan, Korea and the United States, 1970–2010 (unit: thousands)

Year	Japan(1)	Korea(2)	United States
1970	11,605	473	(4)19,381
1975	12,590	750	(5)16778
1976	12,509	846	17,403
1977	12,437	955	19,335
1978	12,383	1,055	19,548
1979	12,309	1,088	20,986
1980	12,369	948	20,095
1981	12,471	967	19,123
1982	12,526	984	18,420
1983	12,520	1,010	17,717
1984	12,464	1,011	17,340
1985	12,418	1,004	16,996
1986	12,343	1,036	16,975
1987	12,272	1,267	16,913
1988	12,227	1,707	17,002
1989	12,227	1,932	16,961
1990	12,265	1,887	16,740
1991	12,397	1,803	16,568
1992	12,541	1,735	16,390
1993	12,663	1,667	16,598
1994	12,699	1,659	16,740

1995	12,614	1,615	16,360
1996	12,451	1,599	16,269
1997	12,285	1,484	16,110
1998	12,093	1,402	16,211
1999	11,825	1,481	16,477
2000	11,539	1,527	16,334
2001	11,212	1,569	16,305
2002	10,801	1,538	16,145
2003	10,531	1,550	15,776
2004	10,309	1,537	15,472
2005	10,138	1,506	15,685
2006	10,041	1,559	15,359
2007	10,080	1,688	15,670
2008	10,065	1,666	16,098
2009	10,078	1,640	15,327
2010	10,054	(3)1,643	14,715

Source: OECD StatExtract
(http://stats.oecd.org/Index.aspx?DataSetCode=UN_DEN). As of 30 June 2011.

Note

(1) Administrative data on total (employed) membership, based on *Basic Survey on Trade Unions* (until 1983) and *Survey on Industrial Relations* (from 1984 onwards), from the *Japanese Yearbook of Labour Statistics.*

(2) Administrative data on total (employed) membership, based on survey of unions and union members reported in the *Korea Statistical Yearbook.*

(3) Ministry of Employment and Labor, 11 November 2011. Available at Korean International Labor Foundation.
(http://www.koilaf.org/KFeng/engLabornews/bbs_read_dis.php?board_no=7481)

(4) 1970 datum based on union returns established by the Bureau of Labor Statistics.

(5) Data from 1975–1981 based on *May Current Population Survey* (CPS). Data from 1983 onwards are *CPS Outgoing Rotation Group (ORG) Earnings Files.*

Table A.4 Union Density(1): Japan, Korea and the United States, 1970–2010

Year	Japan(2)	Korea(3)	U.S.
1970	35.1	12.6	(5)27.4
1975	34.5	15.8	(6)25.3
1976	33.7	16.5	24.4
1977	33.0	16.7	23.6
1978	32.6	16.9	23.9
1979	31.8	16.8	22.4
1980	31.1	14.7	22.1
1981	30.9	14.6	21.0
1982	30.6	14.4	20.5
1983	29.8	14.1	19.5
1984	29.2	13.2	18.2
1985	28.8	12.4	17.4
1986	28.2	12.3	17.0
1987	27.7	13.8	16.5
1988	26.9	17.8	16.2
1989	26.1	18.6	15.9
1990	25.4	17.2	15.5
1991	24.8	15.4	15.5
1992	24.5	14.6	15.1
1993	24.3	14.0	15.1
1994	24.3	13.3	14.9
1995	24.0	12.5	14.3
1996	23.4	12.1	14.0
1997	22.8	11.1	13.6
1998	22.5	11.4	13.4
1999	22.2	11.7	13.4
2000	21.5	11.4	12.9
2001	20.9	11.5	12.9

2002	20.3	10.8	12.8
2003	19.7	10.8	12.4
2004	19.3	10.3	12.0
2005	18.8	9.9	12.0
2006	18.3	10.0	11.5
2007	18.3	10.6	11.6
2008	18.2	10.3	11.9
2009	18.5	10.0	11.8
2010	18.4	(4)9.8	11.4

Source: OECD StatExtract
(http://stats.oecd.org/Index.aspx?DataSetCode=UN_DEN). As of 30 June 2011.

Note

(1) Trade union density corresponds to the ratio of wage and salary earners that are trade union members, divided by the total number of wage and salary earners.

(2) Administrative data on total (employed) membership, based on *Basic Survey on Trade Unions* (until 1983) and *Survey on Industrial Relations* (from 1984 onwards), reported in the *Japanese Yearbook of Labour Statistics.*

(3) Administrative data on total (employed) membership, based on survey of unions and union members reported in the *Korea Statistical Yearbook.*

(4) Ministry of Employment and Labor, 11 November 2011. Available at Korean International Labor Foundation.
(http://www.koilaf.org/KFeng/engLabornews/bbs_read_dis.php?board_no=7481)

(5) 1970 datum based on union returns established by the Bureau of Labor Statistics.

(6) Data from 1975–1981 based on *May Current Population Survey* (CPS). Data from 1983 onwards are *CPS Outgoing Rotation Group (ORG) Earnings Files.*

Table A.5 Harmonized Unemployment Rate: (1) Japan, Korea and the United States, 1970–2010 (unit: %)

Year	Japan	Korea	United States
1970	1.2	–	4.9
1975	1.9	–	8.5
1976	2.0	–	7.7
1977	2.0	–	7.1
1978	2.2	–	6.1
1979	2.1	–	5.8
1980	2.0	–	7.1
1981	2.2	–	7.6
1982	2.4	–	9.7
1983	2.7	–	9.6
1984	2.7	–	7.5
1985	2.6	–	7.2
1986	2.8	–	7.0
1987	2.8	–	6.2
1988	2.5	–	5.5
1989	2.3	2.6	5.3
1990	2.1	2.4	5.6
1991	2.1	2.4	6.8
1992	2.2	2.5	7.5
1993	2.5	2.9	(B)6.9
1994	2.9	2.5	6.1
1995	3.1	2.1	5.6
1996	3.4	2.0	5.4
1997	3.4	2.6	4.9
1998	4.1	7.0	4.5
1999	4.7	(B)6.6	(B)4.2
2000	4.7	4.4	4.0

2001	5.0	4.0	4.7
2002	5.4	3.3	5.8
2003	5.3	3.6	6.0
2004	4.7	3.7	5.5
2005	4.4	3.7	5.1
2006	4.1	3.5	4.6
2007	3.9	3.2	4.6
2008	4.0	3.2	5.8
2009	5.1	3.6	9.3
2010	5.1	3.7	9.6

(B) is Break

Source: OECD StatExtract
(http://stats.oecd.org/index.aspx?queryid=451) As of 14 July 2011.

Note

(1) The harmonized unemployment rates give the numbers of unemployed persons as a percentage of the civilian labour force. The civilian labour force consists of civilian employees, the self-employed, unpaid family workers and the unemployed.

Notes on Contributors and Translators

JENNIFER JIHYE CHUN is an Associate Professor in the Department of Sociology at the University of Toronto, Scarborough. She is the author of *Organizing at the Margins: The Symbolic Politics of Labor in South Korea and the United States* (Cornell University Press, 2009). Her second book project examines community-based approaches to organizing Asian immigrant women workers in the San Francisco Bay Area and Vancouver.

KOSHI ENDO is Professor of Employment and Industrial Relations at the School of Business Administration in Meiji University, Tokyo, Japan. His current research interests are the non-union representation of workers and the development of job-related pay systems based on the principle of equal pay for work of equal value.

HEIWON KWON is Assistant Professor, Department of Business Administration, Dongduk Women's University, Seoul.

JOOHEE LEE is an Associate Professor at Ewha Womans University in Korea. Before joining the faculty at the Ewha Sociology Department, she was a research fellow at the Korea Labor Institute (KLI). Her major research interests are changing collective bargaining structures in a global economy, industrial democracy at the workplace and labour policy for non-regular workers.

MINJIN LEE is a Professor at the College of Sociology, Rikkyo University, Tokyo. Her research focuses on comparative labour relations and coalitions between trade unions and civil society organizations.

STEPHANIE LUCE is an Associate Professor at the Murphy Institute, City University of New York. She is the author of *Fighting for a Living Wage* (Cornell University Press, 2004).

AKIRA SUZUKI is a Professor at the Ohara Institute for Social Research, Hosei University in Japan. His major research interests include social movement unionism and the historical analysis of union involvement in environmental issues. He has edited and co-edited volumes on recent trends in Japanese labour movements, most recently *Neoliberalism and Labour* (Ochanomizu Shobo, 2010, in Japanese).

HIROHIKO TAKASU is Project Director of Research and Education Center for Fair Labor at Hitotsubashi University in Japan. He was an organizer and official of the National Union of General Workers in Tokyo for 14 years. His research focuses on social movement unionism in the United States and Japan.

NOBUYUKI YAMADA is Professor of Sociology at Komazawa University in Japan. He earned his PhD at the University of Tokyo in 1994. His interest is in the historical sociology of industrial relations and capitalist development. He is currently interested in social movement unionism in the United States. He is the author of *Historical Sociology of Industrial Relations* (1996), *Class, the State, and the World-System* (1998), *The World-System in the New Century* (2006), as well as many articles.

CHARLES WEATHERS teaches labour relations and political economy at Osaka City University in Osaka, Japan. His current research interests include problems of female and non-regular workers in Japan and comparative analysis of union activities in Japan, the United States and Australia.

Translators (Chapters 6 and 11)

AKIRA SUZUKI (see above)

SEIICHI YAMASAKI is a visiting researcher at the Research Centre for Labor Education and Media, Meiji University.

Index

Note: The letter *t* following a page number denotes a table.

Trade Unions Past, Present and Future

Edited by Craig Phelan

This series publishes monographs and edited collections on the history, present condition and possible future role of organised labour around the world. Multi-disciplinary in approach, geographically and chronologically diverse, this series is dedicated to the study of trade unionism and the undeniably significant role it has played in modern society. Topics include the historical development of organised labour in a variety of national and regional settings; the political, economic and legal contexts in which trade unionism functions; trade union internationalism past and present; comparative and cross-border studies; trade unions' role in promoting economic equality and social justice; and trade union revitalisation and future prospects. The aims of the series are to promote an appreciation of the diversity of trade union experience worldwide and to provide an international forum for lively debate on all aspects of the subject.

Volume 1 Craig Phelan (ed.): Trade Unionism since 1945: Towards a Global History. Volume 1: Western Europe, Eastern Europe, Africa and the Middle East.
467 pages. 2009. ISBN 978-3-03911-410-8

Volume 2 Craig Phelan (ed.): Trade Unionism since 1945: Towards a Global History. Volume 2: The Americas, Asia and Australia.
364 pages. 2009. ISBN 978-3-03911-950-9

Volume 3 Pablo Ghigliani: The Politics of Privatisation and Trade Union Mobilisation: The Electricity Industry in the UK and Argentina.
293 pages. 2010. ISBN 978-3-03911-961-5

Volume 4 Heather Connolly: Renewal in the French Trade Union Movement: A Grassroots Perspective.
260 pages. 2010. ISBN 978-3-0343-0101-5

Volume 5 Magaly Rodríguez García: Liberal Workers of the World, Unite? The ICFTU and the Defence of Labour Liberalism in Europe and Latin America (1949–1969).
354 pages. 2010. ISBN 978-3-0343-0112-1

Volume 6 Jeffrey Sluyter-Beltrão: Rise and Decline of Brazil's New Unionism: The Politics of the Central Única dos Trabalhadores.
481 pages. 2010. ISBN 978-3-0343-0114-5

Volume 7 Craig Phelan (ed.): Trade Unions in West Africa: Historical and Contemporary Perspectives.
288 pages. 2011. ISBN 978-3-0343-0117-6

Volume 8 Forthcoming.

Volume 9 Tracy Carson: Tomorrow It Could Be You: Strikes and Boycotts in South Africa, 1978–1982.
325 pages. 2011. ISBN 978-3-0343-0119-0

Volume 10 Laura Ariovich: Organizing the Organized: Trade Union Renewal, Organizational Change and Worker Activism in Metropolitan America.
310 pages. 2010. ISBN 978-3-0343-0132-9

Volume 11 Indira Palacios-Valladares: Industrial Relations after Pinochet: Firm Level Unionism and Collective Bargaining Outcomes in Chile.
268 pages. 2011. ISBN 978-3-0343-0136-7

Volume 12 Zhining Ma: The ACFTU and Chinese Industrial Relations.
260 pages. 2011. ISBN 978-3-0343-0205-0

Volume 13 Quenby Olmsted Hughes: "In the Interest of Democracy": The Rise and Fall of the Early Cold War Alliance Between the American Federation of Labor and the Central Intelligence Agency.
218 pages. 2011. ISBN 978-3-0343-0212-8

Volume 14 Hans-Wolfgang Platzer and Torsten Müller: Global and European Trade Union Federations: A Handbook and Analysis of Transnational Trade Union Organizations and Policies.
949 pages. 2011. ISBN 978-3-0343-0744-4

Volume 15-17 Forthcoming.

Volume 18 Akira Suzuki (ed.): Cross-National Comparisons of Social Movement Unionism: Diversities of Labour Movement Revitalization in Japan, Korea and the United States.
355 pages. 2012. ISBN 978-3-0343-0868-7

www.ingramcontent.com/pod-product-compliance
Ingram Content Group UK Ltd.
Pitfield, Milton Keynes, MK11 3LW, UK
UKHW021853100926
8556IPUK00020B/1200